F
HU FENG'S PRISON YEARS

MEI ZHI

Edited and translated by Gregor Benton

VERSO
London • New York

This book has been selected to receive financial assistance from English PEN's
Writers in Translation programme supported by Bloomberg. English PEN exists to
promote literature and its understanding, uphold writers' freedoms around the world,
campaign against the persecution and imprisonment of writers for stating their views,
and promote the friendly co-operation of writers and free exchange of ideas.
www.englishpen.org

This English-language edition first published by Verso 2013
Translation © Gregor Benton 2013
First published as *Hu Feng chen yuan lu*
© Science Press, Beijing 1989

1 3 5 7 9 10 8 6 4 2

Verso
UK: 6 Meard Street, London W1F 0EG
US: 20 Jay Street, Suite 1010, Brooklyn, NY 11201
www.versobooks.com

Verso is the imprint of New Left Books

ISBN-13: 978-1-84467-967-6

British Library Cataloguing in Publication Data
A catalogue record for this book is available from the British Library

Library of Congress Cataloging-in-Publication Data
A catalog record for this book is available from the Library of Congress

Mei, Zhi.
[Hu Feng chen yuan lu. English]
F : Hu Feng's prison years / by Mei Zhi ; translated and edited by Gregor Benton.
pages cm
"This English-language edition first published by Verso 2013"–T.p. verso.
"First published as Hu Feng chen yuan lu"–T.p. verso.
ISBN 978-1-84467-967-6 (hardback : alk. paper) – ISBN (invalid) 978-1-84467-968-3 (ebook)
1. Hu, Feng, 1902-1985–Imprisonment. 2. Authors, Chinese–20th
century–Biography. I. Benton, Gregor, translator. II. Title.
PL2740.K8Z713 2013
895.1'85109–dc23
[B]
2012038655

Typeset in Fournier by Hewer Text UK Ltd, Edinburgh
Printed in the US by Maple Vail

Contents

Contents

Part One

Past Events Disperse like Smoke

1

It Started with a Letter

1965. It was ten years since Hu Feng had been arrested at home and taken into custody. I had been restored to freedom more than four years earlier, but for a decade I had not seen him once, nor exchanged a letter with him. I didn't even know where he was. Immediately after my release, I asked about him at the Ministry of Public Security. They said he was well. I said I wanted to send him some clothes, but they told me it was unnecessary. I asked if they could pass on a letter. They said it might adversely affect his reform. After that, I no longer had the courage even to ask. When friends and acquaintances enquired, I would shake my head and whisper, 'I don't even know where he is.'

In 1962 people started talking. My daughter heard about it on her farm and came home to tell me. She said they might soon deal with the contradictions among the people in the literary world and let him go. That was good news, but I had no way of discreetly enquiring whether it was reliable. All I could do was wait.

In May 1965, I received a letter. It was in an ordinary white envelope with a flower printed in the corner. Unusually, however, the address was written with a brush pen. The hand was dignified and skilled, not slavishly copied from a primer by some young man or woman with a smattering of culture, but the work of a practised calligrapher. It must have been from an old friend, for the writer had used my original name. There was no sender's address, just the words 'posted in Beijing'. Which of my old acquaintances knew where I lived?

I suddenly remembered Mr Sha, who we didn't know particularly well. He looked like a typical intellectual. He was learned, and therefore popular among some intellectuals who had come across from the old society. After we moved to Beijing, he sometimes used to visit us to play chess with F or chat about classical literature. Needless to say, they sometimes grumbled. I didn't know at the time if he ever became implicated when we later got into trouble.

I had gone to the Fulong Temple on the eve of Spring Festival a few months back to buy some small gifts for the children. Coming towards me in the bustling crowd was a familiar face. I realised from the way he dressed that it was Mr Sha. He was still wearing his fine overcoat, tailored from good material. His spectacles, short beard, and classical writer's manner had not changed, but he was more stooped than in the past. He was carrying a big bundle of books wrapped in cloth. Obviously he had just come from the second-hand bookstore. I tried to avoid his eyes, but he had seen me. He came towards me with a look of such delight that I had to greet him. He said in a low voice:

'I hope you're both well. How's Old Hu?'

I answered, also in a low voice:

'Things are all right. I know nothing about his situation.'

Instead of rushing off, he accompanied me to a quieter place, and we ended up in a road behind the temple.

I was surprised to see the little lanes behind Fulong Temple were so quiet and well swept. There were just a few passers-by. It was another world from the road outside. Perhaps the residents did their shopping on the main street.

We walked and talked in the lanes, out of the wind.

He told me how concerned friends had been about us. Later, he heard I had been released. He said how distressed he was when he couldn't discover my address. He said he had been isolated and put under investigation for more than a year because of his association with Hu Feng. Not until later, when it was determined there had been no link, did they decide not to class him as an 'element'.

He made as if to laugh, but his face did not laugh.

I said, 'In 1958, when I was under detention, I heard you talking on the radio about classical poetry. Your recital moved me deeply. It was as if I was back among people. It made me think of my childhood, when I used to read classical poetry. Unfortunately, I never heard any more broadcasts. I thought you must have managed to avoid getting implicated. That made me happy.'

'How long were you in detention?'

'Seventy months. They let me out in 1961 when my mother's remains were placed in the hospital mortuary, so I could take care of the funeral. After that they didn't lock me up again.'

'How about your life now? Is someone looking after you?'

'I'm looking after myself.'

'Nie Gannu and his wife are very concerned about you. So's Old Tian. I heard you'd been released, but the building in which you used to live was pulled down long ago. Later, we heard you were living somewhere around Shaojiu Lane. Old Tian often went there for a stroll, in the hope of bumping into you. Someone said you'd moved out into the suburbs, but no one knew where.'

'That's right. Later, I moved to Chaoyang Menwai.' I wanted to change the topic, so I asked:

'Are you all right now? Why have you not been back on the radio?'

'It's a long story. I'm at Shuangqiao State Farm. They're giving me time off for family business.'

He seemed to notice my surprise, and added, 'It's not important, nothing political. They say I'm a fake doctor and I'm harming my patients. They say I'm practising without a licence. Let's not talk about it. Perhaps it will be over in a few months and they'll let me go home. They're still allowing me to examine reform-through-labour prisoners. I have my own room, only I no longer get paid.' He gestured at his bundle: 'Today I've come to sell my books. I've already sold all the best ones. These are the ones they don't want.'

I looked at the bundle and felt sorry for him, but he didn't seem to mind. He said, 'It's no problem. Mother and the children get living expenses anyway. I'm just trying to get some money.'

I admired his tenacity. However, I felt it unwise to stay too long in the deserted lane. I told him I needed to return to the market to do some shopping. But he held me back:

'First leave me an address.'

He fished a ballpoint from one pocket and an envelope from the other. Indicating the envelope, he said with a smile:

'See, Shuangqiao State Farm.'

I had no choice but to write down my address. However, I told him I never received guests and was living with my younger son. My daughter was working as a farm labourer in the suburbs and usually there was only me, I was often out buying food and not necessarily in the house. We hurriedly parted.

I had given my address to a few acquaintances, including my brother's son, but nobody had ever come to see me or written to me. I had long since forgotten about the encounter at the Fulong Temple.

Now, three or four months later, staring at the careful writing on the envelope, I couldn't help thinking back on that meeting. Perhaps it was from Mr Sha? I opened it. But it was from another friend, Qin, who had probably got the address from Sha.

The letter read, 'Qin asks you to go to the Peace Restaurant at three o'clock on such-and-such a day for a cup of coffee.'

Should I go? The only person I could have discussed it with was my younger son. The child had long forgotten his father's friends, so what could he say? I had to make my own decisions about everything. Even so, I showed him the letter. He thought it wouldn't do any harm. He told me to be careful not to say too much and to be aware of the surroundings. He was trying to join the Young Communist League, so as an ordinary person who had made mistakes I would do well to follow his advice.

I made my way to the Peace Restaurant at Dongan Market. I spied a tall thin man at the door. It was Old Nie. I hurried across and we smiled at one another.

'Did you guess?' he asked.

'Who else could it have been?'

'Let's go in and sit down.'

'Such a luxurious place? Why don't we go for a walk instead. I've never been in such a place.'

'Why not go in and have a look?'

I followed him in, looking timidly from side to side. Noticing, he joked, 'It's rather like when we were doing underground work in Shanghai. But now we're afraid of our own people.'

We both smiled bitterly.

We found a compartment and sat down.

'What do you want?' he asked.

'Just a coffee.'

He also ordered a coffee, together with a plate of Western cakes.

'The reason I asked you to come was because you have an old friend who has gone to great lengths to discover your whereabouts.'

'Who?' I was surprised anyone would dare make inquiries about us.

'Xiong Zimin. I went to see him when he was attending the Third National People's Congress. He asked me if there was any news about Zhang Guangren* or Zhang's family. I just shook my head. Then he said, "How could that be? Surely they can't have locked up his wife and children? What crime have they committed?" All I could say was that his wife had been freed, we had seen her. Then, he told me to find you no matter what, and to tell you to go and see him.'

'Where do I go?'

'Write to the National People's Congress and ask them. I'm worried he might have gone away now the Congress is over. But he left a message telling me to find out about Old Hu and request a meeting. He was furious. He said when we went to prison for the revolution, we were at least allowed to visit prisoners and send them things.'

---

* Hu Feng is Zhang Guangren's pen name.

The conversation upset me. It implied I was to blame for not rushing about on F's behalf. But how was he to know that when I had asked to see F or tried to send him things, the Ministry of Public Security had flatly refused to stretch the rules.

I told Old Nie all this. I also told him about my long-standing secret guess that F was perhaps no longer of this world . . . At this point, I broke into tears.

'That's hardly likely, you needn't worry. I've heard he's been to hospital. We thought they would release him, but they didn't. Nothing is going to happen, they won't do anything. Take things philosophically, don't be pessimistic, things can't get worse. The best thing is to ask again to be allowed to see him, to write to him, and to send him things.'

To contain my emotion, I raised the coffee cup to my lips.

The previous winter, the children and I had gone to see *Dagger Society* at the Tianqiao Theatre. I had spotted Old Nie and his wife. He had just been transferred back to Beijing from the Great Northern Wilderness, where he had undergone reform through labour. He had not yet had his rightist hat removed. He was embarrassed and didn't dare approach us. He just shot us a distant smile, and then dashed off into the auditorium. During the intermission, Big Sister Ying sought us out for a chat. It turned out his daughter had insisted he come to see her perform, it was his first outing. She asked about us, and I answered in as few words as possible. After the performance, I saw them again at the exit and Big Sister Ying again fought her way through the crowd and said she would come to see us in a few days' time. Third Sister (their relative) saw me but gave no greeting. In the past, she had always been warm, and had sympathised with F. But her troubled life over several years had left her cold and haggard. I could understand, so I fought my way to the front and left ahead of them.

This meeting was different. Sitting opposite me was a dignified senior cadre, neatly and fastidiously dressed, untrammelled by convention, a suitable guest at such a top-grade establishment.

'I suppose you often come here,' I said. 'Have you got your old job back?'

'I don't care whether I get it back or not, I wouldn't go anyway, all I do is collect my salary each month.'

'That's good, you can do creative work at home.'

'I no longer write, I just read. Recently I read Zhuangzi. It was interesting, I understood things I'd never understood before.'

I didn't dare reply, I had never understood Zhuangzi.

While drinking my coffee, I looked around. The restaurant filled up. The staff escorted guests to prepared tables. They must have been regulars. I glanced at the menu. Western food was at least three yuan per person and other dishes were two to three yuan. Ice cream was one or two yuan. A meal would have cost at least 10 to 20 yuan. This was an eye-opener. There were still rich people in Beijing.

Seeing how surprised I was, Old Nie said coldly, 'They're spending remittances from abroad. They get a discount.'

'Really? We had better go, then, and let them spend their remittances.'

He paid the bill and asked the waitress to wrap some cakes for me to take back for the three children. I was embarrassed – it had cost him five yuan, and now I was supposed to take the cakes home. And the three children were actually one 16-year-old boy.

Xiaoshan had arrived home before me and was waiting anxiously. I told him what had happened. He thought I should write to Xiong Zimin as soon as possible. If someone was concerned about us, we should say thank you.

I posted the letter. For a long time there was no reply. I thought he had probably returned to Wuhan. I didn't have his Wuhan address, and waiting patiently was no option. So I decided to act on his advice and write a second time to the Ministry of Public Security.

Hu Feng had got to know Xiong Zimin in 1927, during the Great Revolution. After the defeat of the revolution, Xiong and Li Da and others ran a bookshop in Shanghai that published Hu

Feng's first translation, of a Soviet science-fiction novel called *Foreign Devil*, about an imperialist agent in the Soviet Union after the October Revolution. The bookshop was closed down because it published progressive literature. Afterwards, he returned to Wuhan and did some trading. After the start of the war against Japan, the Eighth Route Army set up an office in Wuhan, where he did some jobs, given his past links and the fact that he was a local man. When Dong's wife arrived in Wuhan, she lived in Xiong's house. Hu Feng met Dong there. Xiong was happy to distribute Hu Feng's journal *July*, which played a role in the war. The office helped raise money for the journal and supported its publication. Hu Feng knew Xiong had no money and couldn't even pay his contributors. He himself didn't take a cent for his work. Hu Feng and Xiong remained friends until 1954. When Xiong came to Beijing with his wife on holiday, he came specially to see us. He was not a literary person, but he had a strong sense of justice. He urged Hu Feng to talk less, write less, and find a simple job. But Hu Feng didn't know how to play it safe and always ended up saying what he thought, so he became the victim of an unprecedented onslaught.

I knew Xiong was on the National People's Congress, but I didn't dare bother him. I was feeling gloomy. I didn't believe there was anyone in the world good enough not to fear getting into trouble. I thought it was normal for people to avoid me. Now Xiong Zimin had got someone to seek me out, I was happy and astonished.

In my letter to the Ministry I explained that Hu Feng's old friend Xiong Zimin was a delegate on the National People's Congress and had criticised me for not asking where Hu Feng was being held, since that was both allowed by law and a matter of basic humanity.

To my surprise, there was a response. I received a letter saying I could send some things for Hu Feng, but it repeated the previous message, that he needed nothing.

I prepared some foodstuffs. I thought, who knows where he's being held? Perhaps somewhere outside Beijing. So I bought him some tins of anchovies, red-cooked beef, peaches, pineapple, chocolate biscuits and a pound of toffee. For a normal person that doesn't sound much, but for someone who had been locked up for ten years it would be a feast. (Later, he told me he couldn't even bear to throw away the toffee wrappers or the tin labels. He gazed at them every day, as if looking again at the outside world.)

I went to the Ministry of Public Security at the appointed time and place. I asked the police guard the way and had to walk for a while before I saw the waiting room. The attendant made a phone call, and asked me to be seated. He probably thought I had come to deliver a report or receive a briefing.

Apart from a man called Shi, my permanent contact, an even more senior cadre appeared, also very courteous. He looked at the things I'd brought and said:

'We can get them to him quickly.' He also said, 'Actually, there's nothing he needs. You should trust the Party. We're all committed to reforming him.'

I wasn't prepared to abandon the chance to see Hu Feng, so I asked again. I even said some old friends thought he was no longer alive.

This time, the reply was not completely dismissive: 'I'll tell senior levels. We'll study the situation and let you know.'

On that note of hope, and of joy at the thought that he would receive the food, I left.

A month later, I received Xiong Zimin's reply. The People's National Congress had forwarded my letter, but he was convalescing somewhere else, hence the delay. He expressed his deep concern for the family and urged me to request a meeting with F.

I did so, and I also said the People's Congress delegate Xiong Zimin had blamed me for not daring to show my concern for Hu Feng. You haven't let me see him for ten years, how can I answer old friends' letters, how can I behave as an upright person . . .

I don't know if it was because of a change in the situation or because I mentioned the People's Congress, but a week later Shi and the old cadre visited me to say permission had been granted. Naturally, they urged me to help him by mentioning things that would assist his ideological reform. The Party wanted me to play a positive role.

They gave me the address and a request form for a visit. The old cadre gave me directions on how to get there, where to change buses, and so on. I was grateful, for I'd never been in the remote suburbs. Without his help, I don't know how I would have got there.

2

Reunion

Ten years without ever seeing someone dear to you. What will he be like? Will he be the man in my dreams? Will I recognise him? I don't know how many times I imagined it, how many times I prepared my little speeches. That night, I stayed awake until the sky had turned white and then jumped out of bed and hurried to the bus stop.

I caught the first bus to Deshengmen, but when we arrived the first bus to the suburbs had already left. I waited for the eight o'clock bus to Shahe, where I had to change again. My belly was empty. Luckily, Shahe is a big town with several restaurants, so I had a bowl of soybean milk and a deep-fried dough cake before boarding the bus to Qincheng.

In the Cultural Revolution, quite a few cadres were kept in Qincheng, so it's no longer a mystery. In those days, however, you weren't supposed to talk about it.

The bus was small and rickety. Luckily it was early, so there were still seats, which made it less uncomfortable. The road was smooth, lined on each side by tall white poplars and low willows. Xiaotangshan, my stop, is a market town. A bit further on was an expanse of maize, a bright green curtain. In between were occasional patches of millet, an inlaid decorative pattern typical of the northern landscape. If I'd been on an outing, I would have thought it lovely.

I arrived at my destination. I waited until the other passengers had left before entering a small side road they had told me about. There was an iron gate and a sentry box.

A soldier of the People's Liberation Army stepped out in front of me. I handed over my things. He made a phone call and told me to go in.

Secretary Shi had arrived ahead of me, by car, and came out with a duty officer. He led me along a concrete path lined on either side by flowerbeds. There were small buildings along the way, with drawn curtains. We walked straight on, to a reception point on the ground floor of a high building. Deep inside the main hall, I could see people escorting a man in a blue shirt and trousers in my direction. Not until he was in front of me could I tell that it was F. In the past, he had a ring of black hair either side of his head, now he was completely bald.

Someone who had always been respected as master of the house was now brought to me under escort. I wanted to hug him and weep. But people were watching me, so I resisted the impulse. He walked up, gripped my hand, and looked at me with his sparkling eyes. He was the same man he had always been. His grip was still firm, and so were his eyes. We stood gazing at one another, like people who could never gaze enough.

The duty officer sent us into the reception area, two rooms connected by a small window. Normally, the visitor and the visited were probably separated by the window, but we were allowed to sit opposite one another across a table. Secretary Shi sat in the other room.

Neither of us knew who should say the first word. Finally, I started:

'You're well, I hope. Did you receive the things I brought?'

'I'm well. Yes, I received them.'

'The children send their greetings.'

'Oh!' His eyes widened and began to flash.

'Xiaoshan finishes high school next year. Xiaofeng didn't get into university, she has become a farm labourer.'

'Good. Let Xiaoshan be a worker.'

'They all hope you can come home soon. You must strengthen your thought reform.'

'How can you do thought reform in solitary confinement?'

The secretary in the next room snorted. F shot him a glance and fell silent.

I felt miserable and awkward. When the secretary had told me of the visit, he had made clear I was to help F. But how could I help?

'You can examine idealist literary thought, that's probably the main issue.'

I immediately regretted my remark. All I could see were his two eyes piercing me. In the past, he would have flown into a rage, but now he lowered his head with a pained expression and let out a long sigh.

'You had best not ask about that, that's a problem I can't solve. If I'm wrong about literary thought, that's a question of understanding, not of politics.'

'Wouldn't it be even better to improve your knowledge? Idealism isn't so terrible. Even Hegel needed Marx to correct his idealism. Wouldn't it be better if you yourself were to investigate and correct possible idealism in your literary thought? Who can say he is one hundred per cent Marxist?'

He was really angry, but he managed to control himself. The secretary at the window gave me a look, perhaps to express satisfaction.

F changed the subject.

'I've written a lot of poems – well, not written, but composed and memorised. Some are for you, some are for the children. I'll recite one for you, perhaps you'll understand it. I called the one about you "In Praise of Long-Lasting Love":

'Despite hardship, you are still devoted to your teaching.
When you see young people, it is as if you see spring.
The world is often difficult,
But you delight in people's passion.
You can plant beautiful roses
But you can't buy bread.
You turn myths into children's stories,
Your heart is always young.

'There are lots more verses, ten in all. I called my poem about Xiaofeng "In Praise of Goodness", all I can remember are some bits from near the end:

> 'When you were young,
> You were separated from your parents
> By great distances.
> The Pacific War broke out,
> And families were dispersed.'

I started sobbing.

'Please don't be sad. Let's recite Xiaoshan's. It's called "In Praise of Dreaming":

> 'You asked your daddy when you wanted him to buy you
> books,
> You shouted for mummy when you wanted your pencil
> sharpened.
> Big sister has a loud voice,
> Grandma has hearing problems.

'It also has ten verses.'

'I won't be able to memorise them for the children.'

'It doesn't matter. I have another called "In Praise of the Forget-Me-Not". The prison superintendent asked me to write down my thoughts about revisionism. I'll recite a few lines:

> 'The forget-me-not thinks far ahead.
> It thinks of the past to look into the future.
> Retirement is not the same as degradation,
> It doesn't change one's piety.
> Emotional in battle,
> Your pursuits keep you busy far into the night.
> Strive to avoid being wasteful in your work,
> Be creative but avoid empty talk.
> Do all you can to convey a true sense of responsibility,
> Sincerely explain how to be successors in the cause.'

The cadre barked out, 'No more poems, if you have anything to say, say it quickly.'

F had been happily reciting, I looked at him in confusion. He shook his head and stood up to go, as if humiliated. I could feel things weren't going well, so I pushed him back onto the chair.

'I brought you some biscuits, you can have one when you feel hungry. I also brought you a bag of glucose, a jar of apple purée, and two packets of chocolate. Is there anything else you would like? Oh, I intended to bring you that set of Marx and Engels' *Complete Works* in Japanese, but I was afraid I might get lost, so I left it at home. I'll bring it next time. I also brought a tai-chi chart. I hope you can learn how to do tai-chi from it. You must look after your health, and exercise properly.'

'I will, I can do that in the cell. Next time bring some books, food's not important.'

'I've heard it's not easy to buy good books.'

'Have you finished?' urged the cadre.

'Tell the children I wish them happiness. If my son Xiaogu returns, don't let him come here.'

He was led away. At the door, he turned round and shook my hand, with a smile.

The smile consoled me. It was like the smiles he used to give me.

Holding back my tears, I left. When I reached the entrance, the sentry stopped me. Secretary Shi came rushing over and we stood by the gate until the pock-marked duty officer arrived to sign my visitor's form. Then the guard let me out.

I had set out at six and arrived at ten. Now, it was eleven. I waited for the bus and squeezed aboard. At Shahe, I changed again. It was gone three when I arrived home. I was exhausted and sank onto the bed.

Was there anyone I could share my agony with? Anyone to listen to me cry my heart out? No. Gradually, I drifted into a

lethargic sleep, but I jolted awake at the thought that my youngest son would soon be back. I jumped off the bed, pulled myself
together, and went into the kitchen.

Ten years. Finally I'd seen him and knew he was alive. After
years of numbness, I was unable to calm down. Now I was waiting for my son, so I could share my feelings.

The first thing he asked was 'Did you see father?'

'What do you mean, father?'

He corrected himself: 'You saw him, you saw dad!'

'Yes, I saw him. He looked well. We talked for an hour or
two.

'He recites poems to himself. He recited some to me, but I can't
remember them. The one about me was called "In Praise of
Long-Lasting Love". He composed one about your sister, "In
Praise of Goodness". The one about older brother was called "In
Praise of Sincerity".'

'He chose good names.'

'Yours was "In Praise of Dreams".'

'Why did he call it that? Do I daydream? Do I like dreaming?
I don't think so.'

'I think he meant you've always been as if in a dream. You
weren't even eight. You didn't know anything. I do remember
some lines:

> 'Your heart is as pure as your eyes are bright,
> So naïve and innocent.
> As soon as you finish supper
> You open the door and off you go;
> When the police arrived
> We pretended they were guests.

'That was when they came to arrest us. We couldn't tell you, we
just urged you to sleep. When they took us away in the middle of
the night, we kissed you and wished you sweet dreams.'

I couldn't continue.

One day, Old Tian suddenly turned up. I hadn't seen him in ten years. When I opened the door, I gasped. None of our old friends had visited me for years, mostly because it was difficult to communicate, or they had lost their freedom. I also felt it was unwise for them to seek trouble. But here he was, calm and self-possessed, not caring what might happen. He told me he was going to see a friend who lived nearby, to learn some English. He knew I lived here, so he had dropped by.

He wanted to know about Hu. I told him what had happened. I added:

'He's incorrigible, do you know he's composing poems in his cell? Some are about his family, others about his friends. He chose a beautiful name for them, "Songs in Memory of Spring". He recited some, but I can't remember them.'

'You have to keep up your morale. Then you'll never be defeated.'

We told each other our news of the last few years, and about our friends. I felt as if he had opened a window and a small breeze had blown in from another world. I'd been too out of touch. I knew this or that literary figure had climbed the ladder, fallen into disgrace, or played up to those in power, but I also knew a single wrong word, however true, could lead to the break-up of a family. All these perils left me terror-stricken.

He hadn't been implicated in our case, but he was still wearing three denunciatory 'hats' put on even earlier. Now his entire family of eight people was living on 100 yuan a month.

I was moved most by the case of Old Nie and his wife. In 1955, Hu Feng and his friends were branded a 'counter-revolutionary clique'. I had assumed it wouldn't affect the Nies. Ever since the start of the campaign to criticise him, F had avoided discussing literary issues with Old Nie, for fear that he might say something wrong, so he hadn't let him know about F's 300,000-word memo about the situation in literary and art circles. At the time, Old Nie wasn't interested in such subjects, he was only interested in classical literature. But somehow or another he had got dragged into it, and was even expelled from the Party. Afterwards, he stopped going to work and just read books at home. I suppose you could say he shut himself up to ponder his mistakes.

In 1957, Chairman Mao summoned help for his campaign to rectify the Party. Big Sister Ying was studying at the Socialist College. When she heard the news, she was excited. Inspired by her love for the Party and the country, she resolved to bare her heart. In the spirit of say all you know, speak without reserve, she offered some comments, including about the Hu Feng case. When she arrived home she discussed it with Old Nie and wrote down her opinions. They had got to know Hu Feng in 1929 in Japan. Later, they had worked together in the anti-Japanese movement and had helped F publish a mimeograph, *New Culture*, which propagandised for the resistance and the revolution. As a result, they had been arrested and deported. Later, they joined the League of Left-Wing Writers under Lu Xun. How can you conclude someone is a counter-revolutionary on the basis of a few brief notes? They were at a loss to understand. So Ying wrote down her views and Old Nie revised them. How were they to know that shortly afterwards some students at Beijing University also raised the Hu Feng case and members of the Democratic Party made a lot of criticisms of the Communist Party? The rectification campaign turned into an Anti-Rightist Movement. Ying had to go on stage and receive the masses' criticism. Then the investigation switched to Old Nie, and the pair were branded rightists.

Nie was sent to the Great Northern Wilderness to do manual labour. Ying was removed from her leadership post and transferred to the People's Political Consultative Conference to edit biographical materials written by pardoned Kuomintang officials.*

When I heard this, I remembered how Old Nie had invited me

---

* The Kuomintang or KMT, sometimes romanised as Guomindang (GMD), was the dominant party in the early Republic of China, from 1912 onwards.

to meet him. I was suddenly overwhelmed with respect for what he had done. Would a lapdog or a coward have done it? He was not the man he had once been – he no longer had the carefree air of a literary celebrity. He had been tempered by hardship and become a man dedicated to justice and loyalty, a rarity.

Tian sat for a couple of hours and then said he had to hurry home, to cook for his child. I said:

'I'm really grateful for your visit. But don't come again. You'll get into trouble.'

He gave me a mischievous smile. Gesturing at his aluminium mess tin, he said:

'In it is a steel needle for doing acupuncture. If anyone comes in, I'll say I'm your acupuncturist.'

I laughed.

A talented author ought to wield the pen, not the needle. A warrior on the literary front had become a kindly father who cooked for his child. What a change!

3

A Gaol Visit, Not a Family Visit

Carrying two string-tied bundles of Marx and Engels' *Complete Works* in Japanese, I set out again on the journey to Qincheng. Having learned my lesson, I ate a bowl of noodles before setting out. But there were drawbacks: it was the rush hour, and I had to push my way on and off with my two bundles. Even though I managed to squeeze through, there were no seats left.

At Shahe, where I had to change, I didn't dare leave the parcels unattended. I sat under the hot midsummer sun watching the watermelon sellers on the opposite pavement and the juice dribbling down the chins of their customers. But I couldn't risk running over to buy a slice, so I just sat and watched.

When the bone-shaker from Shahe to Qincheng turned up, it was hard enough to stand, let alone get a seat, especially with the books. I had to keep a tight hold on them and at the same time sway and bob in time with the bus. By the time I reached Qincheng, my hands ached and my leg had gone numb. Luckily, it was the terminus, so I could take my time alighting.

There were some PLA men on the pavement greeting an old lady from the countryside. Some took her parcel, others took her basket. She was probably visiting a relative in the guards' unit. One younger-looking PLA man, perhaps the leader, had nothing to carry and ran over and offered to help me. Without thinking, I declined.

Actually, I was tired and hot, so I dropped behind and hid in the trees. I put the books down and sat on them. Here, I was out of the sun, and in a while a breeze blew up and the sweat on me dried. I stayed sitting there until the PLA men had disappeared through the gate, and then I got up and walked over to it. It was ages before anyone called me in – perhaps they were having a midday nap. I also had to wait in the reception area. I flicked through a list of presents you were allowed to bring. On the last page it said, 'Watermelons – one.' I thought, next time I'll bring one, he's probably not eaten one for years.

The duty officer let him in and left. We sat opposite each other, just the two of us. It was almost like sitting together at home, except I felt so wretched. I told him the children's news, and gave him daughter's letter. He read it and flew into a rage.

'So I'm supposed to learn from Puyi! Who's Puyi? A feudal emperor, who lived a corrupt life exploiting the people. If the Government helped him become a new man, that's because the Party and the people are lenient. Can I negate myself in the same way he did? Was I wrong to study Marxism-Leninism? I loyally followed the Party, everything I did was for the Party, was that wrong too? Of course I know the secret of how to survive under a big hat, but is that being responsible to the Party and the people? Or to oneself? Is that what I should do? I can't admit to things I haven't done, and whether what I have done is wrong or not can't be answered in one sentence. I can only reach a proper conclusion by spending time studying Marxism-Leninism and going deep into the realities of life. That's not something you can do in solitary confinement. Is that my fault?'

He was worked up, like when he used to argue with people in the past. I said:

'Don't get angry. The child means well. All she wants is for your problem to be resolved. Then we can all be together, as a family.'

It seemed like he was about to sound off again, but it was dangerous for him to speak his mind, so I distracted him.

'Today I brought the Japanese Marx and Engels. Two big bundles, it tired me out.' I told him about the journey, and about getting off the last bus, and how the PLA had welcomed the old lady visiting her family, and how difficult it had been for me, on a prison visit. I couldn't help moaning a bit.

He looked surprised. Naturally, he couldn't understand these things. Changing the topic, he asked:

'Are you all right? You look thin. Your complexion is not good.'

'Last year I had neurasthenia. I couldn't sleep and was always dizzy. I took medicine, but it didn't help. Then I learned tai-chi and my spirits picked up. I could sleep peacefully. That chart I brought, do you follow it each day? You've got to exercise to stay fit. Do you need anything else?'

'Sometimes the food here is hard to stomach, a bit of chilli oil would help. What I really need is books. If there's anything worth reading, give me it. You can read the books first. Then we can talk about them.'

'Read? I stopped reading long ago. I subscribe to a couple of magazines, but I have no wish to go deeply into the sort of questions the press discusses, it's enough to know a bit about what's going on nationally and internationally.'

I wanted to talk about the children, the mainstay of my life.

'Xiaoshan finishes high school next year. Last time you said you wanted him to be a worker. Obviously it's something I've thought about. I wanted him to go to technical college. Elder sister was even keener. She sat the exam for university twice and was not admitted, it was wounding. But elder brother said he would go to senior high, where he would get a broader education. Things might change in future, and then he can try to get into university. He said the Party's policy was that parents can't choose, everyone has to make their own choice.'

He looked distressed. Suddenly, he seemed much older. I stumbled on. The duty officer put his head round the door. I thought, it's getting late, I should go. After I had delivered a few more exhortations, he gripped my hand and went.

September arrived. I thought maybe he needed some clothes, so I requested another visit, but no reply came.

Nie visited me. He was wearing a navy blue serge suit and carrying a bundle wrapped in newspaper. He looked debonair. He asked:

'Any news about Hu?'

'None. I haven't seen him in more than a month. The authorities haven't replied to my letter.'

I told him about F's most recent letter and showed him the book list he had enclosed. He said in a low voice:

'So he's still doing literary research. So many books, it's not easy.' He added, 'I bumped into Pan Hannian.* He's living at the Organisation Department. He gets a hundred yuan a month pocket money. It seems Hu's problem will soon be resolved.'

I thought, perhaps the reason they've not let me see him for so long is because a change is in the offing. He told me some other things. I was much more optimistic after hearing him.

I asked about Big Sister Ying. He said, 'She goes to work every day at the People's Political Consultative Conference. I told her to retire, but she doesn't want to. Her morale is low. I don't dare tell her about you two. I'm afraid she'll become an insomniac.'

As he was getting ready to go, I noticed his newspaper wrapping had broken, so I gave him some extra sheets. I saw its contents: a poorly produced lithographic edition of Zhuangzi, on glazed paper. I couldn't help asking, 'Can you understand that? The ink smell gets up my nose.'

'This edition is hard to get.'

'We have a large-character edition engraved on wood.'

He asked me to find it, for an article he was writing. It was in a wooden box on top of the bookshelf. He steadied the table and I put a stool on it and climbed up and got the box. It contained several volumes of Zhuangzi, as well as Guanzi and Han Feizi. He wanted them all.

---

* A leader of Chinese Communist intelligence in the 1930s, accused of treason in 1955 and posthumously rehabilitated.

F had picked them up by chance in Shanghai at the end of the war. It seemed unlikely F would study them. 'A precious sword for a person of high endeavour' seemed a worthy end.

As he was about to leave, I said:

'Give Big Sister Ying my address. I would love to see her.'

'I will. I'll tell her when she's feeling a bit better, physically and mentally.'

Not long after that, I wrote to her. So she would know it was an old friend, I addressed it to Zhiqin, the name she used at school.

Three days later, one wet afternoon, she turned up under an umbrella. As soon as I opened the door, she rushed towards me without even pausing to put the umbrella down. 'My dear Tu, so this is where you live!' I flung myself at her, and the two of us stood exclaiming and laughing in the corridor. When we eventually made our way into the lighted room, I saw she was drenched. I poured her some water so she could wash, and told her to take off her coat. She paid me no attention, but simply told me to sit down so we could talk.

I had never been close to her. She was F's friend. There was a certain sympathy between us, but that was all. But now we were like the oldest of friends. I needed her forthrightness and lack of inhibition, typical of a northern woman.

In her loud voice, she told me:

'Tu, I almost missed your letter! When the old man in the reception office saw it, he said "Zhiqin? That's a girl in my village, there's no one of that name here." I thought that can't be me, but then I saw it was. A near miss! How's Old Hu? Is he all right?'

'He looks all right, but he's gone bald.'

'That's a small sacrifice. He never had much hair anyway.'

We burst out laughing, and our distress ebbed away.

We sat there side by side. Even though her voice and smile hadn't changed, nine years of hardship were etched onto her brow. She was an activist who loved her work and social activities, and suddenly she was consigned to a job of no consequence, with a daily pile of silent documents her only contact. How could she be calm and happy? But her hearty voice and resolute manner remained. She had not been defeated: she was still doing things she was good at.

We talked about many people and subjects, and I took inspiration from her stories. Many people had been entered into the 'other' register, for disreputable people, including some who previously had been powerful. Where did we stand in the scale of things? I was low-level and had never sought fame or wealth, I had never requested anything, and now I was even less likely to have grand hopes. I only wanted what any wife or mother would, to let our family live together.

Xiaoshan was home for the holidays. He recognised Ying and called her 'auntie'.

Ying couldn't hide her delight. 'How big Xiaoshan has grown, he's like an adult.' They chatted about his school. I could see there was nothing that didn't interest her, so I left them talking and went to cook dinner.

After dinner, we again sat for a while. Before we knew it, it was eight. She said she had to go. I tried to stop her, but she had to work the next day. She said she would come again. I took her to the tram stop. She had to cross Beijing, from the eastern outskirts to the western outskirts. This made me anxious, for she was no longer the Big Sister Ying of ten years ago. That made me treasure her visit even more.

4

The Third Meeting

It was deep autumn. The Ministry of Public Security wrote asking me to visit F. The letter arrived in the afternoon and I had to go the next morning, so I had no time for shopping. I took some books I had bought and some apples, and I popped into the food shop to buy some chilli oil. When I reached Shahe it was eleven. I ate a bowl of noodles and caught the bus to Qincheng. I didn't have to wait long. The person on duty led him out and left us alone.

F had changed his clothes. He was wearing a dark blue long-sleeved jacket and trousers, both unlined, with a pullover peeping out from underneath. It was my cream jumper. It turned out that after his arrest he'd written home to ask for clothes and my mother and our son had got my jumper mixed up with his woollen underclothes.

Seeing me shake my head, he chuckled self-deprecatingly and said:

'It's good, it means I can always be with you. I use it as the lowest layer.'

I explained why I hadn't come recently. He turned the criticism on himself. He was too thoughtless, too ignorant of the outside world.

This time everything seemed more natural. He started off by saying:

'Tell me about your lives over the last few years. I've been constantly anxious about you.'

'There's nothing to tell. You just live. At the start, I wanted to die. After you left, they took me away too. They kept me locked up for 70 months. It was thanks to mother they released me. She died, and they had her body in the morgue. Xiaofeng asked the Ministry of Public Security to let me go home to take care of the funeral. They let me. It was the three-year period of hardship, so I kept things simple. I didn't tell the relatives, they wouldn't have been able to come anyway. I cremated her, as quickly as I could. I've got the ashes. When I get the chance, I'll send them back to Changzhou.'

He lowered his head and said in a quiet voice:

'That pitiful old lady, she gave so much and received so little. We should be ashamed. She shared our hardship for so many years. I thought when things improved, we could make her life better, but instead we made things harder for her. I always thought I would see her when I came out and be able to make amends.'

'During my 70 months of introspection, the entire family depended on her. She was almost 80. Xiaoshan had just turned eight, and Xiaofeng was only 16 and at high school. Xiaogu was in Nanjing, at university. Mother looked after everything, single-handedly. I dread to think what would have happened but for her. When she fell ill and went to hospital, she pointed at the door and told Xiaofeng to lock it. She lived with us because she loved me so much. She helped out in everything. We were selfish, we didn't sufficiently value her labour, her dedication to us. Because of me and her beloved grandchildren, she could never bear to go. She couldn't even get her dying wish to see her daughter one last time.'

I choked back the sobs. F wept with me, unable to find words with which to console me. He pulled down his sleeve to wipe his face and tried to wipe mine, but I took out a hankie. Seeing him cry made me think of my mother, how she had cried and wiped away my tears.

There was something else I had to tell him. Otherwise, he might blame me.

'We no longer have that house. You put so much effort into it, but it's been torn down. When I was released, we went to live in a compound in Dongcheng. It was old and dilapidated. Mother got pneumonia. She hadn't eaten well for years. How could an 80-year-old survive that! I'm to blame. We are responsible for her suffering.'

Again, I started crying, and so did he.

I asked about prison life. He said, 'I was interrogated hundreds of times, but I don't think any big problems emerged. I can't think of anything worse, if they had killed me, it would have been fine, because it wouldn't have been my mistake, it would even have brought me some relief. What worries me now is my young friends – I don't know what tribulations they have suffered. I've never acted out of personal interest, I've never chased fame or profit. I acted as any Chinese should. I had no evil intent, and whatever happens I will accept the Party's ruling. I hope you do too. Don't harbour illusions, believe in the Party and the masses. Perhaps I won't live to hear the verdict, but I'm a materialist and I believe history will be fair. But you should prepare for the worst.'

I understood. I could only support him. As he said, you can't barter your principles. Perhaps hardships would beset us, but I could bear it.

He seemed to relax, and there was even the trace of a smile of self-belief. I also felt at ease. The ten years of family dispersal belonged to the past. What more was there to fear?

I looked at my watch – it was almost four. I said it's started getting dark sooner, I must go. He shot to his feet.

'Right, you go. Next time, don't bring any books, the Marx and Engels are enough. Also, I have a premonition things are about to change for the better.'

We shook hands in the hall. Seeing his tragic face pained me. I said, 'Don't be sad. Mother lived into her eighties. She lived her full span. As long as we're all safe, our family is indestructible.' He gripped me with both hands.

I took my visitor's pass to the front entrance, but the guard noticed I hadn't been signed out. I paced back and forth. It was deep autumn and the sun was dropping, so it began to feel cold. The wind blew, fiercer than in the city, and cut into my face. But I had to wait. A long-distance bus started out. Was it the last one? Even though my husband was in that big building, he couldn't come out to protect me. I was on a prison visit. I couldn't go in, nor could I leave. All I could do was stand there, and wait. My feet started aching, but there was nowhere to sit. I got thirsty, but there was no water. I was a prisoner's dependant – who would show sympathy? And this was a prison, dedicated to enforcing the law.

Just after five, the pock-marked duty officer appeared from nowhere. Seeing me standing there timidly, he looked shocked and said:

'What, haven't you left yet?' He tore the form from my hand and signed it.

I took hold of his arm.

'Are there any more buses?' If not, I had to make sure he didn't leave, and that he thought of a way out for me. There were no villages or shops. Where could I go?

He glanced at his watch. 'The last bus leaves at six.' Saying that, he disappeared.

I walked over to the main road. Four or five people were waiting at the bus stop, which cheered me up. Whatever happened, I would have company. The sky turned yellow-grey. Summer's green curtain of crops had vanished. Not a stalk was left, just an expanse of ploughed yellow earth. The seeds were preparing for the long winter.

From somewhere in the distance, a flock of red-bellied birds flew by chirping loudly. Then came a group of young peasants on their way home from a building site. They were riding brand-new bikes and wearing big black overcoats, unbuttoned so you could see the white lining of their cotton-padded jackets and red sweatshirts. They flashed past, leaving behind a streak of dust and peals of laughter.

The sky was dark by now, and there was no sign of a bus. More and more people began to appear – there were more than a dozen of us in the freezing wilderness, chatting or gossiping. The others were probably regulars from nearby villages, waiting to catch the last bus back into the city after their weekend break.

Two distant lights appeared on the pitch-black highway, like dragon's eyes. We cheered up. Everyone stepped out into the road. But the dragon turned out to be a lorry whose driver sped by without a glance in our direction.

Everyone began cursing. 'Do they expect us to walk to Xiaotangshan?' I was the only woman. I became a focus of interest. They asked me, 'What will you do?' One said, 'She'll go back to the farm team.' 'If you're from the farm, they have lots of small buses going into town. Why didn't you take one of those?' I didn't reply.

Just as we were cursing and talking, a bus slid noiselessly to a halt in front of us. Leaving our worries behind, we squeezed aboard. Some demanded to know why it was so late. The driver said the bus had broken down and taken a long time to repair. Only one of the headlights was working, so he'd barely managed to get here. Yet it seemed to me we were fortunate to be sitting in the belly even of a one-eyed dragon.

In this way, we rattled into town.

Although F and I had met three times, we had only been able to talk for four or five hours. I still knew little about his situation, for I felt there were things I shouldn't ask about and things he shouldn't talk about. So I knew nothing at all about how he had spent his ten years in gaol.

5

Warm Current, Cold Wave

In early November, the Ministry of Public Security summoned me. This time I was taken directly to reception. Immediately I mentioned the person's name at the wicket, there was a phone call. A woman in her thirties came out and identified me instantly. She led me to a visiting room. The first thing she said was 'You've not changed, you're the same as ever.' I wondered why I couldn't place her. Then I realised, there were all sorts of ways she could study me.

A short fat cadre emerged. He intoned, 'On the basis of your behaviour over the last few years, we have reached a final verdict.' He handed me a sheet, sixteenmo size, printed in conspicuous type with the words 'No indictment to be laid'. Underneath was my original name, birthplace, and work unit. It said I was a professional writer belonging to the Chinese Writers' Association who had been detained in 1955 for joining Hu Feng's counter-revolutionary clique. Before that I had helped Hu Feng with *July*, *Hope*, and Hope Press. Later, I had helped transcribe the 300,000-word memo, which is why I was considered a core member of the clique. Because I had behaved well in custody, a decision had been taken not to charge me.

Inwardly I felt distaste, like eating sour fruit, yet I also felt our troubles were heading for resolution.

They watched me, as if expecting me to say something. I said, 'Where would I have acquired such ability, you overestimate me. But I sincerely thank the Party for its magnanimity, in future I will strengthen my ideological remoulding.'

'Don't let up on your remoulding. We're confident you can succeed. Help Hu Feng stabilise his position.'

The woman comrade added, 'He's stubborn. He hasn't admitted his guilt. If he doesn't do so, we'll have to use other methods.' I listened in terror. The comrade in charge brought out two bundles from behind the sofa and said, 'These are your old manuscripts, which we confiscated.'

The woman comrade said, 'Check whether any are missing. Then sign.'

I didn't bother to untie them. I just flicked through them and signed. Not without emotion, I said, 'I've long since given up on all that, I no longer intend to do literary work.'

Adopting a severe attitude, the comrade in charge said, 'Such thinking is incorrect. Through ideological remoulding, you can serve the people even better. Try harder.'

I realised that what I had said was wrong under the circumstances. Luckily, they weren't in charge of my case, or I would have got a telling off. All I could do was smile bitterly.

Back home, I read through the decision not to indict me. I knew nothing about the law, but I knew that it would not be of the slightest use to me. Even the Constitution could be amended at will. I remember how happy F had been the first time he got a copy of the Constitution and how he had given an unfinalised manuscript version to our elder son. He said, 'Now our country has a Constitution. Everything has to be done according to the Constitution. Make sure you study it well.' Who would have thought that in 1955 first Pan Hannian and then Hu Feng would be locked up and that the Constitution would be disregarded? Where on earth could I find legal evidence? Although I had been locked up for years and constantly interrogated, I was grateful to them for dealing with me so leniently. But as soon as they mentioned Hu Feng, the tone became threatening. What did they intend to do with him?

In the afternoon, Old Liu from the local police station came to see me. He didn't often come, but he used to call in before every festival. He was extremely courteous. He wanted me to report on the other residents and especially visitors. Apparently that was my responsibility, since I lived on the ground floor. Not long before, he had told me to attend a meeting to hear a report on the general election. He seemed to trust me. In 1961, after my release, I took part in the third general election. By then, my civil rights had been restored.

After we had exchanged conventional greetings, he pulled a long face (this was new) and said, 'We're to deal with you from now on. In future, report regularly to us. We will set up a study class for you people.'

I almost jumped from my seat. 'They said I wouldn't be indicted. Has my freedom not been restored?'

'Not indicting you doesn't mean there's no problem. You're still wearing a counter-revolutionary hat.'

'I'm still wearing a hat?' I unconsciously touched my head.

'That's right, you still have to earn its removal by ideological remoulding.'

I didn't dare say a word. I was like a deflated ball. I collapsed into my chair.

'I've come to tell you to take part in the class we're organising for people like you. Attend the police station the day after tomorrow, in the afternoon.'

He left without saying goodbye. How come it was suddenly even more serious than when I was under detention, how come they had put a hat on me? How could I live here in future? Wouldn't people stab me in the back and curse me as a 'counter-revolutionary'? There were some mischievous young people in the block who had broken a window and run off. When I complained, they said their father was a factory leader, or the leader of a mass organisation, or some such. They told me to mind my own business. If they got to know my status, they would throw dirt at me. The more I thought about it, the more frightened I became. I even thought of writing to the Ministry of Public Security and asking them to lock me up again, for the rest of my life.

I had exchanged a five-room one-storey house for my three ground-floor rooms. Initially, I had thought it was nice and quiet, but now I found it cold and desolate. I felt like bursting into tears. But I couldn't. The window gave out onto the street. I couldn't risk attracting people's suspicion. That could have made things a lot worse. I sat there thinking miserable thoughts, tears dripping down onto my jacket.

It was Saturday, so my son arrived home early. When he saw me sitting there, he said:

'Has something happened?'

'No, I'm just not feeling very well.'

I didn't have the courage to tell him. I longed to share my misery with him, to take him in my arms and cry, but that would have been cruel. I couldn't burden his spirit once again with my troubles. He should be like a normal child, free of worries.

I went into the kitchen. Every Saturday, I used to cook him something special. Usually he would breakfast at home and eat lunch at school – rice with vegetables, re-heated. Only in the evening did we eat proper food, hot and relatively nutritious.

I cooked a smoked ribbonfish, which I had learned how to do from Mrs Jin upstairs. She was a southerner, so we had that in common. We became good neighbours. Being busy with the cooking took my mind off things, and I gradually calmed down. Then, Big Sister Ying suddenly turned up. I was even more delighted than the previous time. It was like meeting your loved one, your bosom friend.

We had known each other for 30 years, but when she came to the house in the past it had been to chat with F. I would make tea or pass round cigarettes and say the odd word, but we had never had a deep conversation. Now, she had come to see me, she had become my friend. How could I not rejoice? The sight of her big broad face and thick lips, the sound of her gruff voice sent a warm current through me. Our shared unhappy lot brought us even closer.

'I've come straight from work,' she announced with a smile. 'So, have you been back to see Hu Feng?'

'Let's wait until we've eaten, then we can take our time over it.' I didn't want the grim story to spoil our appetite.

My son had hidden away in his room to do his homework. That was even better, because we could talk uninhibitedly.

I told her everything, especially today's sudden change. I also told her about my misfortune and misgivings. She was surprised, but she was more experienced than I was, and she said, 'That's not important, it's a formality. We've all worn hats and then had them taken off. It will probably soon be over.'

'I hope so.'

'Two years ago I heard someone in the Political Consultative Conference say Hu might be released, he would have to make a self-criticism before a mass meeting and admit his guilt and it would all be over, but then we heard nothing more. I suppose you've heard about the criticism of *Hai Rui Dismissed from Office*? All it needs is one article by that scoundrel Yao Wenyuan for a distinguished writer like Wu Han* to end up in trouble.'

It was getting late. I wanted her to stay, but I couldn't bring myself to say so. I said, 'I suppose you ought to go?'

'No, not this time. I'll stay if I'm welcome.'

We laughed.

'Do you need to ask? It's what I've been longing for. But won't your family worry?'

'I often stay at friends' houses. I told Old Nie I was coming to see you, he knows where I am.'

We talked all the way from the living room to the bedroom, and continued talking even after lying down. We were two old women, chattering endlessly about things that had happened in

---

* Yao Wenyuan was a Chinese literary critic and member of the Gang of Four in China's Cultural Revolution; Wu Han was a historian and leader of the Democratic League, a non-aligned Third Force in China. In 1965, at the start of the Cultural Revolution, he was denounced for his drama about an upright Ming dynasty official. He died in prison in 1969.

the previous 30 years. I had never talked at length with anyone for ten years, especially not about my innermost thoughts and feelings. I talked with her about things I hadn't mentioned even to my children. In the past, I had known little about her other than what I heard from F. She knew even less about me. That day, I bared all my thoughts to her, all my pain and weakness. I would never again hide away in an impenetrable shell.

When we got up the next morning, we felt relaxed and happy. She went with me to buy some food. I intended to make dumplings, but when she rang home it turned out someone was waiting for her, so she left without eating lunch.

It was not hard to guess that the person waiting for her was probably someone like me hoping for help. She was a warm-hearted woman who would never turn anyone down. One thing she said really touched me. A woman who had got divorced was branded a 'rightist' on account of her famous husband and had suffered greatly. Her neighbours had started bullying her, and she no longer wanted to live. When Ying heard about it, she volunteered to visit her every day. This woman had graduated from an elite Christian college and studied in America. How could she grasp this sacrifice by Ying, a country girl? At night, she let Ying sleep on some planks, while she slept on an iron bed. The story upset me, but Ying said, 'Well, that's her background. What a tragic life!'

Ying had travelled extensively in China. She had once been a famous militant, but now she was an ordinary cadre, capable and homespun. Ten years before, F had said she was a great woman who had developed into a good writer. If she had really wanted, she could have become an influential politician. But she had never given up her integrity or her honest peasant woman's heart. Nor had she allowed herself to be defeated by reverses. She continued to sympathise with people whose suffering exceeded hers. She took pleasure in helping, to the point of selflessness.

She left me a telephone number, told me not to worry, and wished me strength.

6

An Unpredictable Future

I went to attend the study class. The police chief led it personally. He explained the policy, made some encouraging remarks, and then asked everyone for their thoughts. There were six of us, ranging from a young woman in her twenties, nursing a baby, to people in their sixties.

The first to speak was a 50- or 60-year-old man in a neat suit. He had studied at the middle school attached to Nanjing's Southeast University and at Beijing University's law school (a wonderful CV), and had then gone to work in the Beijing court. He had been allowed to stay on after Liberation. However, he came under criticism during the Anti-Rightist Movement because of some things he had done after Liberation, so he was branded a rightist. Then they checked his record and discovered that he had once convicted an underground Party member, so he was classed as an enemy official and an historical counter-revolutionary. He said, 'I've been treated with such magnanimity! They didn't force me to undergo reform through labour. After Liberation, I got an award for studying the Chairman's *On Practice*. In future, I'll study even harder and strengthen my ideological reform, so that I earn even greater leniency.'

A middle-aged man with a fat face, short-sighted and with gravy stains on his jacket, jumped up to get in before anyone else. He had been an economic spy, and had a counter-revolutionary hat. 'In the past,' he said, 'under the enemy and puppet regimes, I provided the press with economic intelligence. Later, I was

registered as someone to be kept on after Liberation. I did some
work and thought it would be classed as meritorious, so I started
to get self-important. During the campaign to eliminate counter-
revolutionaries I was eliminated. Only then did I realise I had
committed crimes against the people. The Government treated
me leniently. I wasn't sentenced, although I was put under neighbourhood supervision. Now, the three of us live off my wife's
wages. My vision is 0.3. I can't even help around the house without making mistakes. I am a good-for-nothing!' He was on the
verge of tears.

The one that interested me most was the young mother with
the baby. She got up to speak. She had studied at the Aviation
School and been retained after graduating. She had a good class
background* and was assigned to the security department.
Unfortunately for her, some students used her room as a meeting
place, and she thought what they were saying was right. She
didn't report them to higher levels and even joined them. When
they were arrested, she lost her job and acquired a counter-
revolutionary hat. Luckily, her boyfriend stood by her. She got
married, and now she was a mother and housewife. She no longer
concerned herself with anything. However, for the child's sake
she hoped to gain the Government's leniency and have her hat
removed.

The rest of us, myself, two other old ladies and one old gentleman, didn't speak.

The police chief again tried to inspire us to say something:
'Young X's family background was good and she had a good job,
but she went with bad people because her standpoint was not
firm. But as long as she admits her mistake, we'll help her, we'll
even welcome her back into the ranks of the people. Don't be
afraid, don't have misgivings.'

I thought, is it me he's trying to encourage? I stood up and
identified myself. 'Some of the things we did, especially the

* A poor, working-class or peasant background.

300,000-word memo, were a great crime. We didn't properly estimate our abilities, we thought it was a question of literary ideology. In future, I'll definitely strengthen my ideological reform and strive to get my counter-revolutionary hat removed.'

I thought I had made a mess of it, I had stammered my way through my little speech. The listeners, all educated people, were amazed, and looked askance at me. My heart beat like a drum. Would I be brought before the masses?

But the police chief seemed satisfied. 'Everyone's spoken very well. I want to meet a few more times before Spring Festival. We'll do our best to ensure that you get your hats removed as soon as possible. The meeting is over. You can go home.'

Like a primary-school student hearing the final bell, I was the first to reach the door. I had attended the class, but was it a disaster or a blessing? Although the police chief had said more than once that he wanted to help us remove out hats, I still looked on the dark side, since they could hardly remove all the hats. They had to leave some on, as a warning to others. In that case, I was doomed.

At first, I thought they might put me under the control of the neighbourhood committee and make me do manual labour, so I went for a check-up in the hospital, to make sure I was in good health. Everything was in order. Even my eyes were 1.5. This consoled me. As long as my health held out, I had nothing to fear.

Not long afterwards, I was again summoned to attend a class. I noticed the old lady who lived in the block behind mine give the police chief a big envelope. I couldn't hear what they said, but I saw the police chief nod repeatedly and smile. He was in a good mood. He said to the young mother, 'It's a cold day, you needn't stay, we don't want your child to catch cold, he's our next generation. No need to come next time!'

As he spoke, he took out the envelope and waved it, saying, 'This is the title deed for Liu XX's land.* She just handed it to me.

---

* In most cases, Mei Zhi uses XX or XXX to disguise the names of officials and other people who might be made vulnerable by their appearance in this book.

She said previously she had never dared to hand it in, because she didn't trust the Government's policy of leniency. Now she knows the truth. She has made up her mind to draw a clear class line between herself and the old landlord exploiting class. We applaud her decision.'

This was like throwing a stone into a pond. An old fat lady got to her feet and spoke. Her husband was a senior army officer in the KMT who fled with his concubine to Taiwan and left his wife behind in Changsha. She had come to Beijing to take refuge with her daughter, who was at university. Her daughter had asked her to take her child home to the village. She said, 'I was never more than my husband's servant. During land reform, I was classified as a landlord, and they told me to hand in my gun. But I had no gun. He had taken it long ago. Where would I hide a gun? My daughter is a state cadre.'

The police chief remained expressionless.

Finally, an old man spoke out. I had often met him while buying food or having breakfast. Not until I heard him speak did I realise that he was a big landlord. He criticised himself: 'In the village, I liked growing flowers and keeping pet birds. I lived the life of an exploiting landlord. Once when it started raining, I ordered my hired hand to help me move the chrysanthemums indoors. I valued flowers more than people. Now, I cook and do odd jobs for my son and his children. Not half as much as what my hired help had to do, but even so I still tell the children off for exploiting my manual labour. That's wrong, of course. Another thing. I really want to serve the people and do things for others. I know a bit of Chinese medicine, so if one of the neighbours gets a headache, I give them a prescription. I only realised later that was against the law, because I don't have a licence. Police chief Liu taught me that it was criminal, so I've stopped treating people. In future, I'll strengthen my ideological reform.'

Police chief Liu said, 'That's good. Wang XX's behaviour is very good, he knows how to criticise his past mistakes and that he has to change, that's very good.'

It seemed to me he was trying to mobilise us to make similar self-criticisms. I was apprehensive. But when I looked at the others and saw them sitting there like Mount Tai, heads bent and pens scribbling, I pretended to concentrate on listening. I also started scribbling, to show I was studying 100 per cent. The man with the 0.3 eyesight was using a home-made magnifying glass to supplement his thick pair of spectacles while he took notes, with a look that was conscientious and Herculean.

This satisfied the police chief, who said with an air of confidence and affirmation, 'We are determined to help. You must also resolve to strengthen your ideological education. We hope to remove your hats at the latest by the Spring Festival. Our job is to turn you into new people who support the Communist Party. We expect you to show you have drawn a clear line between yourselves and the reactionary classes. XX's behaviour is worth studying, because it shows she has split from the landlord class and drawn even closer to our Party.'

All of us were close to tears, constantly nodding.

I hurried off, not wanting to talk, and slowed down only when I reached the main road. I started to ponder what to do at the next meeting. How could I demonstrate that I had drawn a line under my erroneous thinking?

The first idea that entered my head was 'learn from the workers, peasants, and soldiers.' I should do manual labour. That would be the best way of showing my resolve.

The man next door worked for a building company, and the old ladies in his family used to greet me courteously. Some families did appliqué work, others took in children. It didn't seem a good idea to take in children, for I might be accused of corrupting them by spreading bourgeois ideology. The alternative was appliqué work. My eyes were still good. I couldn't do cross-stitching or flower embroidery, but I could sew and mend. I hurried over to discuss it with one of the old ladies, who agreed to give me some work.

I also went to see Mrs Jin, on the floor above. She had always been very good to me. She was by herself during the day, and so was I, so we used to sit and chat. A decent and kindly middle-aged woman, she was timid and over-cautious. She used to invite me to accompany her to meetings of the neighbourhood commit-tee or to do voluntary labour. She was a good needlewoman and could do embroidery on the sewing machine. Her aim in life was to ensure her husband and children lived and ate well. I explained my plan. She said, 'Even if you only earn ten yuan a month, it's better than nothing.'

Her husband worked for a big company. According to her, he was a fine man who stayed aloof from the world. It seemed unlikely he would try to stop me.

People's Daily used a whole page to reprint Yao Wenyuan's 'Criticism of the New Historical Drama *Hai Rui Dismissed from Office*', prefaced by an editorial note. The note suggested a new turn of events that did not look encouraging. Reading the ominous portents, I had the feeling we were in for a period of instability. Was a change in the offing, as Big Sister Ying had predicted? Did it augur well for us, or not?

7

An Uncompleted Mission

Beijing is coldest at the start of winter. The Slight Snow and the Great Snow were still ahead of us. We had not yet reached December, so the central heating was still off. Outdoors icicles were forming, and the north wind cut to the marrow. Even when you got home, it was still icy.

I received a summons from the woman comrade. She told me:

'Our Party has done everything possible to save him, but he's stubborn. We would like you to cooperate. Tomorrow I'll go with you to Qincheng.'

We arranged for her to fetch me.

However, I was due for a study session. I told her, and I explained they were preparing to remove our hats. I was hoping they would choose another date.

The cadre in charge of the case listened in surprise. After thinking for a bit, he said, 'You don't need to study any more, we have our own plan.'

I told them that I had to go to hear the report on the general election. I had been in detention during the second general election, so I had been unable to cast a vote. Between my release in 1961 and the third general election in 1963, my name had been restored to the list. When I went in trepidation to read the list and found my name on it, I wept tears of gratitude, for that meant I had the right to exist, as a citizen. I was part of the Chinese people, not its enemy. Now I was once again invited to hear the report on the election. How could I not go?

The two cadres were at a loss to understand me. All they could do was shake their heads and say, 'Listen to it at the next election!'

The next morning, a car came to fetch me, and we sped along the highway into the open countryside.

The woman comrade said, 'Did you bring food for Hu Feng?'

'A bit of braised beef and smoked fish.'

'Did you cook it last night?'

I smiled faintly. 'That's my duty.'

She also smiled.

She spoke most. She dropped lots of hints, repeating her suggestion that I help Hu Feng acknowledge his guilt. She said, 'We've waited a long time. He should show some awareness. The Party is never wrong, he must recognise his guilt.'

I couldn't think of a reply.

'Then we can deal with him leniently. Otherwise, we will have to leave it to the law.'

'The law!' The word scared me. What law had he broken? 'What can I do to help him? Is he likely to listen to me?'

The car drove right up to the main building, without stopping. F had been alerted, for he came towards us. We met in the usual room. He was wearing a black quilted jacket, clumsily done up with some buttons in the wrong holes. He looked untidy. But he was animated. The woman comrade sat there, but he ignored her. He asked, 'Did you get the letter?'

'Yes, but some of the books were hard to find.'

'No longer any need, I've got no time for reading.'

Something must have happened.

I said, 'Don't be pessimistic. All you have to do is admit your criminal behaviour, say why you wrote the 300,000-word memo, explain the origins of your thinking, that sort of thing, and you will be granted leniency. Think it over for the sake of the family. Admit your guilt.'

I clumsily rushed out my prepared speech.

He stared at me, radiating such an air of dignity that I lowered my head. I realised my speech would not have the desired effect. But he kept his temper, and simply smiled coldly.

'You think I haven't admitted my guilt? Wherever possible, I've assumed responsibility.' His voice soared, like in the old days.

'You can't deny facts. After all, the Party can't be wrong!'

'I know I've committed crimes against the Party. They can chop my head off, I won't complain. They might bring me to trial, but you mustn't worry, it's nothing to do with you, it's me that implicated you, you're just an obedient wife, I'm the guilty one.'

I looked down, tears streaming.

'Don't be sad. I can stand it, you needn't worry. They wanted to find me a defender, but I refused. I've defended myself and lots of other people for the last ten years, and still I haven't gained the Government's confidence. Could anyone defend me? What a joke.'

The mission I had been given seemed to have failed. I had been unable to convince him. I didn't blame him, and I had no regrets. Neither he nor I could have acted differently.

'If you don't want a defender, then don't accept one. Whatever the case, we hope you'll be found not guilty and set free.'

He smiled, and then asked me how things were at home. In my previous letter, I had told him about Xiaofeng's wish to marry.

'If she wants to, then let her. I just hope I won't implicate them.'

The woman comrade stood up, indicating the visit was at an end.

F came towards me, grasped my hand, and said:

'Whatever happens, stay strong. It doesn't matter if they bring me to trial. What worries and grieves me is that I might implicate others. I've already implicated enough people.' He let go of my hand.

'Go back, don't worry, if anything happens, I'll write to you. Get me a pair of thick cotton-padded trousers, made of coarse cloth.' He gestured at the quilted clothes he was wearing, stitched together with crude needles and thick thread, which came unbuttoned at the slightest tug. 'Out of doors you couldn't survive the winter in this.'

The woman comrade and the secretary came to return him to his cell. I handed him the food I had brought. I reached into my shopping-bag and took out a dozen Sichuan tangerines. His hands were already full of paper bags, so I stuffed them into his pockets, and when his pockets were full, I balanced the rest on the bags. He mouthed noiselessly at me, smiled bitterly, and left clutching the food.

The woman comrade and I got into the car and drove back into the city.

No one had summoned me to any meetings, and I thought perhaps they had cancelled my right to vote. I was worried. I had already guessed F would not achieve a good outcome.

I got out the appliqué work I had received the day before and took up my needle, in the hope it would calm me down.

They were tea cloths, probably for a foreign market. I had to lockstitch a dogtooth border, with embroidered corners. The stitching had to be quite fine. I worked out that if I did five a day, I would earn 15 yuan a month. I wanted to find out how many I could do in a day. An experienced needlewoman could earn 30 or 40 yuan a month.

The work failed to calm me, and I kept pricking myself. I became even more agitated when another letter arrived from the Ministry of Public Security. I was to go to see them the next morning. Would it be bad news or good?

The old cadre handed me a statement of charges. Before I could study it, the woman comrade said I should follow her to fetch some things. Secretary Shi dug out a big rattan bag full of letters and books and a medium-sized leather suitcase, confiscated when our home was searched. There was also a piece of cloth with some of F's things. They were giving me back my things — that meant they had wound up my case.

Looking at those two huge packages, I didn't know what to do. However, people usually recover their wits under pressure, so I opened the rattan bag, put the suitcase in it, removed my scarf to use as a string, and tied it all together. It was heavy, but I could still lift it. I signed for it, ready to leave.

Perhaps they took pity on me, or perhaps they were worried bystanders would disapprove, for the woman comrade said to Secretary Shi in a wheedling tone, 'Couldn't you take it on the back of your bike?'

Secretary Shi didn't look too pleased, but nevertheless he loaded up the bag and case.

To signal his status and authority, he put on a hard look and said, 'These incorrigible elements. We still have quite a few to sentence. We'll bring them to trial and make it known to the public. Maybe it will even be reported in the press. That will educate the masses.'

He was going to do me a small favour, but at what a price. I almost fainted. I followed them wordlessly to the main entrance. He unloaded the case and they left.

I made my way to the No. 9 bus stop. I don't know how I managed to get there, or how I got aboard. Luckily, there was a free seat. In a daze, I made my way home.

8

At Around the Time of the Sentencing

I felt terribly alone. I needed someone to talk with about what had happened, but there was no one. Daughter could not come home from the farm; youngest son was at school, and even if he did come home, he was so young, how could I discuss it with him? I racked my brains. The more I thought, the less I understood. I knew nothing about any of the charges, nor did I believe them. Sitting there alone, I screamed silently: Is this really happening?

What new humiliations would be heaped on our heads? Would F, with his passionate temperament, be able to bear it? Would I?

Suddenly I thought of Big Sister Ying. She would give me strength. How I longed for her to be by my side. Then I remembered she had left me a phone number. A young girl answered. She said auntie had not come home yet, so I asked her to tell auntie a friend in the eastern suburb needed to see her urgently.

I took out the jumper I was making for my son, in the hope that knitting would calm me down. But I couldn't stop imagining things. I don't know how many times I missed a stitch or had to unravel a line and start again. Reading was even more impossible. The best thing would be to go into the kitchen and prepare the evening meal.

There was a knock at the door. It was Ying, an angel come down from heaven. She was out of breath. She said, 'The girl told me. You're the only person I know in the eastern suburb, so I hurried over.'

When she arrived, I was kneading dough. I took the bowl into the sitting room, kneading and talking simultaneously. When she saw the charges, she looked puzzled, and angry. She said, 'So this is counter-revolutionary? In that case, there must be a lot of counter-revolutionaries.'

I fought back the tears, and didn't dare reply. I was afraid my anxieties would cause me to break down if I opened my mouth. I simply lowered my head and continued kneading. But the dough got the better of me, and was too hard to pound. I got up to add water, but she stopped me and took over. Miraculously, the dough immediately became soft and smooth. She divided it into separate lumps and rolled them into dumpling skins. I marvelled at her skill: 'I had no idea you could do that, I always imagined you scorned housework.'

'I learned it at home when I was a child. All the girls can cook in the Hebei villages.'

With her by my side, I seemed less fearful. I asked her a few questions, but she knew as little as I did. However, she was more experienced than I and more abreast of events. She explained that even if the worst happened, we shouldn't be disappointed or depressed, it would simply mean a few more years behind bars. She thought there would probably be a big change soon, and whether they kept him or released him, it would all be over.

What she said had a big effect on me. I stopped thinking of a public trial and verdict as a mortal attack. I had to learn to face up to suffering, to confront it with fortitude.

She again stayed the night. It was as good as a tranquilizer. Inwardly, however, I felt uneasy, for her daughter and son-in-law had to go to work, and she was supposed to look after her grandson.

While we were in bed, she said, 'At night I have to get up to change the baby's nappies. Third sister is afraid she'll oversleep. When I do the changing, I'm always afraid he'll catch cold because his bottom is bare and he's only got his vest on.'

I had always thought of her as a social activist, but it turned out she was also a conscientious grandmother.

I said, 'Can I help? . . . I'll knit him a vest, then he won't catch cold.'

She was delighted. So the two of us, old ladies in our second half-century, chatted away, and my inner grief subsided without me noticing.

The next morning, she told me to phone her if any problem arose. She also told me to stay calm. I took heart from her matter-of-fact way of speaking. I was like a deflated ball reinflated.

The Ministry of Public Security again contacted me. They took me to a small house next to the main entrance. A cadre in his thirties entered. He opened a briefcase and handed me a written judgment. The first paragraph repeated the indictment. I skipped to the next section, which said, 'We sentence the accused, Hu Feng, to 14 years in prison and six years' deprival of political rights. The counter-revolutionary secret letters and other proof of guilt submitted in relation to this case are attached. If he rejects this verdict, he can lodge an appeal within ten days.'

The cadre scrutinised me, head to one side. 'If you don't accept, you can appeal.'

I didn't respond, but he continued to wait, so I said, 'It's the Party's verdict. He's unlikely to appeal.'

He seemed pleased. Tucking his briefcase under his arm, he hurried off.

Secretary Shi and the woman comrade took out two big bundles of books and newspapers, opened them, and asked me to check and sign for them. They were things that had been taken away when my home was searched in 1955. I couldn't help smiling as I flicked through a scrap book I had stapled together for our youngest son from strips of paper salvaged from F's cigarette packets.

'So this is proof of guilt?'

'We can't explain everything.'

They took their responsibilities seriously. Nothing escaped their attention. The care with which they approached the case was evident.

The two bundles contained books taken from our desks and bedside tables. I asked whether they still had the clothbound copies of *July, Hope, July Poetry Collection*, and Belinsky's *Selected Works*.

'We know nothing about that. Perhaps they kept it for the archive.'

The books and journals that they set no store by were faded chrysanthemums. I too no longer had any use for them. They were just another burden. I lugged them to the bus stop, pausing every third step, and finally got them home.

I was tired, but I suddenly remembered that Big Sister Ying had written inviting me to meet her at the Zoo for lunch. A scale-five wind was blowing from the northwest and I was reluctant. But when I remembered that her sole aim was to distract me from my troubles, how could I let her down? Also, I'd finished knitting the jumper and wanted to give it to her.

It was one o'clock by the time I got there. She rushed over to me, her silver hair blowing all over the place. I was overcome by emotion. I had once told her I always arrived early for appointments, so she had arrived early too. She had already been there an hour, what an amazing woman.

We entered the Moscow Restaurant. It was getting late, and the restaurant was emptying. We ordered a bowl of ox-tail soup, fried fish, and vegetables, which arrived cold. The conversation got round to the borscht we used to eat in Shanghai – 20 cents a bowl, but much tastier than this. I was unable to find my appetite. Toying with my food, I told her of the morning's events. She became agitated, but still she tried to console me: 'The Party's policy is to be strict and then lenient. Think of the war criminals – they're all guests of honour!'

'Maybe they'll let him go to a farm to do manual labour. That wouldn't be so bad. He only has another three and a half years to go. But I'm afraid it will affect the children. Can they cope? Youngest son finishes high school next year. Will they let him go to University? Our daughter is getting married. This might be a big blow to them.'

'Yes, our daughter suffered because of us. She missed her chance to go abroad.'

The waitress was waiting to clear the table, so we left. Ying went to buy tickets for the cinema. I realised she didn't want me to stay at home moping. We weren't in the mood to watch the film, we just wanted somewhere to sit for a while. After the show, I suddenly remembered the woollen vest. She was delighted, and I cheered up a bit.

After dinner, I showed the verdict to our youngest son.

'I didn't expect this,' I said. 'But it doesn't matter. You're not responsible for your family background, you can choose your own way forward.'

'If I can't continue with my studies, I'll be a worker or a peasant, it's all the same to me. Don't worry, it's no problem.'

But I knew it was a blow to him. How could it not be, with a father labelled a 'counter-revolutionary'?

I remembered an incident I had witnessed in prison. I was feeling miserable and unable to sleep. One of the menials started quarrelling. He felt he was being unfairly treated, and spewed out his grievances. But he said, 'Who cares, it's not such a big deal, you can overcome anything if you want to.' This inspired me. Nothing was so terrible you couldn't get over it. I had developed a capacity to gloss over criticism or ridicule. Perhaps that's what my son was doing.

My next task was to prepare for F's departure for the reform-through-labour farm. I dug out the cotton-padded trousers the Government had given him when he was working in the liberated areas in the northeast and a heavy woollen pullover I'd knitted for him. I also made him a cotton-padded jacket. Being busy calmed me down.

I asked the Ministry of Public Security whether I was right to assume that his case would be administered by the court, now that he had been sentenced. Which farm would he be sent to? Would the arrangement be for monthly visits? What preparations should I make? What did he need? They replied that his case would still be administered by the Ministry of Public Security.

9

Welcoming the Prisoner Home

Out of the blue, I was notified of a phone call. That very rarely happened. It was from a Comrade Huang in the Ministry of Public Security. He told me to go to the Ministry. He would be waiting for me at the entrance. I said I don't know you. He said you will recognise me. I said all right, I'll carry a black briefcase so you know who I am. Actually, I was extremely naïve. When I arrived, he came out to receive me. He was in his thirties. He had been present at the first interrogation.

He took me to the reception room, where the cadre responsible for maintaining contact with me was sitting. Huang introduced him to me, as Director Wu. The fact that I was being treated as an equal overwhelmed me.

Director Wu came straight to the point: 'I've read your letter. We passed on your letter to Hu Feng. We've decided not to send him for reform through labour. How about if we send him home?'

I must have looked astonished, for he added, 'Our Party's policy has always been to treat people leniently. Leniency and severe punishment mutually combined. So we're going to release him and create the conditions for him to reform. That requires your cooperation.'

Comrade Huang said, 'When you get home, prepare some clothes for when he comes out. Don't tell anyone. We'll let you know what happens next.'

They asked me about my home circumstances and the other members of my residential unit. They said they would come to see me the next day. Then they politely escorted me from the building.

Shortly after I arrived home, Big Sister Ying rushed in, carrying a big fish. I told her what had happened. She was delighted, but unable to fathom the outcome. Would he be allowed to stay, or would they send him somewhere else?

After dinner, she left, although she had planned to stay the night. She said, 'I must go back to tell Old Nie the news. Perhaps in future it won't be so easy to come. If you need anything, phone me.' She took a big bundle of wool from her bag and said, 'The vest fits perfectly. It will soon be Spring Festival. The child will continue growing. If you have time, knit him a jumper.'

As I looked at the ball of fiery red wool, my depression lifted.

I hadn't told my son about F's imminent release, because he was busy with his end-of-semester exams. I didn't want to distract him. Better if I undertook this venture on my own.

The next day, they didn't turn up, but in the afternoon they phoned to say they would fetch me by car the following morning.

Such were the last two days of 1965. At eight o'clock the next morning, a black sedan car stopped opposite the building, a rare sight in our neighbourhood. I had slept barely a wink. When our son was helping me lift the chest containing his father's overcoat, I told him what was happening. He said, 'Daddy's coming home, that's wonderful!' That's all he said.

Dragging a suitcase and dressed in an old cotton suit and a long scarf, I hurried out.

I noticed that the Director was also in the car.

'Why the suitcase?'

'Didn't you say I should bring some clothes?'

To the driver, 'Hurry, we have some formalities to go through after we arrive.'

Even though I was travelling in a luxury vehicle, comfortably upholstered and air-conditioned, I felt uneasy. For more than half a year now, I had rushed through this same scenery, which swept through my head like scenes from a film. Would I really no longer have to toil back and forth along this route? There were practically no pedestrians. The countryside was bleak. There was no sign of vitality, just like in my heart. I was on my way to fetch my beloved from prison, but I couldn't feel the requisite joy, because everything had happened too suddenly.

The car sped straight up to the metal gate. The guard waved us through. We got out, and I was escorted to a guest room. The others were led away by a cadre.

The guest room was tiny. There were two small sofas but no heating. My feet began to ache. This was the outskirts and much colder than in the city. Luckily, I had brought F's thick cotton shoes and a leather overcoat. At least he wouldn't freeze. Thinking this, I calmed down. I stood up and paced around, to exercise my legs.

Through the window, I saw him in the middle of a group of people headed my way. He was wearing the clothes I'd brought. He seemed to have become taller. From a distance, he looked like he had looked ten years before. I hurried out and helped him into the car. The others started putting the suitcase and various bits and pieces into the boot. We were alone. He gripped my hand, squinting and smiling like he used to, but without the sweet joyful smile I knew from the old days.

The car sped off. It became stiflingly hot. Director Wu, sitting at the front, wound down the window so the cold wind blew in. My head became clearer in the fresh breeze. F, sitting next to me, was as if in trance. He said nothing, and showed not the slightest emotion. I knew he must have been full of thoughts, so I started to talk, in an attempt to drag him from his reverie. I said, 'This road is beautiful in the summer. It's green, dark green, with white poplars and willows on either side.' As we passed through Shahe, I showed him the restaurant and said, 'I ate here twice.' He mumbled a reply. Not until we entered the city, with its broad bustling streets and ceaseless flow of vehicles, was his attention finally caught.

'Why are there so many people in Beijing, how come it's so lively?'

We arrived home. I helped him from the car and was about to fetch the case, but I was told to enter the house. Carrying a bundle of books in one hand and supporting him with the other, I went to the front door. Neighbours peered from their windows.

We entered the living room, just the two of us. I didn't know whether to laugh or cry. My nose began to tingle. Stifling the tears, I helped him out of his overcoat. It was hot indoors, so he asked me to help him remove his woollen suit. Only then, doing things like that, which I'd not been able to do for a decade, did I really feel my beloved had returned.

The driver and Comrade Huang helped bring in the suitcase. I was about to make some tea when the Director said, 'No need, you must take it easy. We'll come in the afternoon.'

They left through the back door.

I lived in a three-room ground-floor flat. Normally I was there by myself during the day. I showed F the house. He spent a long time looking round his son's room, flicking through his books. When he had left, his son had been in the first class of primary school, and now he was reading all these books. He would no longer be pestering dad for children's books.

I sat him down in the living room on the swivel chair. He had bought the chair second-hand. I showed him some letters from friends. Then I went into the kitchen to make him his first meal since arriving home.

I had got the food ready in advance. I had bought him a bottle of bamboo-leaf wine, his favourite, but I didn't dare give it him yet, because the Director was returning. I watched happily as he took big mouthfuls of food. It felt like we had regressed ten years. In those days, whenever he came home from his travels, even if only after a few months, I had felt the same joy when we sat down together to eat. He used to say he often ate banquets when he was away from home, but it never tasted as good as my vegetables and beancurd.

I let him go for a nap. I told him, 'I have to go out. I'll lock the door from the outside. If anyone knocks, don't open it.' I added, 'I want to buy you a toothbrush. Also some nice tea, so if anyone comes, we've got something other than boiled water to offer. And some cigarettes.'

He told me he hadn't smoked for ten years and had given up, that was his reunion gift to me.

I went to buy the toothbrush and some other things, and I also bought him a razor. When I got home, he was sleeping. I was afraid they would soon turn up, so I woke him. Just at that moment, there was a knock at the back door.

The first thing the Director said on entering, with a big smile on his face, was 'Why did you lock him in? And such a useless lock!'

How did he know the lock was useless, and that you could open it without a key?

He said, 'It doesn't matter, if there's a crime, we can easily solve it. But don't use that sort of lock, don't cause us unnecessary trouble.'

F was baffled and I was ill at ease, so I left to make tea. I thought it best to leave them to chat with him.

Comrade Huang took out a list of five or six rules. The gist was that he shouldn't talk with strangers or meet foreigners, go out by himself, or leave the neighbourhood.

Director Wu added, 'This is for your safety, you must cooperate. I'll introduce you to two comrades who are coming to help you. If you need anything, ask them.'

All I could do was nod earnestly, to show I supported the measures they proposed.

Comrade Huang went onto the balcony and shouted across at two men, who then entered the building. The thin tall one was Old Chen and the short sturdy one was Little Zhang. He introduced Hu Feng to them, as Old Zhang.

Liu from the police station also turned up, and shook hands with Hu Feng. Then, the two other comrades went to find accommodation.

Hu Feng had spent ten and a half years in prison. Director Wu formally announced he was being allowed to serve his sentence outside prison as an act of leniency, but his movements would be controlled by the public security organs.

10

Family Reunion

Director Wu and the others left. One thing worried me: how F would deal with meeting his younger son. He was applying to join the Young Communist League, and had been asked repeatedly to draw a clear class line with his father.

I heard him pushing his bike up the steps. His father opened the door. Our son looked awkward, and went into his room.

I said, 'You recognised him?'

'He's become a young man. I couldn't resist kissing him on the forehead. I can't stop seeing him as a child.'

The child reappeared and called out to his father, 'I hope you're all right. I've made you a cup of tea.'

I cheered up. I still had a close and harmonious family.

When the two of us retreated to what was now our bedroom, I felt a bit at a loss. He was no longer the same man. In some ways, he had become a stranger. More than once he said, 'I've let you down, I've harmed you, I've treated no one else as badly as I've treated you, I can never repay my debt to you. I ruined the second half of my life, but I also ruined yours, I dragged my whole family into it.'

He put his head on my shoulder and wept.

'Don't say any more, I know all that, I'm never going to blame you.' I lifted his big, heavy head and wiped away the tears.

He pulled me to the bedside and held my hand tight.

'You can forgive me, but I can't forgive myself. Whenever I thought of you and the children, I suffered agonising pain. I also felt guilty about the friends I implicated, but they had their own ideas and ideals. But in your case, you were innocent. What I most fear is that they will drag you out and expose you to the masses.'

'Yes, I've also feared that.'

'When I think of the friends I implicated, how they were locked up all those years, how they had to bear witness against me to my face to gain their freedom, I feel anguish. I haven't seen them for ten years. They must have gone grey. Some have started wearing glasses, some have become fat and can no longer button up their clothes. A flogging by the masses would be easier to accept. How could I know it would continue for more than a decade, that they too would waste their finest years? They were so talented. I would rather go to the gallows than see them wrongly punished. But did I have a choice? It was like a drama, with me as the tragedian. I hope they can put their sufferings behind them.

'In the interval between judgment and pronouncing judgment, they gave me soup and two dishes with two bowls of rice. That counts as special treatment. But a comrade from the Ministry of Public Security sat watching me, to observe whether I was afraid, whether I was heartbroken, whether I had lost my appetite. I gulped it down as always, to show they couldn't defeat me. They had too simple a view if they thought they could damage a person's spirit by such means.

'Later, the prison authorities asked me to write down how I felt about the sentence. I said, "My heart is at ease but reason has not prevailed." This surprised them. They moved me to an unheated cell. It was not until a few days ago that they moved me back to a big cell. But I ignored their petty measures.'

'So, the food was not so bad?'

'Each morning I received a cup of powdered milk and a steamed bun with jam. The food was sufficient in quantity. Sometimes I got boiled meat. But sometimes someone had put a lump of soil or an insect on it. I ignored them. I fished it out and ate the meat as usual.'

'Do you know why that happened?'

'The people who brought the food were in a bad mood. During the period of natural disasters we didn't get meat for months on end. Sometimes we only got vegetables and steamed corn-bread, and on one occasion we got onion skins. Even that cost 20 yuan a month. You were lucky to be an official prisoner, for I wouldn't have been able to pay for your provisions. You don't know how lucky you were.'

We laughed.

There were no words to describe what had happened. We needed sleep, but there was one question I had to ask him. 'When I got out of gaol, I heard rumours that you wanted to kill yourself. I thought maybe you could no longer bear it, because I also had the same idea.'

'Do you remember what we talked about that night, when Shu Wu* published the private letters I had written to him before Liberation? You said that if the freedom of correspondence laid down by the Constitution couldn't be safeguarded, what is left? You yourself mentioned suicide. I thought about it and said people might think we killed ourselves because we feared punishment, that we had alienated ourselves from the masses, who would dare to speak up for us after that? You also thought of mother, who was nearly 80, and our son, who was eight. You could only weep. So we decided to grit our teeth and suffer all attacks. That oath kept me going. However, I did waver. In 1957, after reading Chairman Mao's *On the Correct Handling of Contradictions Among the People*, I said I hoped I could have a down-to-earth discussion about my case, that I wouldn't just be left in the dark. I was always being told to confess, but I had nothing to confess. No one listened, so I went on hunger strike. Obviously, they couldn't let me starve to death. I won't go into details.' He opened his mouth. 'Look, they knocked out my front tooth so they could pour the food in.'

'And then?'

---

* A writer and friend of Hu Feng's.

'The judge promised to show me the incriminating evidence and discuss it with me. But when I resumed eating, nothing happened. Now I've been sentenced to 14 years, but where's the evidence? To uphold the Party's name, I didn't appeal or even try to defend myself. "My heart is at ease but reason has not prevailed" – that was the best way of putting it!'

I started to think back on my own experience, the torment caused by never-ending demands that I confess. A brief moment of pain seemed preferable to protracted pain. Death would put an end to my troubles. I forget how many times I approached the hard corner of the rosewood table, but each time my heart softened when I thought of mother and our children.

'Let's not talk about it. As long as we live together, nothing can defeat us. We must treasure what is left of our lives. I will make life worth living, so you can work.'

'Do you know what I've been thinking all these years? I used to think that when I was released I would ask you for five yuan and go to Tanggu in Tianjin. The boundless sea would be my final resting place.'

We fell into each other's arms weeping.

We spent the night crying and laughing.

I woke at six when our son went to fetch the water flask. Later, he crept out with his bike. I was pleased he was so sensible.

When Director Wu returned that afternoon, the child was at home and the Director had a chat with him. Perhaps it was to help him put his relations with his father on a good footing. Before leaving, the Director said, 'I hope you have a happy New Year at home. The offices don't reopen until the third. Then we'll organise some visits for you. You can see how much progress the country has made over the last few years!'

'The Ten Great Monuments are wonderful,' I chipped in.

'Yes, we'll see everything.'

The winter holidays started, and our elder son returned from Xi'an. I had written to him about his father, so his visit was not unexpected. However, the sight of him shocked me. He had hurt his leg at work and they had only just removed the plaster, so he walked with a limp. He said, 'I decided not to tell you, so you wouldn't rush up to Xi'an. Dad needed you more.'

Perhaps Director Wu knew my elder son had come home, for he too turned up. It was partly to discuss the visits with us, but the main reason was to talk with our son.

Apart from rushing around preparing meals, I also had to keep an eye on F. The children seemed reasonable and not as 'leftist' as I had feared. Xiaoshan dragged his father off to play chess. Xiaogu talked with him about the domestic and the international situation and about university. Even though F had been locked up for ten years, he still managed to express some opinions. But about his son's future he felt nothing but regret.

'If it hadn't been for me, you could have studied abroad.'

'So what? I can hear lectures by Soviet experts. No one has obstructed my career. I've been promoted to a lectureship.'

On lunar New Year's Eve, when families get together for dinner, I prepared a rich assortment of food and drink, and our daughter hurried over from the home of her husband's family. I suggested we each talk about our innermost thoughts and feelings. I was hoping the alcohol would loosen our tongues, so we would get to know what was on each other's minds.

Sadly, the children remained ill at ease. F told his daughter to go to the bookcase and find Lu Xun's translation of Arishima Takeo's 'To Young People'. He read:

'I have loved you, and I always will. It's not because I expect to get any reward from you as your father, that's not why I say I love you. My sole request is that you accept my gratitude. By the time I have raised you to adulthood, I may well be dead; or perhaps I will still be alive and working hard; or in my dotage. Whatever the case, I am not the one you have to help. You cannot waste your fresh energy on my generation. It would be better if, like lion cubs, you endeavoured to build up your strength by eating the flesh of your dead kin, entered into the stream of life, and tried to shake off your memories of me.'

The room fell quiet. Again, father spoke, in his calm, dignified voice. 'That's how I feel. I want to give you my body and mind. You are young lions. You are strong and animated. You can leave me – then I will be at peace.' Everyone felt the grief contained in those few words. Xiaofeng said, 'The last tram will soon leave, I must go.' That broke the silence. We got up to see her off. Afterwards, I blamed him for affecting the children with Arishima Takeo's despair. He said, 'Xiaogu suffered a lot because of me. They thought it would convince me. It's been a burden for him, he's in the Party. I want to be the victim. Let them step across me and go their own ways. They have the Party to lead them, they can be happy. When I see how sincerely they heed the Party, I will no longer worry.'

11

Visiting in Beijing, Heart of the Ancestral Country

Visiting Wangfujing shopping street, Beijing Hotel and Dongan Market after ten years' absence, F had the feeling he knew them but didn't know them. I took him to a department store to buy a woollen overcoat. Navy blue with a velvet lining and a good fit, just 200 yuan. I decided to buy it. He stopped me, saying it was too expensive and he didn't need one. I said, 'You've never worn nice clothes. You always bought old suits and old overcoats. This time, you will dress presentably.'

He wore the new coat when Comrade Huang took us to the Great Hall of the People, and looked quite imposing as he stood outside the magnificent building. The assistant, a young girl, seemed enthusiastic and even respectful. How was she to know that F was still serving his sentence?

The girl's voice, posture and gait made me think of a person lightly dancing, filled with the beauty of youth. I thought, the assistants in the Great Hall of the People are bound to be out of the ordinary. After all, not just anyone could enter the Great Hall of the People. I had only seen it on a news documentary. I was delighted F could go there in person.

I had heard the dome at the Great Hall of the People was designed in the shape of a sunflower. Unfortunately not all the lights were on, to save electricity, but although we saw only the sunflower and not the sun, we were satisfied.

Treading that thick red carpet leading to the Great Hall, I

noticed with what solemn steps Hu Feng walked, striding along like the master of the building. I have a vivid recollection of how joyful and jubilant he was at the First Session of the National People's Congress. The silly thing is, he thought he was a representative of the people and ought to speak for the people, so he submitted his 300,000-word proposal to the Central Committee and was branded a counter-revolutionary. There's no medicine to cure regret. But Hu Feng did not blame and censure himself on this account, nor did he repent.

One can gauge his feelings at the time from something he wrote after his return home:

> I walked solemnly up the steps of the Great Hall of the People and through the main entrance and into the Great Hall.
>
> I felt it was tall, big, firm, heavy, strong, solid, thick, fixed.
>
> As I advanced, my steps soared.
>
> I felt harmony, composure, balance, unity, dignity, radiance,
>
> I was at the centre, touching the firmament, reaching the remotest areas;
>
> I felt the centre governing the parts.
>
> I felt the parts bowing to the centre.
>
> I felt a massive image towering before me, all around me;
>
> the image of revolutionary political power;
>
> the image of the ancestral homeland;
>
> the image of the Party;
>
> Mao Zedong Thought.

'That this great work of art was built in just over ten months, including the period of its design, demonstrates the power of the people led by Mao Zedong Thought; it shows how the revolution is advancing by leaps and bounds, at an unstoppable speed.

'The Great Hall of the People, a melody in space, symbolises the greatness of the Party, the greatness of the ancestral homeland, the greatness of Mao Zedong Thought, which turns matter into spirit and spirit into matter.'

Back in the car, Old Chen asked me where we wanted to go. It was lunchtime, so I suggested we go somewhere to eat. I remembered there was a restaurant in Nanchizi where I had eaten dim sum on one of my visits to the Ministry of Public Security, so I said, let's go there.

It was not full. Along the sides were Shanghai-style compartments. We found one that seated four, and I ordered the food. Sitting there reminded me of the Cantonese restaurants in Guilin and Chongqing. Braised pork in red beancurd gravy had been Old Nie's and Old Yu's favourites, so I ordered braised pork in red beancurd gravy, beef with oyster sauce, flowering cabbage in white sauce, fish in tomato sauce, and soup with meat balls. F was not to know I made my choice on the basis of my memories of those years and that I was trying to make him forget his present situation, so he could eat and drink as in the past, amid the merry shouts of his friends. He tucked in happily.

Later, Old Chen said, 'I thought you would want to go to Senlong's instead.'

'It gets too full. And we might have bumped into someone we knew. After all, he's not supposed to talk with people.'

Chen gave an awkward smile. He decided we would pay two more visits.

First we went to the Revolutionary History Museum. A female guide showed us round. We listened and looked, as events we had personally lived through were re-enacted on the pictures and photographs and in the guide's narration. F paid close attention and asked questions. More and more people gathered in our wake, surrounding F and the guide and squeezing me to the back. At times, there were so many people that F and the guide became separated. The guide tried to push them aside, but she and F were re-surrounded in an instant. Most of the visitors were from outside Beijing. They chatted incessantly. Although it was midwinter, the hot air they gave off aggravated the atmosphere in the hall. When we saw the two doors of the peasant association preserved by the people of the revolutionary Soviet area, the guide pressed them and they opened. She led us in and the doors closed behind us.

Inside was a tiny guest room. F flopped down on the sofa. He was drenched in sweat. The guide poured us some tea, and we rested. In next to no time, we had witnessed the overthrow of imperialism, feudalism and bureaucratic capitalism, and the birth of new China.

When we left, the sun was sinking, but Tiananmen Square was still bathed in the diminishing light. We walked towards the Monument to the Heroes of the People. Hu Feng enjoyed the carvings, not so much intoxicated by the artwork as lost in thought at the revolutionary commitment of the people.

That was his first time in public in ten years, his first encounter with that rich and magnificent tableau. After returning home, he lay down. I boiled some congee and made some pasties, but he preferred a bowl of gruel. In the middle of the night, he started coughing. His temperature was more than 38.

The next morning, I told Old Chen. He said, 'We must take him to hospital for a check-up.'

It turned out he had a slight fever. The doctor recommended sleep and lots of water, and discharged us. Old Chen had been planning to negotiate a hospital bed for F. Once outside, he rebuked me for making a fuss about nothing: there was no high temperature, and I had made it up. I said, 'I didn't say he had a high temperature, I said it was 38.' I don't know how he reported the matter to his superiors.

We decided to stay home for a few days. F stayed in his room, copying out the poems he had composed in gaol. The children were worried he would get tired, so they got him to play chess with them. At first, even the youngest almost beat him. Xiaoshan was afraid father would be embarrassed so he said it had been a draw, but F laughed and said his son played well. Xiaoshan was pleased. It was not until a few games later that he realised his father was an old hand at the game and could win if he chose to.

Comrade Huang arrived to see F on the third day. He asked a lot of questions about his health and said, 'Tomorrow we'll visit some factories.'

We were driven off into the remote outskirts. It was completely deserted – a vast expanse of yellow earth. There was no snow, just the occasional patch of frostwork on low-lying land. These scraps of white added to the bleakness. I was puzzled by the absence of buildings – where was the industry? The car drew to a halt in front of what looked like an honorific arch. A man jumped out of a parked car and said, 'We'll go ahead, you follow.'

After another stretch of yellow earth, crossed by a railway line, we arrived at an official entrance, consisting of two square columns made of red bricks and a sentry post, where PLA men were standing guard. Inside was a busy road lined by small shops.

The car parked outside an old-style building, probably the reception area. The comrades who received us told us the history of what turned out to be an iron and steel works. F listened attentively, and I made notes. They took us round an exhibition. There were lots of photos and articles of clothing and daily use demonstrating the cruel exploitation by the imperialists and the pillaging and slaughtering by the Japanese. There were bloodied clothes and instruments of torture, as well as a mass grave with piles of bones.

We toured the furnace and the rolling mill, where the fiery ingots were placed under the rollers to produce a bright red steel plate that got longer and longer, as if by magic.

We entered a small building in which there was a green rockery, a haven of tranquillity. The floor was waxed and thickly carpeted, and there were wall lamps and a chandelier. It had been a club for Soviet experts, with a dining room and even a dance floor. They must have had advance notice of our arrival, for there were dishes waiting. They looked, smelt and tasted wonderful.

We then drove off to the Qinghe Wool Mill. We saw all the stages, from carding to the finished product, including bolts of variously patterned fine wool, soft, densely textured material for overcoats, and wool of all colours.

The next day, we visited the No. 1 Machine Tool Plant. There was a pile of logs in the square, which I later learned marked the entrance to the air-raid shelter. The big factories were already building defence works in case of war. The comrade who took us round was a technician. He carefully explained the name of each lathe, its function, and the names of the things it produced. There was a contour lathe alongside a small model of it. The lathe could turn out enlarged versions of the model by copying the pattern. It was very advanced technology. Several big lathes had been put to one side. These were Soviet-made, but they required too much power and compared badly with our own products. I was over-joyed to learn of our progress.

In the afternoon, we visited Beijing's No. 3 State Cotton Mill. At F's request, we saw the nursery and the kindergarten. Inside the courtyard was a slide, a seesaw, and other playground equipment. It was cold, and the children were playing indoors. Some lay sleeping on the beds. The older children were inside watching slides. When they saw an animal, they laughed and shouted bois-terously. They had chubby faces and reacted with curiosity to our presence. They weren't shy, and some were quite talkative.

F was delighted, and I rejoiced at seeing him so happy. Spring Festival was almost upon us, and the whole family reunited in celebration. For ten years, we had been unable to gather.

12

Farewell Beijing, Farewell Dear Ones

We spent Spring Festival in a 24-hour hubbub. Director Wu and Comrade Huang came to wish F a happy Spring Festival. Then they got round to the purpose of the visit: we were to leave Beijing and make a new home in Chengdu in Sichuan. F's face fell and any trace of a smile vanished from it. I was also shocked.

Seeing us dumbstruck, Director Wu gave a small lecture: 'Chengdu is, as you know, a land of plenty, with a good environment and beautiful scenery. It's a far better place than here. We've made arrangements. They'll find you a nice house. As for work,' he said, pointing at me, 'we've arranged for you to join the archive section of the Provincial Cultural Bureau. You'll be a cadre under the Ministry of the Interior. There'll be no problem about your son changing schools, he can join any school you want. Sichuan University is very famous.'

He had probably already discussed it with Xiaogu, our elder son, who said, 'Sichuan University is famous nationwide. I can travel down from Xi'an to see you.'

Younger son said, 'It's only a few months before I finish school, I want to complete my senior high here.'

Everyone waited for F to speak. He said, 'I would prefer to stay in Beijing, even on a reform-through-labour farm. Beijing is the heart of the nation, here I can feel its beat. It's easier to study in Beijing, it will help my thought reform. The southwest is a long way away, we would have to start from scratch. I'm already 64. My remaining years are precious, I would like to do some research and translating. In Beijing there are libraries I can use. If I go to the southwest, I will be old and useless, an old criminal.'

'We've thought about it from every angle. We can create excellent conditions for you to work and study. The provincial Department of Public Security can help you.'

Comrade Huang said, 'If there are problems, you can write to us.'

They asked me what I thought. I said, 'It's good of you to find me a job, obviously I'm grateful. But I too would prefer to stay in Beijing. If it's not convenient for us to live here, we can go somewhere more remote. I don't need to be a cadre, I would like to be a worker.'

'We want to ensure your safety. This is a decision of the Central Committee.'

Xiaogu said, 'It's true, mum, you should have a new life, you shouldn't stay at home looking after us. You've spent half a lifetime caring for us. Dad's still in good health. The time has come for you to serve the masses, to give free rein to your talents.'

F felt as if he were being banished. He would never again be able to do literary work. In his lonely cell, he had continued to recite poetry to himself and had worked out in his mind drafts of the articles he intended to write. Now all his hopes were shattered. There were no words to describe his grief. I understood, but had no way of consoling him.

I made a suggestion. What about if he wrote a personal letter to Premier Zhou Enlai asking to be allowed to stay in Beijing? He didn't accept my proposal. Instead, he said I should insist on not going to Sichuan. 'I've lost my freedom. I'm not qualified to make requests. But you are a free person.' I was also reluctant to go to Sichuan, where I had no one. And I had an additional reason: the police station had promised to remove my hat, but I had stopped attending the study sessions after F was let out and didn't know where I stood. Here it would be easier to remove the hat. So I had good reason not to want to go to a place where I would have to start all over again.

We spent the whole time moping. It was snowing, and although it wasn't cold indoors, we no longer took pleasure in sitting together by the stove. When the weather cleared up, I suggested F and I climb the Jingshan. He had never been to Jingshan Park, and had never seen the scholar tree from which the Chongzhen Emperor hanged himself. We followed the path to the Wanchun Pavilion. He hadn't walked or climbed for ten years, but he was not in the least exhausted, and he even out-walked his elder son. The red bricks and green tiles of the Forbidden City were covered in snow. Some of the shrubs that grew out of the cracks between the roof tiles were still upright, their withered branches fluttering in the wind, as if announcing that 'Spring is coming, and I'll put out new leaves, emerald green, towering proudly over you', because it's a shrub growing on an imperial roof. But little does it know that one day it will be hacked down and uprooted.

Old Chen suggested we visit the Art Gallery to see Rent Collection Courtyard. The Ministry of Public Security had got us some invitation tickets. During the war, we had spent six or seven years in the countryside in Sichuan. Now that they were again talking of sending us to Sichuan, it was interesting for us to see Rent Collection Courtyard. I don't like clay sculpture, but it re-awakened my wish to re-study old issues and materials. The tenant farmers' life of cruel exploitation reappeared before our eyes, together with the sight of girls and boys labelled for sale on market day. We had never seen the illegal punishments meted out by the landlords or the dungeons filled waist-high with water.

In the afternoon, we went to see *The East Is Red*. Old Chen told F to write down his feelings about it. He wrote, 'Ancestral country, I heard your heartbeat – thoughts after my visit.' He added that to study even better and strengthen his thought reform even further, he hoped to be allowed to stay in Beijing, under whatever mode of life.

Director Wu came to see us, accompanied by Comrade Huang. He said, 'The leadership has concluded that it would be best for you to go to Sichuan. Originally the idea was to send you to Yunnan, but then it was judged unsafe, because of the Vietnam War. But Chengdu is a lovely place, and a house has been arranged for you there. They're even preparing a toilet. You can do your writing. But the main thing is to strengthen your thought reform. You can look up old friends, as long as you tell the organisation.'

F said, 'The people I'd like to see would not necessarily want to see me; and I don't want to see those who would like to see me.'

'Why?'

'I'm afraid of implicating them.'

'You worry too much. Isn't Nie Gannu your old friend? You can see him.'

After that, he took me aside. I was looking for a chance to explain why I didn't want to leave Beijing. The main thing was my hat. I even said let him go, and I'll join him when the hat has been removed.

'This is a directive from the organisation, you must obey it. We can send on the materials. They can remove your hat there. You must help us talk Hu Feng round. You can write to me directly if anything happens.'

'I'm already over 50. It would be better not to work at all than make mistakes and get criticised.'

They had separate talks with the children. We were left with no room for doubt: 'Don't be irresolute, forget your misgivings. Go to Sichuan. It's been decided, the Central Committee has agreed – what's more, they hope you can go a bit earlier.' Looking out of the window, 'This isn't safe, we're doing this for your sake.'

The children, including our new son-in-law, all urged us to go. The son-in-law even said that he and our daughter would also go, that Director Wu would help them get jobs and they could look after us. Younger son would finish school here and elder son would go back to Xi'an. I was in a fluster, unable to make a decision. The children wanted me to get a job, but F suspected that I wanted to go to Sichuan so I could become a cadre, that I didn't want to help him stay in Beijing. He didn't realise it was a Central Committee decision.

I suggested that F see Old Nie and Big Sister Ying and hear their views. Big Sister Ying promised to come the next afternoon.

When old friends meet for the first time in ten years, it can be both happy and bleak. Each has gone through hard times. Each has progressed from the promise of youth to the decline into old age. Each says, you've grown old. The wrinkles and white hairs of a decade, the bitter memories.

F said to Old Nie, 'I never thought you would be implicated, that they would take your Party card away. I should have been less gullible. My friends paid a big price!'

'There's no escaping fate.'

They talked about things that had happened after their separation, and started discussing poetry. I steered Ying away and poured out my worries. Perhaps she could help me find a way of talking F round.

She thought aloud for a while, unable to make up her mind, and then surprised me by saying, 'I think you should go to Sichuan. Beijing is not a good place. They may launch another movement – those left behind could easily get into trouble. If you have the chance of leaving, take it – the further the better.'

She saw how surprised I was. 'You don't know. The row surrounding *Hai Rui Dismissed from Office* might deepen. The Beijing Municipal Party Committee might not be able to stay out of it. It's not a simple issue, that's obvious from the Editorial Note.'

We returned to the small room. Old Nie also thought it would be better to leave Beijing. He even said, 'When you're settled, we'll come too.'

F told Old Nie with deep feeling, 'You should continue with your Zhuangzi and write your novel, for example by adapting *Journey to* the *West* or *Legend of the White Snake*. Bai Suzhen is a strong woman opposed to feudalism, she is worthy of a book. Research *Dream of the Red Chamber* from an aesthetic point of view.'

Big Sister Ying butted in, 'Don't be so pessimistic. You've been beaten and punished, what else can they do? If they let you out, they're bound to let you work. Look at those war criminals, some are commission members and even commissioners. I spend all my time filing away materials for them, can you believe that?'

Everyone was moved by what she said. Our pent-up feelings seemed to dissipate.

'Old Hu has one big fault, he thinks too much, and ends up creating anxieties for himself.'

The two men who in the past had drained glass after glass now sipped sparingly. I had bought a bottle of their favourite bamboo-leaf wine, but neither showed much interest. They were old men, in their sixties. When they talked of old friends, each sighed. Quite a few of them had been branded rightists. Big Sister Ying said, 'You stayed out of trouble in 1955 but in 1957 you couldn't escape. There are so many movements, it's not surprising. I felt my heart was in the right place. By raising criticisms, I was trying to help the Party rectify itself. How was I to know I would be called anti-Party? But I learned from the experience. Old Hu, in future do as you're told and you can't go wrong!'

'What do you mean, do as I'm told? Don't you listen to the Party?'

'Of course! But listen or not, we don't understand, so we're bound to go wrong.'

All things considered, we enjoyed a lively evening.

Before leaving, Old Nie said, 'Old Tian would love to see you. Is that all right?'

'No! His situation is not much better than ours. Don't get him into trouble again on my account. He can write a letter.'

Shortly afterwards, I phoned to tell Old Nie and his wife the date of our departure. The same evening, Old Nie arrived, to see us off.

He and F had a long talk. From it, I sensed Old Nie had changed a lot. He thought deeply about things and boldly expressed his opinions, which was not easy. He had learned caution and was no longer negligent and unworldly. He had become a thinker.

From a paper wrapping he took out a poem he had written. It moved F greatly, and the two of them discussed it. He also gave F a set of the 80-chapter *Dream of the Red Chamber* edited by Yu Pingbo and some volumes of *Romances of the Red Mansion* and *The Resolution of the Dream of the Red Chamber*, for F to do some studies on it.

They took affectionate leave of one another. I watched Old Nie vanish into the cold air, a windcheater on his thin, tall frame, along the sparsely populated road.

F was depressed at the thought of going to Sichuan, and suggested visiting the Lu Xun Museum. I hadn't dared go ever since it opened, but now was an opportune moment.

He inspected the photos from which his image had been erased. He betrayed not a flicker of emotion. He asked the guide some questions. Where were the manuscripts kept? Were all the books kept here? How many visitors came? Did they include young people? It was midwinter, and the exhibition hall seemed deserted. But the guide said students usually came in groups and quite a few people came from outside the capital. That cheered F up.

Finally, F agreed to go to Sichuan. All that remained was to fix the date. The Ministry of Public Security pressed us to leave at once and said letting the family spend Spring Festival together had been a special favour and there could be no extension.

I saw off elder son and then got some bedding and luggage ready for younger son's school. It was heartrending, especially for Xiaoshan, who had been alone for more than five years following his eighth birthday. I had only been able to dream of him, and would wake in tears. For the last few years, we had depended on each other for survival, and now he was off to fend for himself and I was to follow F to far-away Sichuan, to face an uncertain future. Packing his clothes, I wept.

I only intended to take a few clothes and books, and then request a permanent transfer back to Beijing once F had completed his sentence. However, he was determined not to return to Beijing and wanted to take everything. I couldn't deal with his extremist attitude, so we even took his four shelves of books. The Ministry of Public Security engaged some packers to help. Four women packers packed dozens of pieces of luggage in wood and cardboard. I admired their efficiency and sense of duty. The only thing I worried about was whether the glass bookcase would survive. It had cost 80 yuan and was F's favourite possession.

On February 15, the Ministry of Public Security sent a station wagon to take us, our daughter, our son-in-law, Comrade Huang, and two other comrades to the station. On the platform, our younger son rushed up to us. We were escorted to a soft-sleeper compartment. Two men jumped down from the upper berths and introduced themselves. They had been sent from Sichuan to fetch us. I could speak Sichuan dialect, and we had a friendly chat. Comrade Huang went to say hello to the carriage attendant, and then politely took his leave.

We were left alone in the compartment. Our two short months together as a family had come to an end. We were about to leave Beijing, where I had lived for more than a decade. Again, I couldn't stop crying. Xiaoshan put on a manly air and did his best to cheer me up: 'Mum, tomorrow you'll see elder brother, I've already told him to meet you at the station. The sleeper doesn't look bad, I've never been in one.'

'Of course you have! What about when we came to Beijing from Shanghai?'

'But I was small then.'

When he said small, again the tears welled up, so I turned away to look out of the window. It was not so bad with my daughter and son-in-law. They weren't long married, so our separation was not so unbearable. That made us feel a bit better.

The attendant came. 'The train is about to leave, get off if you are not a passenger.'

Farewell Beijing, farewell loved ones. Once more I tasted the bitter sorrow of separation. Outside, Xiaoshan shouted, 'I'll come and see you in the summer holidays, everything will be all right!'

Everything will be all right! Holding back my tears, I silently watched them. I wish you a good life, grow up healthy! Strive to make a way for yourselves!

The train set off. We lay on our bunks, choked with tears.

Part Two

Living with a Prisoner

13

An Uncertain Future

We left Beijing grieving. The train sped into the countryside, where neat rows of urban housing gave way to small towns and villages and the grey-lime roofs of peasant dwellings and then to expanses of yellow-grey wind-blown sediment and roads lined by withered trees. What fate awaited us?

The public security men from Sichuan entered the compartment. I hastened to wipe away the tears and tried to greet them as if nothing had happened. The senior of the two was Department Chief X and the other was Section Chief X. They explained they were travelling back to Chengdu because of another matter. A colleague was travelling in a hard-sleeper berth. We were to call him Old Leng. He was our official escort.

The Department Chief was just two years younger than F, already in his early sixties. He had a thick head of hair that had remained largely black and sideburns that made him look even younger. Section Chief X was in his forties. It was clear at a glance that he was shrewd and capable. Old Leng spoke irritatingly slowly: he seemed honest but dull.

It was a long time before dinner and even longer before sleep, so the Section Chief took out a pack of cards and said to F, 'What about a game?' F waved his hand. 'I don't know how to, I've forgotten.' 'We'll play Chase the Pig. It's fun, you'll soon get the hang of it.'

F didn't like to decline, so they played, with F learning as he went. Sometimes he made a mistake and almost became the pig, and everyone laughed.

I sat there finishing the woollen vest for Big Sister Ying's grandson. Chugging along in the direction of unfamiliar people and surroundings, I sought solace in remembering old friends and loved ones in Beijing.

The following afternoon, we reached Xi'an. The station was painted bright red. Scanning the platform, I spotted Xiaogu. A fine drizzle was falling. To see him standing there all by himself pained me. Glancing sideways at F, I knew he too had seen his son, but his face betrayed nothing. He just sat there staring dully.

Our son entered the carriage, looking happy. He said again and again that he would come to Chengdu to see us: 'From here to Chengdu takes half the time it does from Beijing. I've always wanted to go to Chengdu.' He was trying to cheer us up.

F took out a pack of coloured postcards he had bought in the International Bookshop after his release and told him to choose some, but he simply flicked through them. His father tried to encourage him: 'Choose the ones you want!'

I could tell Xiaogu was embarrassed, but the comrades from public security were watching us, and it was hard for him to say no. I took over, choosing a couple and saying, 'Look, these are really nice, a single bud, standing proud and alone, it shows spirit.'

As he mumbled his reply, the attendant came to tell him to leave the carriage, so he said a hurried goodbye and left clutching his postcards. He watched the train chug out of the station.

This didn't mean much to me, for I was used to seeing the children come and go every winter and summer. However, F started sobbing. He had been holding back his feelings. I didn't dare try to console him – that would start me off too. I knew I should hide my grief, but I didn't know how to, so the tears flowed anyway. Had my feelings become fragile? Had my tear glands slackened? In the past, F had never cried easily. The best thing was to let him cry his heart out.

The attendant arrived to ask what we wanted for dinner, and whether we wanted it brought to the compartment. I ordered some cold dishes and beer.

A big plate of food and two bottles of beer arrived. The five of us sat chatting, eating and drinking, like friends. The atmosphere grew more relaxed, and F's state of mind improved. You could even say F spent his night on the train in quite a good mood.

When we reached our destination, it was already seven o'clock in the morning. So why was it not yet light? I asked if we had arrived ahead of schedule, and was informed that the sun here didn't rise until eight, unlike in the north.

A group of people arrived to receive us. By the time we got outside, the sun was up. Two jeeps awaited us, one with a trailer. When they saw there were only two of us, they seemed disappointed. 'What about the children? Why only two of them?'

Chengdu really was a land of plenty. In Beijing, nature was bare and barren. The trees lining the roads were leafless and rattled in the wind. Green leaves and red flowers were confined to greenhouses in the parks. But in Chengdu, the flowerbeds outside the station were full of brilliant dwarf evergreens. A purplish red creeper spread across the ground, which on closer inspection proved to be a variety of cabbage. Between the beds were stretches of grass and sago palms, each supporting a head of symmetrically arranged spikes. The sight nourished beautiful thoughts in me, including the wish that we might live forever in such a colourful world and never again suffer cold.

The car drove along through the first rays of the morning sun. After leaving the main road, it entered an area of small lanes and turned many corners, until we finally came to a halt in one of the alleys. We were led into a house with a small courtyard behind a black-painted gate. The main room faced the southern gable wall. The front and back rooms on the western side were ours, but we could use the back room to the east if the children came. After giving us these instructions, they left.

We were the sole inhabitants of the courtyard, with its five or six rooms. Fortunately we had been given a bed, a desk and chairs, and a square table and four stools in the main hall where we could sit and rest. I tidied up the things we had brought with us and saw from my watch that it was almost ten. We had been busy the whole morning, so we were hungry. No one had told us what to do, and I didn't dare take the initiative. When we were leaving Beijing, Xiaofeng had bought us some bread and snacks for the train, but we hadn't finished eating them, so we ate them now, to allay our hunger.

This 'meal' counted as lunch. F was in the habit of taking a midday nap, so I spread a blanket on the bed and let him sleep, using my overcoat as a pillow. He dropped off immediately. The ability to sleep was an essential asset he seemed still to possess.

He didn't wake until two o'clock. No one had come yet, so we sat chatting and thought we might as well eat the remaining bread. At three, they returned, and Department Chief X said in a loud voice, 'Have you eaten?' We pointed at the scraps of bread left on the table and told him we had just finished. He looked embarrassed. 'We were very busy, we made you wait a long time. All right, take it easy for a few days, in any case your luggage hasn't arrived. For the time being, you might as well eat out. But Old Leng must go with you. If you need anything, tell him. If Zhang Guangren feels like going out, Old Leng can go with him.' He introduced a little old man seated to one side: 'This is Old Wang. He got the house ready for you. He will stay here. If you have any problems, tell him.' He and Old Leng asked us about Beijing. They wanted to know what the Ministry of Public Security had decided. We showed them the stipulations and Old Leng wrote out a copy. Department Chief X said, 'All right, Old Leng can go out with you for dinner.' Old Leng said, 'Someone should bring a bedspread, they haven't brought enough bedding.' On his way out, Department Chief X said, 'I'll let them know.'

So we had permission to go out for our evening meal, with Old Leng.

Our side street led to a bustling main road. We walked round the area for a while, noting where the restaurants and general stores were. At first we couldn't make up our minds, but then

Old Leng mentioned Mrs Pockmarked Chen's Beancurd Shop, which we had often heard people talk about in Chongqing during the war, so we were curious. It was just down the road. Now we could enjoy the beancurd we had heard so much about. This was our first meal in Chengdu, and we had Old Leng with us, so I ordered three portions of beancurd and two vegetable dishes and a soup. The beancurd set our mouths watering: the brown pepper powder and chopped green onion sprinkled over the white bean-curd and surrounded by a ring of red oil was a sight to behold. But when I put it in my mouth, I gasped, for it was scorching. I could barely keep it in my mouth, although I was too polite to spit it out. The second mouthful went down more easily, and I could taste the flavour. With rice, the beancurd seemed less peppery. All the dishes were spicy so we asked for less chilli, but even then everything was still quite hot, except for the spinach and soup. There was nothing like this in Beijing, where all you could get at this time of the year was cabbage and turnips. The beancurd made up for our two missed meals – and it only cost two yuan.

This went on for several days, while we waited for the luggage. Because it didn't get light until late, we lay in bed and waited for the sun to rise. I went out by myself to fetch breakfast, but Old Leng had to accompany us to lunch and dinner. After a few days, all that fatty and pungent food began to seem monotonous. F had piles, and spicy food was bad for him. I asked for greens, but they had none. How we longed for some of the spinach and kale on sale in the vegetable market. If you eat with a stranger, you have to rack your brains for things to talk about. I found it hard to balance what to eat. If I ordered good food, it wouldn't accord with my status. If I ordered poor food, I'd feel embarrassed about our guest. I didn't know what he would say to the authorities in his reports, so whenever we ate I first asked him what he thought. I wouldn't even buy F a drink unless Old Leng wanted one. Old Leng was reserved, which made me even more uncomfortable. So I found the food less and less palatable.

When we got off the train, it was early spring in Chengdu, with flowers everywhere, but on the third day there was a sudden cold spell. The sky hazed over and a wind blew. Even indoors it was hard to avoid the chill. Again, we couldn't help thinking of Beijing, where the houses were heated.

The cold and the enforced idleness were hard to endure. With each hand in the opposite sleeve of his padded jacket, F would pace up and down in the house. I also had nowhere to go and no one to talk with. I said, 'We should discuss what to do. We can't just sit here in the cold.'

'There are countless things I would like to do. We haven't got our luggage. There's no one to talk to.' He paused, and then started up again: 'I'm going to sort out the poems I composed in prison.'

He stood up and freed his hands from his sleeves. He began to talk, a mixture of reminiscence and soliloquy. His spirits lifted and he began to recite, in a louder voice. He became more and more passionate, and I too was infected. The room no longer seemed like an ice cellar. It was as if his verses had loosed a current of warm air. He was moved to tears and his voice deepened and became hoarse. My eyes too grew moist as I thought of his years in gaol, relying for warmth on his poems.

I said, 'Let's buy some paper, then you can write them down. Can you still recall them all?'

'I think so. There are several thousand poems in all, and several tens of thousands of lines.'

'When did you begin composing?'

'In 1958. The officials talked with me hundreds of times, and then suddenly stopped coming. I thought, we must have talked about everything they needed to discuss, the only thing left is the final disposition. If there's nothing left to do, I'll go mad sitting by myself in a cell ten metres by ten. They brought me *People's Daily*, but even if you read it from start to finish it only takes a few hours. As I paced around, poems started to form in my mind. At first they were in free verse, but that was hard to remember and I had no paper to write it down on, so I switched to classical poetry. They kept on coming. After a few experiments, I created a series of poems in the traditional style. I only had to recall the first line and then the rest came easily. Each section had eight or ten lines. I did my best to use characters that are easy to understand, unlike in real classical poetry, which uses literary allusions. My hope was that people would be able to read and understand them. Each poem or song was aimed at a specific person. Some were friends or acquaintances, others were imagined. They accompanied me in my lonely life.'

'Did they keep you in your cell for the whole ten years?'

'Sometimes they took me away for interrogations. Every day they checked up through the peephole, but I couldn't see them.' Adopting an even more serious tone of voice, 'That pock-marked official who brought you in observed me for the full ten years. I was allowed out once a day for exercise, but the time was never fixed. In summer, they sometimes let me out when the sun was at its peak. In the winter, they let me out late in the afternoon, when it was bitterly cold. But I didn't mind. The main thing was to get in touch with nature. The exercise yard was a brick-paved square, a dozen metres across. You could do what you wanted. It was divided into four segments. Sometimes I could hear people across the wall coughing, other prisoners who had been let out for exercise. There were watchtowers manned by armed PLA men. If you stretched your neck, you could see mountains. They were almost completely grey. You couldn't see a single tree or blade of grass. Once, I spotted a blade of grass on the yard floor in a crack between the bricks. You can't imagine how delighted I was! It was drooping, so the next day I went out with my mouth full of water and watered it. I did the same day after day, and it lived for ages. It grew big and strong and turned into a small clump. I couldn't help admiring its vitality, that it could take root and sprout in that tiny crack. I also thought that without water it would have died. Wasn't it the same with me? Would I have survived the rigours of the old society if I had not studied

Marxism-Leninism? If I lacked confidence in the Party, I doubt whether I could have survived.' He seemed to lapse into a depression.

I changed the subject: 'Couldn't you read?'

'Yes, but not for a few years. They let me read books they chose for me, but I didn't have a pen or paper and I had no way of making notes.'

'Surely you must have written some confessions?'

'Of course. I only left the cell for interrogations and exercise. The door was inches thick, and there were bars. When they wanted me to write confessions, they brought in a small table. All I had was a six-inch high bed. I had to sit on it cross-legged to write. Perhaps that's why I got piles. I used to bleed regularly. The water in the slops bucket turned red. I told them and they gave me some ointment. It got so bad, I couldn't stand. I even gave up my exercise. I used to spend all day lying on my bed. It was torture. I used the time to sort my entire set of poems in my mind, reciting them one after the other. Some people came to life inside my head and we did antiphonal singing. That lifted me out of my misery. They didn't send me to hospital for an operation until 1962. Even that didn't put an end to it. I still get piles, and walking hurts.'

'So that's why we heard you'd gone to hospital.'

'One day a young man came in and threw a wheatgrass hat-ribbon and a bundle of wheat-stalks at me and said, "You eat but you never work, you must learn to weave straw." I said, "Who said I didn't want to work? It's you who won't let me. My job is not to weave straw, it's to write." I left the stalks where they were, and later they took them away.'

'Didn't they punish you?'

'No. Perhaps they thought they should be a bit more polite to political prisoners not yet sentenced.'

'So you were never punished?'

'I was once. The director in charge of the interrogation asked me a question and I said I didn't know. He said sarcastically,

"Aren't dogs supposed to have a good sense of smell? Can't you sniff it out?" I returned the compliment: "You're the dog, not me." His jaw dropped. He whispered something in the note-taker's ear. The note-taker left and returned with a pair of iron handcuffs. He handcuffed me and took me back to my cell.'

'How could you eat? How could you get dressed and undressed?'

'At meal times the official unlocked them.'

Then he said to me, 'You were locked up for 70 months. What was it like?'

Actually, I didn't want him to know. My inability to decide whether to tell him how much I had missed the children and my old mother had cost me a lot of sleep over the previous three months.

'Let's not talk about it for now, it brings up too much hurt. Did you see the materials I wrote?'

'Yes. They used you and Lu Ling as weapons against me.* I said you were the mother of our children, of course you would write that.'

'Do you know how I saw the light? One day, the cadre in charge of the interrogation showed me some handwritten notes – "Exposing XX's anti-Party opinions". I was scared, but I managed to hide it. Then he started to educate me. He said my progress was slow, I wasn't thinking of the children, etc., etc. He came up with all sorts of arguments. Finally, he told me to confess about your counter-revolutionary crimes. I said, all I know is he opposed Zhou Yang's sectarianism. His criticisms were about literary issues. "But didn't you know Zhou Yang is a minister under the Central Committee?" I didn't answer. "Surely opposing the Communist Party is counter-revolutionary?" When he put it like that, I saw the light. I was really grateful for his "help". But when it came to writing my confession, I wasn't allowed to write about myself or you, I had to write about "us", in the plural,

---

* Lu Ling (1921–94), a writer and pupil of Hu Feng's.

because I personally didn't have anything to confess. According to the chief interrogator, if I didn't say anything I would be covering up. I said that I opposed your 300,000-word memo. The interrogator said, "Why didn't you report it to the organisation?" That frightened me to death. I said, "How could I do that, unless I wanted to break up the family? And what should I have told them? He hadn't killed anyone, he hadn't robbed anyone." He snorted. "You really are backward!" "That's why I said I was just a housewife." "Don't take refuge in the kitchen, you're a backbone element, after all."

'I confessed about us for three months. Then they started asking me about other people. That was even worse. What did they mean, counter-revolutionary? If they really were counter-revolutionary and I didn't say so, I would be deceiving the Party, but if they weren't and I came out with nonsense, wouldn't that be deceiving the Party even more? So I used words like "apparently", "I've heard that", "if this and if that", and I was told off for it. Especially when they started on about Zhang Zhongxiao.* How was I to know the letter by Zhang could cause so much indignation? I stuck to the facts: he was a young student, his lungs started bleeding, so people put him on a plane and sent him home to Shaoxing, where he lay on his bed for five years. When they operated on him, they cut away five ribs. He didn't know anything about changes in the outside world. He was susceptible because of his illness. Also, his family situation was not good. Because of all that, he easily got angry. Hu Feng sent him a letter of advice, etc., etc. The interrogator said I was covering up for him. Later, he asked about the burning of Zhang's letter, that was also a crime, because you weren't allowed to burn correspondence, even your own letters. They demanded I recall its contents, so I made up a standard courtesy letter. Actually, I had only a vague memory of it, I remember it praised your theories but disagreed with your behaviour towards the authorities. He discussed with

---

* A victim of the campaign against Hu Feng.

you about copying it and sending it to the Central Committee, but you didn't agree. Later it was burned to avoid implicating him. He was ill and had a quick temper, so he might not have been able to withstand a fierce attack. But once the letter was burned, it became a big problem, and there were endless investigations. The questioning drove me mad. I wrestled with my conscience. I couldn't simply shift the blame onto others. In my cell, I wrote on a sheet of paper, "They have started to force a confession." The next day, it was confiscated, and there was another interrogation. He wanted me to say in what way I was being forced. All I said was, "About Zhang Zhongxiao, if you carry on interrogating me like that, I will have a break-down." He replied, "If you think it's inappropriate you can retract your confession. We want a truthful confession." That was good, it meant I could ask to be allowed to say things more vaguely. I couldn't cause people harm by pretending to know things. They agreed, and my insomnia cleared up.

'They kept asking me, "What was your purpose in writing the 300,000-word memo?" I said, "We hoped the Central Committee would adopt it, so everyone could work better." "The Central Committee has so many people, do you mean they're unable to work? Did Hu Feng want to become a minister?" I almost burst out laughing. I said, "Hu Feng wasn't even a Party member, how could he become a minister? His biggest wish was to be allowed to run a magazine." You know I haven't the slightest experience of these things.'

F said, 'That was a perfect way to answer. If I'd wanted to be an official, there were thousands of jobs in the early years. I could easily have wormed my way in. Zhou Yang used to say, "As long as Hu Feng makes a self-criticism, there'll be no problem in employing him." Should I give in? Should I denigrate myself? All I wanted was to be free to write. I was no longer interested in literary theories. All I wanted was to praise the Party and the people.

'You saw the light after three months, I was plunged into darkness after three months. I was blindfolded with a black cloth. My

14

First lesson

One afternoon, a few days after our arrival, someone from the Department of Public Security came to see F. He was in his forties. He seemed to be an intellectual. He treated us civilly and cordially.

First he asked about F's health. He said he should see a doctor for a check-up, since it was essential to stay healthy. He added that they had recently opened a stomatological hospital with advanced equipment, and that it could do false teeth. He asked politely about our life in Beijing, how we had lived after F's release from prison, etc., etc. Noticing that we were both wearing overcoats, he said, 'The winters aren't cold here, it's just that we don't have central heating. In any case, we can install a stove for you. It will be spring in a few days. It will soon be better.' He asked F whether he had any friends in Sichuan. 'If you want to meet them, we'll help you get in touch. If you want to see any senior leaders, we'll arrange it, as long as they have time.'

F replied, 'I'm a prisoner awaiting punishment, I wouldn't dare bother them.'

He introduced us to two cadres who would share our lives. Section Chief X was a Red Army veteran; charged with guarding the house was Old Wang, a skinny ex-Red Army man in his early sixties. Both were handpicked to help us reform. We should do our best to learn from them. F indicated his esteem.

The cadre again told Old Leng to accompany us on our outings, and to contact the hospital and get F cured. The conversation went on for more than an hour. He kept on saying we should let him know if we needed anything, and that he would come frequently.

The next day, Section Chief X handed F a note adding a new instruction to those laid down by the Ministry of Public Security in Beijing. Every month he was to submit a thought report.

That afternoon, we suggested going into town to look round and do some shopping. After living in seclusion for three or four days we at last got to see Chunxi Road, Tidu Street and Zongfu Street and the big department stores in the city centre. F went to the Xinhua Bookshop, but failed to find what he wanted. We bought a green hardback diary and a bottle of ink. We tried to buy some squared paper, but none of the stationery stores had any.

We also toured Chengdu's well-known scenic spots with Old Leng. We visited the ancestral temple of Liu Xiang, the Sichuanese warlord. It was in the style of the Three Kingdoms period. The rows of cypresses and shrubs leading up from the main gate were meticulously laid out. The first great hall was probably used for memorial ceremonies. In front of the tomb is another smaller hall with incense burners and altar tables. The tomb itself is large and circular. The coffin had long ago been removed, so we were able to enter the coffin pit. People used to call Liu Xiang the King of Sichuan, and his temple and vault confirmed that he was no ordinary man.

The vault was surrounded by rare flowering plants. They included a night lotus, which I had seen as a child in the courtyard of a gentry family in southern Jiangxi. I had never again seen it in any park, and here it was growing along both sides of the temple. It was a green shrub, a little higher than a person, with greenish blue peach-shaped buds that produced white lotus flowers after dark and scattered a faint fragrance. After flowering, it left behind a tiny seed in the shape of a finger citrus.

We had a group photo taken under a scholar tree. There are very few scholar trees in the north, and even in the south they are rare. F enthused about its soaring trunk and spiky foliage. He praised its character: especially its refusal to blossom to please the sightseers. However, I would love to have seen it produce flowers.

After a fortnight, the luggage arrived. When old Comrade Wang went to the station to enquire, he was told that it had been there for a while, but they hadn't known who to tell. Cadres from the Reform Through Labour Bureau helped bring it over. We were surprised: why didn't they get someone to do it for them? But we didn't dare ask. All we could do was stand around with a guilty conscience and thank each of them.

The women workers from the Beijing removal company had done a good job. All the glass in the bookcase remained intact. Only the wardrobe had lost a leg, but it was easily put right with a couple of bricks. We gave the wooden pallets and a few things we didn't need to Department Chief X, who was setting up house in Chengdu.

Now we had our pots and crockery, we finally felt we had settled in, and we stopped our visits to the restaurant. F loved home cooking and Chengdu's rich assortment of fresh vegetables. He shovelled them into his mouth, as if rejuvenated. In Beijing, such vegetables could not be bought in the winter, and F had not tasted the like for ten years.

Old Leng dropped repeated hints about the ideological reports F was supposed to write, and implied that the authorities were keen to see them. So F wrote his first account of his impressions. To give an idea of his state of mind at the time, I copy them here:

IMPRESSIONS (FROM BEIJING TO CHENGDU)

1. While moving from Beijing to Chengdu, we were first looked after by the leadership of the Ministry of Public Security, and then the leadership of the Sichuan Department of Public Security showed us consideration: we were taken care of en route, and the house was repaired and put in order in advance

of our arrival. The careful and attentive help and guidance from which we have benefited since our arrival means that at every turn we have felt the warmth of the Party. Besides two sincere and honest veteran comrades with a long experience of the life of revolutionary struggle to keep us company, we have received frequent visits from comrades in the direct leadership, so that even though we are living in solitude, we still enjoy the opportunity to learn from old revolutionaries and 'take lessons from the lives of others'.

2. Despite this big change, I feel inwardly stable and even happy.
3. However, this stability and happiness is that of a lazy person and even of a 'mediocrity'. Since last December, I have begun noticing that my mental ability to respond to objective phenomena has weakened and I have become ideologically lazy. When the leadership of the Ministry of Public Security decided to move us to Chengdu, our mental outlook was that we felt we would henceforth be far away from the heart of the ancestral country and the Party, in Beijing, and we experienced a sudden attack akin to despair; after that, I realised it was our duty to submit to the decision of the organisation, so my state of mind stabilised. After I arrived in Chengdu, my state of mind stabilised even further, so I started to become happier: but my ideological laziness became even more obvious. Age and physical deterioration meant that my original awareness of objective reality had slowed; now, because of the weakening of my mental powers, it seemed that ideologically my exploratory power was lost or paralysed. I could no longer raise questions about objective affairs. Even worse, I felt there were no problems, i.e., ideologically there was no demand for discovering problems and no sense of responsibility. For example, after arriving in Chengdu, we felt we should visit historical sites like the Wuhou Temple and Du Fu's Thatched Hut to evoke the past and grasp through concrete phenomena the influence these two historical figures exercised on millions of people and the attitude of different ages and classes towards

them. Given my circumstances, this was for me a permitted activity. But even though the luggage did not arrive for ten days and I was at leisure, I had no interest in sightseeing. When we visited Wuhou Temple, I had some thoughts and feelings, and when we returned home I took out the *Records of the Shu* to see how Chen Shou recorded it and to compare it with the account in the *Romance of the Three Kingdoms*; I was even more interested to see how the three-volume *Zhuge Liang*, published for young people after Liberation, introduced these historical personages. But up to now, I have failed to do even that small thing. Which is why I say that although I am stable and even happy, this is the stability and happiness of a lazy person or a mediocrity.

4. Such a mental state is not good. When I think of the leadership's concern for me and the way it has looked after me, I feel guilty about my laziness and mediocrity. From now on I am unlikely to get any further chance to commit errors or damage the prestige of the Party's literary leadership, which is a consolation, yet given the national and international situation, a Chinese of the Mao Zedong era cannot but feel conscience-stricken. At the same time as eliminating my physical exhaustion, I must find ways to restore my mental powers and overcome my ideological torpor, by reading new books and re-reading Marx, Engels, Lenin and Stalin to see if I cannot try, by applying Mao Zedong Thought, to do some preliminary research into my predecessors' works. At the very least I would hope to avoid an even more erroneous understanding of the Party's policy and line, of the mainstream trends internationally and nationally, and of major events.

5. I have only been in Chengdu for a short while and have not been able to get in touch in a deep-going way with the masses, but I do have some impressions. Compared with the period of the Resistance War, the mental outlook of the Sichuanese people has undergone a revolutionary transformation. Even compared with their mental outlook at the time of land reform,

in which I participated, there has been a gigantic and qualitative change. Chengdu, which in legend and imagination was a city of landlords and bureaucrats, has become a city of workers. Its streets are practically void of parasites; particularly eye-catching is the widespread participation in labour of women. Public morality is good: this is clear from the level of street hygiene. The people's political enthusiasm is high: I was happy to observe this from the sensitive reactions of the audience to good people and bad people when watching a film. They have deep faith in the Party and Chairman Mao. The *Quotations from Chairman Mao* are everywhere to be seen. This intensely moves me.

13 March 1966, in Chengdu.

He said, 'I hope that this will put an end to their belief that I have some sort of "wild ambition". I'm already totally worn-out. All I want is to do a bit of work so I don't become a living corpse. All I want is not to make any more mistakes.' He was impossible to cheer up.

After we had bought some red squared paper, F started copying out the 'Songs in Memory of Spring' he had silently intoned in prison. He immersed himself in memories of the past and poetic sentiment. He would only let me read them when he had finished transcribing them all. All I could do was watch him pondering, remembering, copying.

I returned to the routines of everyday life, buying food, cooking and doing housework. Food was easy to get, so things went smoothly. However, it was obvious from the press that a storm was blowing up in Beijing concerning art and literature. Could it spread even to our apparently peaceful southwest? I watched anxiously. They had hinted repeatedly that I should report to the provincial Cultural Bureau. But how could I both go to work and cook him three meals a day? I asked if they could get us a female help to do the cooking while I was away. Department Chief X didn't think so. He said, 'Let Zhang Guangren do his own cook-ing.' 'He's never cooked before.' 'Let him learn, it's not so hard.' 'I think it's a bit late. It would be better if you could find a way of helping.' 'All right, we'll see what we can do. But don't forget to get ready to report for work.'

For decades, I had longed to be able to work. F's lack of a permanent job in the old days had meant that we had no settled home, so again and again I had missed the chance, and could at most snatch a moment here and there to do some of my own writ-ing, especially children's stories. All things considered, I can't say I wasted my life. I persevered with my work, and I could claim to be part of the world of literature. To put me in the Cultural Bureau would mean I was publicly employed, I would have more opportunity to be near others and learn things. The children urged me in their letters to stop being a housewife. How could I not seize the opportunity? But the political situation was complex and unsettled. The world of art and literature was about to be plunged into troubled times. If I got drawn in, would I be able to cope? I was apprehensive and irresolute.

F was attending hospital almost daily. He mainly saw tradi-tional doctors, so every day I had to decoct medicine for him. For years he had had a bitter taste in his mouth and ringing ears. He used to say there was a small insect near his ear, which buzzed or chirruped. It was not too bad during the day, when he had some-thing to concentrate on or people to talk to, but at night he could hear it especially clearly; and first thing in the morning, his mouth tasted bitter. The doctors put it down to liver heat and feeling ill at ease, and prescribed antipyretics and medicine to calm the spirit and ease anxiety. He took the medicine but said he could still hear the noise, so the old doctors prescribed some herbal remedies. I had to buy an ear herb called *xiang'er cao* and stew some pork kidney. I went to lots of medicine shops before I eventually found the herb, which turned out to be grass about a foot long with small bells on it. I had to stew it with the kidney. Perhaps the idea was that the little bells would drown out those ringing in F's ears.

The stew turned pitch-black. I couldn't help admiring F when he swallowed it in one go.

Department Chief X again urged me to go to work. He told me female helps were hard to find, and cost 40 to 50 yuan a month. Moreover, in our case it wasn't convenient.

I understood what he meant. Outsiders weren't allowed into our building. A woman brought milk into the courtyard, but I rarely saw her, let alone talked with her.

F was adamant: I should not go to work. He said, 'The situation may turn out a lot more complex than in 1955. We're cut off here, and we don't know what winds are blowing in the outside world. If you insist I won't stop you, but I would no longer dare discuss opinions with you. Also, you should never talk about me. If some campaign starts up, you won't be able to resist. You would blurt out whatever was in your heart. You're too naïve. You don't know how cunning people are nowadays, how servile.'

I knew what he meant. Our credulity had often cost us dear. It was not easy living together. What would be the point in once again bringing trouble upon ourselves? So I decided to give up my chance of working as a state cadre and instead dedicated myself to helping F finish his research on *Dream of the Red Chamber* and other classics.

Comrade X, who was responsible for us in the provincial Department of Public Security, talked with F about what he had written: 'The Central Committee is busy with cultural questions. You must do your best. There's no room for pessimism. You must work even harder to reform your thinking, don't sit idly by. Actively examine your thinking. In the current excellent situation, you should go all out to do your best.' F again stressed his incapacity: he had been detached from society and the world of art and literature for more than ten years, he was unable to grasp the Party's policies in a comprehensive way, his main preoccupation was to do everything possible to avoid committing errors, to commit fewer errors, to serve his prison term without getting into further trouble. Obviously such a response would not satisfy the leadership, but the visitor did not criticise F and was even polite. Finally, he turned to me, and asked why I hadn't reported for work. 'It's April already, surely you've got the house sorted out by now. It's not often people get the offer of a job.'

'I've considered it, but I had better not. It would be better if I studied at home.'

'The work would hardly exhaust you. You could find time to study. At work you can listen to reports and read documents. Then you can transmit them to Hu Feng, that would help him too, would it not?'

For my own progress, to strengthen my ideological reform, I ought not to refuse. I could hardly tell him that I feared getting drawn into quarrels and disputes. All I could do was say that I wanted to stay at home to care for F during his illness, to study with him, to reform ourselves together. I said I was grateful to the Government for taking care of our lives and getting me work, but we still had a bit of money that we could use to supplement our living expenses. I had gone over this answer again and again in my mind. When they gave me the job, they told me the pay was enough to cover my needs, but they hadn't said how much. We had only F's living allowance of 50 yuan, which we shared, and I had no way of predicting how things would turn out in future. But I thought, if it gets worse then it gets worse, we'll just have to economise and dip into our savings.

To my surprise, he agreed. However, he also said, in a more serious tone, 'If you won't accept the job and prefer to shoulder the burden yourselves, so be it, but it's your decision.'

With that problem resolved, we both calmed down a bit, and F's morale began to lift. He carried on copying out his poems – he had already filled more than 200 sheets. I was full of admiration for his memory, but I couldn't help asking him, 'Didn't you ever think of writing them down? What if . . .'

'They would just have rotted away inside me.' He paused, and said, 'There was one opportunity, in the summer of 1962. The cell door flew open and a senior cadre walked in. He addressed me courteously, not like the interrogators. He enquired about my health and what I was reading. I answered his questions. Then he asked, "Is that all you've done?" "I've also composed some poems." He looked surprised, and said he would like to read them. I explained that they were only in my head. "Why didn't you write them down?" "I had no pen or paper." "That's easy to arrange. I'll tell them to bring some." I didn't say anything, since I couldn't work out who he was. He said, "It's up to you. If there's anything you want, just ask."

'Later, the cadre supervising me told me it was Xu Zirong, a vice-minister of the Ministry of Public Security, who was also Director of the Office of Internal Affairs in the Prime Minister's Office. I felt a current of warmth slowly thawing my long-frozen heart. It even occurred to me that he might actually be in charge of my case. However, I made no requests, not even for a pen. I decided to wait patiently, until the Party reached its verdict. I always believed I would gain the Party's comprehension and be released. But I spent more than three years waiting. I was too confident, too simple-minded.'

His poems eventually took up more than 400 pages. I seemed to recognise the people in them, but some things puzzled me. He explained that here and there he had added fanciful details. In that way, he could cherish the memory of leaders and dear ones who had influenced him or had feelings for him.

After he finished his copying, he relaxed. It was late spring: the parks had donned their gaudy raiment, and I suggested we take a walk. But he wanted me to go with him to the bookshop to look for some materials on *Dream of the Red Chamber* and ask whether he might be allowed to borrow some rare editions. Old Leng accompanied us. How were we to know that such editions couldn't be fetched from the depository without a letter of introduction? So we left disappointed. We asked Old Leng to get us a letter, but they told him the stack room was under reorganisation and they couldn't help us for the time being.

We received letters from family members and friends in Beijing. The children were disappointed I had not gone to work. I couldn't blame them, for if I had taken a job, they would be able to say on official forms that their mother was a cadre. But how were they to know my troubles? Old Nie and Big Sister Ying also wrote. They said they had started to envy us. They envied our access to fresh vegetables and our quiet life, and they even asked us to find them accommodation so they could move to Chengdu and become our neighbours. Old Xiao wrote about scenic spots and historic sites in Sichuan that he had visited in the past, and sent F a book on health care and massage. That was something F definitely needed.

We didn't live far from the sports ground, and in the mornings we went there with Old Leng and saw people doing tai-chi. F told Old Leng he wanted to learn tai-chi and so did Old Leng, but we needed a supporting document. We asked Old Leng to organise one, but we were told to exercise at home instead. When we received the book on health care and massage, he followed the exercises every morning. He wanted me to join him, but I didn't.

F had forgotten about the thought reports he was supposed to write. One day, Department Chief X came to see us. He asked whether F had any friends in Chengdu he would like to see. 'You can suggest people you would like to invite. It's a nice time of the year in Chengdu, you can go to the park and sit for a while.' He added, 'I was planning to organise a car to take you to visit Liu Wencai's landlord residence in Dayi County.* But there was no car.' Finally he asked, 'Have you begun writing your thought report this month?'

So F hurriedly wrote 'Recent Developments', his thought report for April:

---

* The former residence of the Liu family, converted into a museum in 1958

In my March 'Impressions', I explained that my inner life had undergone a loss of motive power and collapsed into an 'indolent' mental outlook, so that my response to objective circumstances became paralysed. Is that a product of ideological (intellectual) pessimism? Investigation suggests that it is not. The same is true of my present state of mind.

First, in regard to general trends in the world revolutionary movement and the forward march of history, I am not pessimistic – quite the opposite. As for the twists and turns in this or that stage in certain countries, or even marking time or marching backwards, such things are inevitable – otherwise, it could not be considered a revolution, especially not a world revolution. As for the actual situation, my political level may be low, but I am not so impractical as to imagine that the world revolution can sail to victory in just a few decades or centuries.

Second, regarding the domestic situation, the opposite is even more true. The ancestral country is in mid-spring, with its leafing and budding, and even those who are experiencing difficulties or partial defeats in the course of reform are moved and excited.

Third, someone like me who once stood on the literary battle-front has, over the last couple of years, entered the stage of all-out and deep-going revolution. Since the May Fourth Movement, the main trend has been to adapt to the revolutionary tradition of realism as part of the revolutionary struggle of the working people led by the proletariat.* However, the anti-feudal tasks have not been thoroughly carried out, not to speak of the poisonous feudal pus of its component parts and the elements of the semi-colonial bourgeoisie that are massively present. Because of this, there are unresolved problems and endlessly troublesome big and small swindles that cannot be overlooked.

---

* The May Fourth Movement was an anti-imperialist, cultural, and political movement protesting against China's weak response to the Treaty of Versailles in 1919. It sparked national protests and an upsurge of Chinese nationalism.

He couldn't help saying what was on his mind, and it took him a long time to calm down after he had finished writing. He said to me, 'First of all they accuse me of a big crime and now they want me to talk about ideological questions. I'm not saying anything more. The Central Committee has switched its focus to literary issues. If this means clearing up improprieties in art and literature, all well and good. It was really difficult, if you touched on one thing, it affected all the rest. Would they be able to reach such a decision? Immediately they started, Yao Wenyuan's article came out, which is a bad omen. So I've decided to steer clear of literary issues. In the past, I laid bare my heart by writing out my opinions for the Central Committee, but it turned out I was wrong. If they are rejected, it means I've committed a cardinal error and I'm reprimanded even though I had no evil intent. The chief interrogator said I wanted to become a minister, what a joke! How would I, a non-Party democratic personage, have qualified? The result was my views were seen as a savage attack on the Party, I was a counter-revolutionary, and I was sentenced to 14 years in prison. And now I'm supposed to dare to discuss ideological questions again?'

15

Ominous Portents

It was May, and the start of summer in Chengdu. The midday sun was scorching. Our main room faced southwest, so that by the afternoon the front was unbearably hot. The back room was cool and shady, but it became musty. Except for sleeping, we tried to avoid it. F often sat together with me, helping me sort out the vegetables or chop kindling. He seemed to like it, especially shelling beans or peas. He told me about how he used to help his mother shell beans when he was a child in the countryside. He narrowed his eyes and smiled, as if back in those happy days.

However, our lives were imperceptibly changing. A middle-aged man lived in the courtyard, perhaps he'd been sent to help us. He told us about life in Chengdu, even about how to cook Sichuan food. He told us that one of his relatives was a top chef and had gone abroad. Things like that. Apart from letting him teach me a few essential techniques, I ignored the rest. However, he also taught me that you couldn't wash away the blood of finless eels with water and that first you had to dry them in a hot pan and then cut them into shreds. That was a useful lesson, for F liked eels, which were cheap and plentiful in Chengdu. Not long afterwards, they transferred him elsewhere and replaced him with a young newly demobilised PLA man. He lived with Old Leng in the house opposite. A small glass room jutted out from it, and from there he watched me coming and going through the entrance. The presence of a uniformed soldier (even though demobilised) made me a bit anxious.

Department Chief X called for a talk. He was an old cadre who had joined the revolution when the Red Fourth Route Army passed through his hometown in the thirties. He had recently been relieved of his post as director of a tea plantation under the Reform Through Labour Bureau, and now he had been put in charge of us. He saw himself as a man of experience where prisoners are concerned. It wasn't long before he came to the point:

'It will soon be three months since your arrival, but your progress has been slow. You must work at having your sentence reduced.'

F asked, 'How should I do that?'

'Admit your guilt and submit to the law. Our policy is that those who tell the truth receive a lighter sentence and those who render meritorious service are rewarded.'

'I don't recognise my guilt and there's no meritorious service I can render. The best thing for me is to sit out my sentence.'

'You are stubborn, you refuse to listen to correctional advice.'

'Haven't I conscientiously submitted to the law?'

'Damn you! Don't you realise you're dishonest?'

'If I'm stubborn, you can shoot me, but can you swear at me as well?'

I could see his hands shaking. I was afraid he would be unable to control his temper, so I ran over and whispered, 'Calm down, you're not well.'

Old Leng started trying to mediate: 'That's how they speak in Department Chief X's native town, he's not swearing at you.'

Finally, the plantation director wriggled out of the situation by saying, 'Since you're ill, perhaps you should first see a doctor.' Then he left, looking put out.

I could hardly blame F for the clash. He said, 'They couldn't get me to say it after ten years in prison, and now he thinks he can make me say it at the drop of a hat.'

The Department Chief really was incompetent. I learned from someone else that he had also behaved crudely in the plantation. Senior levels had concluded that he was an old man and things could only get worse, so they had transferred him to the Bureau. And now this happens. When two elderly and irascible men meet, such clashes are inevitable.

Fortunately, things simmered down, even though there was no further mention of visits and when F said he wanted to go out, he was told 'there's no time'. Even getting a haircut was a problem – he had to queue for two or three hours at the barber's, so I bought a pair of clippers and did it myself. Luckily, he didn't have much hair anyway and wasn't particular about the style. Borrowing books from the library and buying new books was a far greater trial. It seemed as if people had no interest in such things. They were too busy doing other things, although we could never find out what.

Yet we were not completely cut off. When I went out in the morning, I could see slogans strung up along the street attacking *Three-Family Village* or denouncing *Evening Chats at Yanshan*[*] or whatever. Crowds of residents, old and young alike, took wooden stools to the square to hold meetings and hear endless speeches. I didn't dare hang about.

My hands came out in blisters, perhaps because I hadn't got used to the new environment. They started to turn septic, so I had to go to hospital. There I saw lots more slogans. So Old Nie and Big Sister Ying were right when they said a new movement was in the offing.

Sichuan closely followed Beijing, and during the campaign in Sichuan to denounce *Evening Chats at Yanshan* Li Yaqun, Head of the Ministry of Propaganda, was also criticised. Li Yaqun had come under F's leadership in Guilin and after Liberation they often met. Li was good to F, and when he was deputy editor of *People's Daily* he published my children's book, *How Little Redcap Escaped the Danger*. At first he was transferred to Xikang Province to head the Ministry of Propaganda. Later he was sent

---

[*] *Three-Family Village* and *Evening Chats at Yanshan* were literary targets of the Cultural Revolution.

to Sichuan. F had intended to ask to see him. Luckily, he never did.

We were able to read *People's Daily* and *Sichuan Daily*, and we could increasingly smell the gunpowder. Many of the formulations were no longer about art and literature. We had no way of knowing what was going on, nor could we ask. All we did was quietly observe developments. F said, 'I am on record as an imprisoned criminal. What more can they do to me? I'm simply hiding away in my little room doing my best to manage my life.'

The storms in the outside world grew in frequency, but F's mental safe haven was the letters he received, especially the poems. His correspondence gave him moments of joy, as he put his heart and soul into composing poetic replies and writing words to set lyric patterns. Sadly, his friends' poems were confiscated and never returned, and I wasn't even able to keep all his.

A letter from Xiong Zimin took F by surprise. Xiong was an economist, and F had never imagined he was interested in literature. So his comments in a letter about Romain Rolland's *Jean-Christophe* were unexpected. Here is what he wrote:

> While reading *Jean-Christophe*, I came across two paragraphs that are enlightening for the way in which we think about problems: 'Each one of our threads of thought represents just one period in our lives. If living is not in order to correct our errors, overcome our prejudices, and broaden our thinking and mental horizons, what then is it for? Every day that passes will, we hope, bring us nearer the truth.' Another passage went like this: 'I myself have also taken leave of my past soul; I cast it off like an empty shell. Life is a seamless whole of death and resurrection. Christophe, we die together in preparation for our rebirth!' The human organism is ceaselessly renewed, and it is the same with new thoughts. Let wrong thoughts die, let Marxism and Mao Zedong Thought mature. I wish you every happiness in making progress in your ideological reform.

F didn't believe that Zimin had written it. He thought someone must have told him to quote those passages to help F sort out his ideas. He got out the original volume and re-read it (it was the old edition), and wrote back to say:

Older Brother Zimin: When we first got here, the spring chill was on, but before long it got warmer and flowers began to blossom. Copying the ways of persons of refinement, we visited the Wuhou Temple, Du Fu's Thatched Hut, and the River-Viewing Pavilion (built in memory of the Tang Dynasty poet and concubine Xue Tao). They are Chengdu's three best-known sites.

Six or seven years ago, emperors, generals and ministers were extravagantly praised and people in power and authority rebuked those who opposed emperors' merits and achievements and disrespected them. Over the last couple of years, things have come full circle, and it is no longer considered correct to praise emperors, generals and ministers. I wouldn't dare pass judgment on such things, I simply joined in the visits to the Wuhou Temple and Du Fu's Thatched Hut. As for Xue Tao, she was nothing more than a 'famous concubine', yet people in ancient times did not bury her in oblivion and the scholar-literati thought she was elegant and refined. Even the common people did not throw bricks at her. Today, the Xue Tao Well, the Poetry-Recital Tower, and the River-Viewing Pavilion continue to attract visitors on the strength of her name.

In early May, we had another visit from the cadre from the Department of Public Security. Department Chief X also came. He seemed embarrassed and sat silently to one side.

The cadre left no room for doubt: a 'Great Cultural Revolution' led by the Central Committee was in full flow and we should throw ourselves into it. 'You usually pay close attention to the newspapers. We are happy to see that you wish to achieve progress by means of careful study. However, in the course of this movement you must examine your past errors and thoroughly reform yourself.'

F seemed shaken. Frowning, he paused before saying:

'I've been away from the world of literature and art and lived in solitude for more than ten years. My sole source of information is the press. I am unable to follow Chairman Mao's injunction to discuss issues by "proceeding from outside to inside, from one point to another". My task is to serve out my sentence. My health won't allow me to think too much about problems.'

Again and again, F made clear there was nothing he could say. Thankfully, the cadre was a cultivated man. He didn't fly into a temper but spoke tactfully and politely. He said, 'Commission Chief Guo Moruo has written an article declaring where he stands. You should at least say where you stand.' With that, he left.

Deputy Chief Commissioner Guo Moruo's article (actually, a speech) had been republished in *Sichuan Daily*, so we read it. When he had finished, F laughed and said, 'So let's learn from Commission Chief Guo Moruo and say where we stand!'

WHERE I STAND

Regarding this Great Cultural Revolution, although I lack the ability and the conditions to understand issues concretely and in depth, I can nevertheless take note of general trends within the limits of my competence.

I support this revolutionary movement with all my heart. Very many years ago, I thought it was essential for an opening to be created on the literary front, under the leadership of the Central Committee, for a big struggle to purge away the poison. Obviously, this was no more than a muddled not to say superficial and unrealistic hope, so my understanding and the manner of its formulation inevitably contained numerous errors. Today, when the struggle has already developed in an all-rounded way and objective conditions have matured, I believe: it is directly led by the Central Committee, it takes command on the basis of Mao Zedong Thought, its means and methods are definitely correct, and its victorious future is guaranteed.

In the past, I took my place in the realm of art and literature and wrote some jumbled essays, but although I lack both the ability and the conditions to make a concrete investigation, I wish to learn from the example of Guo Moruo, Deputy Chief Commissioner of the Standing Committee of the People's Congress. I would like to say my essays should all be burned, none has the slightest value. I would go even further: thanks to the literary leadership, they were all literally burned more than ten years ago, thus slightly lessening my present mental burden. And to go further still: the things I have written not only have not the slightest value from the point of view of their active meaning but also contain numerous errors from the point of view of their passive meaning. They are harmful, so the fact that they were burned a long time ago makes me even more thankful.

I ought and most fervently wish to receive instruction from this great revolutionary struggle and to transform my literary ideology. However, I lack the conditions to do so, from the point of view of my state of mind and health, and I do not need to do so from the point of view of my status. But given the right conditions and help, my state of mind and health might recover, in which case I will strive to carry out a concrete investigation of my past views on literature, using Mao Zedong Thought as correctly expounded by leading literary comrades in the course of this great revolution and as developed through practice, as well as to learn wholeheartedly from the workers, peasants and soldiers. Even though I probably lack the ability to do literary work, I will at least assume responsibility for my errors.

As a Chinese of Mao Zedong's era who stands outside the literary front and the ranks of the people, I can only 'say where I stand' in this way, which I profoundly regret.

8 May 1965, in Chengdu.

After he had handed it in, one might normally have expected him to feel relieved, since at least he had said where he stood on the 'Great Cultural Revolution'. But he was still ill at ease. I told him his fears were groundless, but what else could I say? Would we succeed in escaping simply on the grounds of 'laziness'? I didn't dare think about it. The only thing was not to think anything, to be a mediocrity without any interest in human affairs.

Apart from studying Chairman Mao's *Selected Works*, we read Tang and Song poems. Xiong Zimin sent us a letter in which he had copied Su Dongpo's 'The Immortal by the River' ('At the Mid Autumn Moon Festival I drank until dawn, and wrote this for Ziyou while drunk'). While checking the original we discovered a witty song. After getting drunk, Su Dongpo had arrived home late and the county magistrate had mistaken him for an escaped criminal. The magistrate was about to issue a warrant for his arrest when he found him lying in a drunken stupor outside the gate. We had a good laugh.

After F had handed in 'Where I stand', Department Chief X was no longer so concerned. He even promised to let the young PLA man go shopping with us. This young man was a simple soul, and there was nothing F and he had in common. Old Leng, on the other hand, was an old public security man. Although he usually had little to say, once he did start talking it was clear that he had rich experience of life, had travelled widely, and knew lots about local conditions and customs. He told us that during the three years of natural disasters many people starved to death in Sichuan. However, he never once uttered a word of criticism. He was a cultivated man who rarely betrayed his feelings. Whenever I bought something while out shopping, he would watch from the corner of his eye. We always did as he said.

It got hotter and hotter, and I had to buy F some summer clothes. Old Leng told the young man to go with us. I looked in the department store and some small shops, but they didn't have F's size, so I went to the people's market, but they had nothing suitable for an elderly person. We slipped into a bookshop, leaving the young man at the door. It didn't have many books – mostly just rubbings from stone inscriptions. Another door led into a newly opened 'ice-water parlour', screened off behind a beaded curtain. It emitted coolness. Our mouths parched and our bodies drenched in sweat, we were ineluctably drawn in. F looked backwards and briefly hesitated, but in the end he followed me.

We were practically the only customers. We chose a place near the window and ordered orange juice with shaved ice. We couldn't help but smile. We were thinking back to more than 30 years before, a similarly sweltering day in 1933. F had invited me to discuss my work for the League of Left-Wing Writers. We met at the entrance to Shanghai's Paris Theatre. He was sweating profusely. He steered me towards an 'ice-water parlour' and he ordered two glasses of orange juice with shaved ice, just like today. I listened to him while sipping through a straw. He said I had been assigned to the southern part of the French Concession in Shanghai and gave me his address. As we were leaving, I opened my handkerchief and took out a silver dollar to pay. He laughed, and reached out for the bill. Afterwards, he always made fun of our visit to the ice-water parlour. He said my bashfulness was silly and immature.

Who would have thought that more than 30 years later we would be sitting opposite one another in an ice-water parlour in Chengdu. Even though it evoked feelings of nostalgia, they were diluted by pain and sadness at the thought that those days were gone forever.

F remembered the cadre and looked out of the window. I said, 'Don't worry, rest for a bit longer. If he comes, I'll invite him for a drink. He's hardly likely to tell the authorities that we tried to escape.'

We laughed. That was the only time in ten years we enjoyed a brief moment of pleasure, two carefree and happy people. I would have given anything not to have to leave.

We returned to the bookshop and bought some letter-paper with coloured watermarks and hurried out. The young man was waiting. He came over, looking relieved. I told him the bookshop was crowded and we had looked at the calligraphy and painting and tried to buy some books, and thus we talked our way out of it.

In June, the political situation hotted up relentlessly. Even in our little back street you could hear members of the neighbourhood committee shouting at people to attend meetings. I hadn't seen the slogans so I didn't know who was being criticised. It was much more mysterious and serious than the criticism of *Three-Family Village. Sichuan Daily* had published articles criticising novels by Sha Ding and Ma Shitu: the spearhead still pointed at art and literature. Luckily we were already a mass of bruises and living at the very bottom level, so perhaps the storm would miss us.

F couldn't resist reminding me that he had known best: 'I was right to say you shouldn't go to the Cultural Bureau. Otherwise how would you have been able to say where you stood once the movement started up? These present criticisms are almost the same as those against me in 1955. We must study the Cultural Revolution well. It's so hard to understand. First they criticise *Hai Rui Dismissed from Office*, then *Three-Family Village*, then something about "right-opportunist elements attacking the Party", "rightists complaining about being dismissed from office", and then up a further notch to "a tit-for-tat class struggle", and suddenly Deng Tuo and Wu Han turn into class enemies. Such reasoning takes no account whatsoever of the facts.'

I was even more confused than he was. I considered myself lucky that I had never joined the cultural hothouse and was a nobody. At first we had held high hopes of the Great Cultural Revolution. It seemed as if the Central Committee was finally paying attention to literary problems that had existed for years. Only now did we realise the aim was to 'sweep away all demons and monsters'. Had so many people really become class enemies?

We couldn't help shuddering. Yet most of the full-page articles and directives were written personally by Chairman Mao. That meant we dared not entertain the slightest doubt. The Great Cultural Revolution was no longer directed solely at culture: the fire had spread to other areas, it was 'touching people's souls'.

On June 2, *People's Daily* reported on the big-character poster put up by the Beijing University student Nie Yuanzi and six others demanding to know what leaders of the University 'were actually doing in the Cultural Revolution'. A *People's Daily* commentator noted: 'All those opposed to Chairman Mao and Mao Zedong Thought, all those who oppose Chairman Mao and the Party's Central Committee's directives, regardless of what flag they hoist, regardless of how exalted their position or how long-standing their qualifications, in reality represent the interests of the toppled class of exploiters. The people of the entire country will rise up against them, overthrow them, and destroy the black gangs, black organisation, and black discipline!' What did that refer to? A couple of days later, an editorial posed the question: 'To be a proletarian revolutionary or a bourgeois royalist?' By then, F had begun to grasp what lay behind it. He said, 'This has turned into an inner-Party struggle. What's all this about revolutionaries, royalists, emperors? Who's the emperor? It's a big muddle.'

On June 18, *People's Daily* published a decision to reform admission procedures for higher education and to postpone admission by half a year. It also reported that Beijing No. 1 Girls' Middle School and No. 4 Boys' Middle School had responded to the call by demanding the abolition of the old system of moving on to the next level of schooling and enrolment by examination. Our younger son was in the twelfth grade there. What would become of him? We received a brief letter from him saying he wouldn't come to Chengdu during the summer holidays and would write to us less frequently. That was earth-shattering. We had wanted Xiaoshan to go to a good university and come to Chengdu for a reunion. But now he was not going to take the exam or continue his studies. We would receive fewer letters – did that mean he had drawn a class line with us? I was distressed. F, however, stayed calm: 'It's a good thing. The child has grown up. He can decide his own fate. It's better if he doesn't come here and if he writes less. On no account must we implicate him.'

16

The Tempest

The weather became unbearably sultry, leading to storms accompanied by thunder and lightning. The road flooded and we were unable to leave the house. When I eventually went out shopping, there was no food available. The vegetables had been washed away or damaged. All I could buy was pickles and beancurd.

The political storm was even fiercer. The old saying 'the louder the thunder, the less the rain' did not apply to the Great Cultural Revolution. The newspapers became ever shriller. We had been through movements of this sort before, but because of our arrest we had not been given access to newspapers, so we hadn't been able to taste their flavour.

In July, Chairman Mao's *Talks at the Yan'an Forum on Literature and Art* and *Red Flag*'s editorial note were republished, together with an article exposing the 'literary black gang'. The biggest accusation against F had always been that he 'opposed the *Talks*' and had not written articles supporting them (actually he had, but they weren't published). He had always worked in areas under Guomindang rule, where in his view the situation was different from that in Yan'an, so you couldn't apply the same standards. The methods he favoured therefore didn't conform to the views of the literary leadership and he was seen as being 'against the *Talks*'. However, he and his comrades had always remained in step with the Party and enjoyed Chairman Mao's trust. They never stopped discussing the *Talks*. They saw explaining the Party's literary policies as their duty and prided themselves on upholding them. So why were they suddenly a 'black gang'? It seemed as if everything they had ever done was wrong. Their work was comprehensively negated. The article borrowed some terms from Lu Xun to criticise and censure them. What was going on? If they were the 'black gang', who were the 'red gang'?

We only talked about these things when there was no one else in the courtyard. F appeared indifferent, as if he had seen too much and gone through too much. However, I could see from the care with which he scrutinised the paper that he took the situation extremely seriously. Political prisoners like us under house arrest could not know what was really going on. All we could do was hope the storm would not engulf us.

The comrade from the Department of Public Security came to see F. This time there were no polite preliminaries. He said in a severe tone, 'Recently Chairman Mao's *Talks at the Yan'an Forum on Literature and Art* and *Red Flag*'s editorial note on the *Talks* were republished, with an article exposing and criticising Zhou Yang and the others. What are your views?' F didn't answer immediately. The cadre said, 'This is a test for you. You can talk about your attitude towards this Great Cultural Revolution. You've worked with Zhou Yang and the rest since the thirties. You can expose them. You can accuse them. This is a revolution to touch souls. You must show yourself in a good light, or you'll be in trouble.'

'I'm a convicted prisoner. It's a long time since I was qualified to discuss literary questions.'

'This movement will touch everyone's soul. How can you remain indifferent?'

'Of course I support it. I'll write a thought report hailing and supporting it.'

AN ACCLAMATION

This month an epoch-making event took place: *Red Flag* republished Chairman Mao's *Talks at the Yan'an Forum on Literature and Art* and *Red Flag*'s editorial note 'A Compass for the Great

Proletarian Cultural Revolution', together with articles exposing Zhou Yang, the ambitious schemer and leader of the black line and the black gang who for the last 30 years has usurped the name of the Party and Mao Zedong Thought to carry out a 'dictatorship' against progressive and revolutionary art. This is an outcome of several months' great struggle, and the starting point for a deeper-going struggle.

I hail the republication of the *Talks* and *Red Flag*'s note. However, due to my status and level, I do not dare nor am I able to use it against others as a demon-detecting mirror, nor am I able to use it as a bugle call for advancing into battle. Even so, I will use it as a compass and, when the day comes, as it certainly will, rigorously investigate my literary work and literary viewpoint and, as I have already said, accept the verdict passed on me by the new literary leadership and take responsibility for my errors. Although a convicted criminal outside the literary front and the ranks of the people, I will correct the wildly arrogant errors I committed in relation to those great works that I considered I had understood and use them as a compass, see if I can manage despite the difficulty to engage with some literary phenomena, to avoid being cheated as often as in the past, to reform myself, and strive to become at least minimally a Chinese of the Mao Zedong era.

Although great changes have happened in the objective situation, I will under no circumstances offer any explanatory comments on the judgments made in my regard by Zhou Yang, Xia Yan, Tian Han, Lin Mohan, He Qifang, Shao Quan and others. Unless at some future date they are investigated by the Central Committee, I will not offer any explanation or raise any questions.

On September 9 Vice-Premier Zhou and alternate member of the Political Bureau of the Central Committee and Secretary of the Secretariat of the Central Committee Kang Sheng, alternate member of the Political Bureau of the Central Committee and Head of the Cultural Revolution Small Group of the Central Committee Chen Boda, and Secretary of the Secretariat of the

Central Committee and Minister of Propaganda Tao Zhu hosted a reception at an emergency conference of Asian and African writers. These three leaders are assisting the Central Committee and promoting the Great Cultural Revolution and from now on will lead literary and artistic work. I rejoice that my confidence in the Party Central Committee and Chairman Mao has been realised. Although a convicted criminal, I hail the inevitable victory of the great revolution in culture and ideology, I hail the brilliant future of the new socialist literature. Long live Mao Zedong Thought!

12 July 1966, in Chengdu.

He wrote more than 1,000 characters, carefully weighing each word. We had no idea what was going on. F said, 'I don't care what terrifying things they say in the press, I must maintain my own opinion, on no account will I simply say good or bad things about people. Zhou Yang has been dragged out before the masses, but I don't feel like clapping. Theories of art and literature are a grave issue. They require careful attention and a free discussion. They can't be resolved by mass repudiation. Criticising Zhou Yang and the others in this way will convince no one.'

The muggy atmosphere ahead of storms in Chengdu made it hard to remain cheerful. F read on silently or copied out his poems. He seemed uninterested in anything. Department Chief X had stopped coming and only Old Leng, Little X and Old Wang were in the courtyard. No one spoke much. It was as if everyone was waiting and watching. No one seemed to think about excursions or shopping. Apart from my trips to the food market, I barely left the house. Along the road I saw slogans calling on people to 'Overthrow this or that', 'Repudiate this or that'.

When night fell, Old Leng sometimes suggested a stroll. That was when people took their walks. The park was crowded, so we went to the Wenshu Temple to relax and take tea.

The lotus throne on which the Wenshu Bodhisattva used to sit had changed owners. It was now a bed for a group of youngsters who lay stretched out in all directions. It was cool inside. I'm not surprised people went there for a good sleep – especially those who lived in the houses facing the street. At the back of the hall was the refectory, which the neighbourhood committee had turned into a room for studying and holding meetings. Old Leng showed us the cauldron the monks had used for cooking and the big wooden fish they beat at meal times. He then took us into the back courtyard, now the teahouse. It was spacious and there were trees everywhere – huge ones that reached into the sky and covered the courtyard with a panoply of leaves, so people could enjoy the cool and escape the last rays of the sun. In every nook and corner were clumps of bamboo that added to the coolness. We sat down on stone stools and a Daoist priest came over and poured tea. It cost just ten cents, and you could sit there until closing. That was the only time we lived among the people. Those taking tea were mostly old ladies and gentlemen from the neighbourhood. There were not many young people. Some had grandsons and granddaughters with them. F hadn't seen small children for more than ten years, and he watched in delight, his eyes following their every move. Some of the bolder children ran over to where we were sitting and F gave them sweets. Watching their little smiling faces and shining eyes, F laughed out loud and cheerfully stuffed the sweets into their pockets. We were at our happiest and our most relaxed, for we were living among people. We could hear the old folk gossiping endlessly. We heard lots of lively stories we could talk about after returning home. F said, 'You should observe them more and learn their language, and then when you've lived in Sichuan for a few years it won't have been in vain.' He was thinking about my creative work. I didn't know what to answer.

Sometimes Old Leng took us to the Yulong Teahouse, where we heard Sichuanese storytelling, arias and crosstalk. It cost 20 cents. You could sit there for hours among the local people, and laugh together with them. All that stuff about criticising, exposing and settling accounts was cast into the remote distance. It was as if all was well.

But such moments could not be allowed to last. Before the month was up, Department Chief X called in person at the house. He told F to stay at home and study. Looking stern, he said, 'Read more of Mao's *Selected Works* and examine your thinking. The Great Cultural Revolution has reached its climax. You must stop being so stubborn. Our policy is to reward truth-telling with lighter sentences. The emphasis is on behaviour – you know that. You must reveal all.' After delivering his lecture, he stalked off.

In the past, F would have shouted a retort, but now he calmly acquiesced. Old Leng said tactfully, 'It's chaotic out there. It's for your own sake that higher levels forbid you to go out. When things have calmed down, you can go out again.' F smiled.

A letter arrived from Xiaogu saying he wouldn't after all be coming to Chengdu in the summer holidays. He also said that he wouldn't write, and that Xiaofeng would tell us about him and younger brother. We understood: it was chaotic in the outside world, and his relations with his father might be investigated. We completely agreed with his decision.

17

A Bleak and Chilly Autumn Wind Arises

Normally, the cold winds should have started, but that year the autumn tiger roared loudly and it was hard to breathe in the midday heat. F hadn't handed in his thought report. He waited for them to urge him on, so he could get a clearer indication of the required content. He decided to copy out a poem he had written, following the rhyme sequence of Chairman Mao's 'Jinggang Mountains Revisited' and written in the form of 'Prelude to the Melody of Water' when Mao revisited the Yangtze.

The lead story in the newspapers was about 'Chairman Mao's braving the wind and waves in his seventies and swimming the Yangtze'. The press announced: 'The Chinese people rejoice that Chairman Mao is in such good health! The peoples of the world rejoice!'

After he had finished, he recited it to himself and got it ready to hand in. He was confident it would get full marks. I couldn't help splashing a bit of cold water on him: 'Do you think that's a thought report? They'll curse you as an old diehard. They don't want you to write eulogies. They want you to join in the chorus against the "black gang". A bit of abuse will do, that's what they mean by progress.'

'I know how to deal with this. When I was in prison, the chief interrogator told me the Ministry of Public Security doesn't hear cases to do with thought questions. Not long after that, they sent me to a normal prison.'

He added, 'In 1962, when the supreme procuratorate interrogated me, the first thing they talked about was investigation. When we had our last talk, nearly ten years later, they told me the supreme procuratorate investigated legal questions and warned me not to deviate into thought questions. I've made repeated pledges to the organisation. In May 1955, I declared that I sincerely accepted the decision of the Presidium of the Federation of Literary and Art Workers to expel me. In 1959, in a letter to the Premier, I pledged to accept any verdict by the Party in regard to literary thought. In 1965, when I was being sentenced, the secretary told me the supreme procuratorate wouldn't hear my case. I thought maybe it was because it was a thought question. So in the end I wasn't sentenced on thought grounds. Even so, the charge related to the "300,000-word memo". I was supposed to be "plotting the overthrow of the people's democratic dictatorship", "aiming to usurp political power over art and literature", and violating the Ordinance for Suppressing Counter-Revolutionaries. I didn't even want to ask, it was beyond my competence. I submitted my opinions to the Party's Central Committee openly and sincerely, with both hands.'

'The interrogator said it was a bomb you made for the Central Committee.'

'Deliver a bomb with both hands? Even a time-bomb would easily be detected. I may be a fool, but I'm hardly such a fool. "If you want to condemn someone, you can always trump up a charge." That's why even if Zhou Yang is let off the hook on literary questions, there are bound to be lots of other charges. I'm not prepared to be an activist of that sort. But I hope you stand by me, whatever the circumstances.'

That went without saying. But how to support him? All I could do was strive to keep him healthy and cook him nice things to cheer him up, what else could I do? A few days earlier, Department Chief X had told him, 'Stop going out. Things are chaotic on the streets. We're thinking of your safety.' To me he said, 'You can go out, but increase your vigilance, don't speak irresponsibly. If you get beaten, we might not be able to help.'

So F could no longer go out or take a walk in the park. I had not only to look after his daily needs but to keep his spirits up.

Two people depending on each other for survival and making the best of their pitiful 'happinesses'.

In August, Chairman Mao's letter to the students of the middle school at Tsinghua University was published and China gave birth to the Red Guards. Chairman Mao had his first audience with them.

Crowds of youths started appearing on the streets of Chengdu. They looked no older than 17 or 18. They were destroying the 'four olds', old customs, old culture, old habits, and old ideas. Every evening a group came to our street. They pushed their way into a resident's house and started crashing around and digging out a pile of earth. Later, we learned it had been a temple of the earth god. The earth god and the earth goddess had gone, but their thrones remained, and the little generals had come to smash them. They daubed black ash on the five bats (indicating 'five blessings have descended on this house') and the good-luck signs asking for 'riches and treasures to come in' (a big mock tinfoil silver ingot) that were painted on the walls. They even smashed the animal tiles on the roof and the little stone lions at the entrance.

One day, I heard a row and rushed out to see what was happening. An old man came out of the 'four olds' house clutching a big vase and looking tearful. He said to the youths, but as if addressing himself, 'Didn't you say you would smash the "four olds"? No need, I'll smash them for you.' He lifted up the vase, and smashed it. There were bits everywhere. On some of the shards you could still make out the heads and clothing of beautiful women. The youngsters looked on agog, and then they left.

A few days later, big-character posters appeared along the busy main road, mostly copied from posters in Beijing. One attracted my attention. It was a poster by a leader of the Hubei Provincial Committee quoting a poem by Mayakovsky. When I told F, he also found it strange. He said maybe something would come out of the Hubei Provincial Committee, because Li Da, President of Wuhan University, had objected to the 'peak theory', which said that Mao Zedong Thought was the highest plane of

Marxism. (He had said, 'Do you mean there will be no development beyond this peak? That isn't in accordance with the laws of Marxism.' I'm just giving the gist.) Li Da was an old Party member. His pamphlet 'Reading "On Practice" and Reading "On Contradiction" ' was very popular and Chairman Mao had praised it. Now he had courageously stated his own view. F saw it as a fruit of the Great Cultural Revolution and a good omen.

New things became ever more commonplace. Chairman Mao talked of 'people like Khrushchev nestling beside us' and said 'it is right to rebel against reactionaries'. We had no way of knowing what that implied. Things seemed to have transcended the 'cultural' sphere. It couldn't be resolved simply by dragging out a few cultural officials.

Apart from the guards, we had little to do with anyone, so there was no one to discuss things with. Old Leng and the others always came up with the same answer: 'No idea. We don't know who they mean either.'

As for the family, our only contact was with Xiaofeng. She told us Xiaoshan was not qualified to be a Red Guard, so he spent all day riding round on his bike reading posters. She said Beijing was abuzz. Some units had moved their posters from the courtyards to the outside walls, and the exposés were getting more and more bizarre. Xiaoshan and some of his classmates had gone to Shanghai and other places to establish revolutionary ties. We hoped he would be able to come to Chengdu, where Red Guards were already beginning to appear. Some wore armbands saying 'Red First Company', 'Red Combat Regiment', etc. Their rebel spirit was much more pronounced than that of the local youths. The walls of the old Imperial City in Chengdu were covered with posters calling for the bombarding of the headquarters and the burning down of the Provincial Committee, and for the bombarding of named targets in the Provincial Committee. Everyone started wanting to burn and destroy.

The weather started to cool, and people were making what they could of the clear, crisp autumn weather. I could no longer go out with F, and even ordinary people no longer sat around in the teahouse or took strolls in the park. Every afternoon I took my food pail round the crowded streets to read the posters while buying F some fat duck, smoked rabbit, etc., and some wine to stop him getting depressed. Every day he read the paper, making lots of red and blue underlinings with his pencil. But he still couldn't make out what was going on and was always ill at ease, unlike at the start, when he had pinned his hopes on the movement.

F received a letter from Xiong Zimin telling him to ask for his case to be resolved and for the original sentence to be reduced or revoked. F answered:

> My state of mind is as it has been for the last ten years or more. I believe in Chairman Mao and the Party Central Committee's leadership, I won't explain anything. The Party's sacred principle is to conform to reality, my confidence in this is unshakeable. If the Central Committee inquires directly of me, I will make a statement, but I will on no account criticise or make demands on units or individuals, such has been my bitter experience over the last ten or more years. For several months now, organisations here have hinted I could voice my opinion, but I have diplomatically declined.
>
> I've never trusted XX and the others, because they never trusted me, so I've never 'cooperated' with them. However, I've never 'opposed' them either, I've simply done everything possible to evade their authority. Now the Party is making inquiries about my literary and artistic aspirations over the past 30-odd years, which have been rendered completely redundant. I have not changed: I submit to the verdict and will live out my remaining years in peace. It is not pleasant to be sentenced thus, but few people have a pure conscience.

Trapped in his tiny room, he could not understand what was happening in the outside world. I, on the other hand, could witness the changes, which drove me into a panic.

The Red Guards wore old army uniforms and attacked bourgeois fashions. They clipped girls' plaits, hacked off their perms, and even slashed one young girl's shorts. They surrounded people on the streets to scare them, roaring with laughter. It was hard to remember what age we were living in. Luckily I looked like an ordinary citizen out shopping. Also, I always kept my distance and observed things from afar.

Sometimes I went to the old Imperial City to read the posters. There were two big stone lions at the entrance, which had been painted red. Some Red Guards scrutinised them. One said, 'They're slaves of the emperor.' Another said, 'We should sweep them away, with all the other demons and monsters.' A crowd gathered round and pushed, but the lions stayed where they were. A worker said, 'I know how to do it. They're made of sandstone, it's not hard. I'll come back tomorrow with some sledge hammers. If that doesn't work, we'll use a steam hammer.' A couple of days later, they had been reduced to two piles of red sandstone, as if sprayed with blood. A result of the 'cooperation' between the Red Guards and the workers, their elder brothers. I heard no expressions of regret, but one person said, 'Good heavens, what an enormous pile. It will take two lorries to remove it.'

I discussed the lions' fate with Old Leng. He said the arms had been knocked off some of the statues at the Wuhou Temple. It wasn't easy to ask the Red Guards to leave, so they had to close the temple gates. Luckily the temple authorities had advance notice and shut the gates before the Red Guards arrived.

I replied, 'Well, the Chairman said it's right to rebel.' Old Leng remained expressionless, as if he hadn't heard me. That evening, he told me to avoid crowds. If anything happened, he wouldn't be able to help.

The cadre from the Public Security Department and Department Chief X turned up. They gave F an order: 'Prepare immediately to leave Chengdu at any time.' They didn't say where we were going, simply that we should pack some bedding and luggage. I asked Department Chief X whether we should take a cotton quilt and padded clothes. He said, 'OK, but not too much.'

I sorted out the bedding and packed some autumn clothes and F's lined overcoat. Old Leng said I hadn't packed enough. He said I should take a mosquito net and another quilt, and more clothes. He also said I should take some pots and pans. The only thing he didn't say I could take was books. So we had the mistaken impression that we wouldn't be away for long, perhaps just a couple of months. We calmly ate our evening meal. I got some leftovers ready and put the other things back in their places. I put the kitchenware back and put the kettle on the stove, as if we would be back in a few days' time or even the following day. F tidied up the books on the table. He didn't touch the reading notes and letters that he kept in the drawer, except for a few he took along to answer in the course of the next few days. He believed that he would be back soon and could resume his reading and writing. We waited, calmly oblivious.

After ten in the evening, some people arrived from the Department of Public Security. They checked our preparations and told us to take more clothes. I emptied the bag I had put the clothes in and packed a small suitcase, but I didn't pack F's overcoat and woollen suit, since I was convinced that we would soon be allowed back. Even though it wasn't paradise, our home of the last six months protected us against the storms of the natural and human worlds. I knew it wasn't a real home – it was actually a gaol – but I wanted F to stay there until he had completed his sentence.

F sat silently on his chair. I had no way of knowing what was in his mind. His eye was on the Seagull Alarm Clock we had brought with us from Beijing, slowly ticking its way towards midnight. Outside, we could hear noisy voices, as if a great throng of people had arrived. Then the cadres walked in, and said without pausing, 'Are you packed? OK, let's go!'

Old Leng and Old Wang helped carry the luggage. I was embarrassed to see Comrade Wang do this, but all he said was,

'Don't worry, we've come to see you off!' I was moved by his solicitude. I thanked him again and again for taking care of us.

A jeep was parked in the lane. The back door opened and two PLA men leapt out, carrying loaded guns. Old Leng and Little X boarded first, and the PLA men brusquely ordered us to do the same. Then they got in. It was a refitted prison van. F and I sat opposite one another, sandwiched by a cadre and a soldier. The canopy was canvas and wind-resistant. There were plastic windows on the back doors. You could see a bit of the outside world through the driver's windscreen. The cadre from the Department of Public Security turned round to ask, 'Are you properly seated?' Then the driver drove off.

We sped through Chengdu in the quiet autumn night. Most of the residents were safely asleep, but from time to time a bike rode past in the opposite direction, almost grazing us. Probably it was workers coming off shift, for they wore scarlet armbands. The cyclists became ever fewer. The further we drove, the darker it got. Finally, the yellow street lights stopped. The jeep's headlights lit up a yellow-grey strip ahead of us.

The jeep drove at high speed. Either side, leaves rattled in the autumn wind. The cold air blew onto us. How will we cope with this biting cold?

18

Snake and Mouse

The jeep was frequently engulfed in fog, and the wind turned ever colder. F and I sat face to face. I wanted to reach out to touch him, but the presence of the others inhibited me. He suddenly stood up and indicated he wanted to leave the vehicle. The PLA men raised their guns. I was frightened to death. Fortunately, the cadre got the driver to stop and told Old Leng to get out with F and told me that I could get out as well. I was glad to stretch my legs, which were numb and cramped after the journey.

We were on a small road between two mountains. There wasn't an electricity cable in sight, and an ice-cold wind howled through the valley. F stood for a long time by the side of the road without moving. I realised he found it hard to pass water, given his prostate problems and the fact that he had been sitting still for such a long time. Finally he finished. The cadre urged him to get in quickly, for there was still a long way to go. I could see F was having difficulty in walking, so I went to help him. So did Old Leng, and between the two of us we got him in. I asked quietly, 'Are you feeling unwell?' He shook his head. 'Are you cold?' Again, he shook his head. But his hand was frozen. This scared me. If he got ill, what could we do?

The vehicle continued along the bumpy mountain road. From the windows you could see nothing. We could only resign ourselves to our fate, and go wherever they intended taking us. Suddenly the driver slammed on the brakes and a man jumped aboard, like in a scene from an American thriller. He said, 'I've been waiting ages, where have you been?' 'We didn't leave until after midnight.' He twisted round to take a look at us.

He was middle-aged, and sounded like a northerner. He told the driver to drive on. After a lot more driving, we finally stopped. We were told to get out and our luggage was unloaded. There were no people or houses in sight, and the driver drove the two soldiers back. The middle-aged man carried the bedding, Old Leng took the suitcase, and I took some bits and pieces. The newcomer used a torch to light our way along the mountain track. I intended to give F a hand, but he managed to keep up without help. Instead, it was me that stumbled. Instead of me helping him, he helped me. After climbing up and down again and again, following them mindlessly, we finally reached a grey-brick house standing alone on a hilltop. It was empty except for a double bed, a table, and two chairs. The man threw the luggage onto the bed and told us we would be staying here for a while.

His name was Jiang, and he was the director of a tea plantation. 'Fresh ginger,' he said, in a reference to his name. The cadre chimed in, 'Old ginger – all the spicier!' Everyone laughed. The laughter seemed to dispel the hours of cold, and we all suddenly felt warm. F asked where we were. 'This is Miaoxi Tea Plantation, there are lots of fruit trees, it's a nice place. Tomorrow I'll bring you a pound of tea. There's plenty of fruit, you can eat as much as you like.' They seemed to have found us a happy retreat.

I got out the bedding, and Director Jiang asked me if we had brought a mosquito net. I showed him our domed net. He took the rope I had used to tie the bedrolls with and swung it over the roof beam, so we could hang the net. Outside the window, a pale light slowly appeared. Seeing everything was in order, one of the two men said, 'Hurry up and go to sleep. We'll send someone over with breakfast.' Old Leng came in. They asked him, 'Is everything done?' He nodded. The cadre said to F, 'Old Leng will be in the room beneath. If you need anything, ask him.'

F was exhausted. I got things ready for us to sleep and told him to eat some biscuits. He shook his head. Seeing his worried look,

I thought maybe he needed to pass water and took out the spittoon. I was right, but it took a long time. He said, 'It's taking ages. Perhaps the urine's blocked.' I got him to massage himself with his hands, and he finally managed to pass water. Then he flopped onto the bed.

I slept until broad daylight. It seemed as if we were on a big boat, just the two of us, travelling across the sea. The wind and waves rose and fell, and so did I. Suddenly a big wave crashed down and I woke with a start. I could hear voices outside. Inwardly, I was still afraid. F was deep in sleep. I thought, he has had a terrible night with all that jolting, I'll let him sleep a bit longer – the last thing I wanted was for him to fall ill. I too could have done with some more sleep, but it was already nine so I quickly got up. I opened the door and saw someone had left a bucket of water and two thermos flasks. I woke F and rinsed his mouth and washed his face. Just as I was about to go out, someone started up the path below. First he went to the room below and then he came up together with Old Leng.

It was the plantation director, who had ambushed us the night before. He was in his fifties, and looked like a soldier. He had the forthright manner of a northerner. He seemed very concerned about us. He asked whether we had slept well. The comrade in charge said, 'What do you think, it seems to me it would be too much to ask people of their age to go every day to the plantation canteen.' 'How about if we get the kitchen to send it over?' Old Leng interrupted, 'No need, I can bring it back.' The problem was solved. Just before leaving, the plantation director said, 'Don't go walking around all over the place.' His tone was that of the director of a reform-through-labour plantation giving orders to a prisoner.

Old Leng brought someone over with our food – three fried dishes and a bowl of rice. The dishes included stir-fried meat and pork liver. It tasted good, although it was a bit cold. F said it was too greasy and he wasn't hungry. I added some boiled water to half a bowl of rice and urged him to eat it. I also had no appetite and I just picked at the food. I was worried, eating like this would never work. I said, 'Perhaps we can ask them to cook gruel?' F waved away my suggestion: 'You can't go bothering people. You know what sort of a place this is, you know my status. Try to put up with it. I've got a bad headache, let me get some sleep.'

He very soon dropped off. There was nothing for it but to wish him a good sleep and a quick recovery, and to forget the misery and inconvenience.

After I had tidied up the room, I went out for a walk. It was a bit like Robinson Crusoe. I was determined to study the lie of the land.

We were in an isolated house on top of a small hill covering a few dozen square metres. On the ground floor was Old Leng's room. Further off was an apple tree and at the bottom was a road, among paddy fields and small hills. It was a modern road with cars and pedestrians. We were the hegemons of this small hill. Fortunately, there were no masses, so we were unlikely to be denounced. But how would we live? I had never fantasised about living happily and had never known happiness. I was used to a life of hardship. But for F, this sudden ambush would add to the intolerable pressure on his body and spirit. I hoped he could stick it out. On no account could I betray any sense of flinching. I must seem optimistic and impart a touch of romanticism to the challenge.

From the top of the hill, I saw Old Leng returning from the Plantation Headquarters, so I went to meet him. 'Could you buy us a small stove so I can boil water and warm up the food? It's cold when it arrives, and it's quite fatty. It's hard to digest. I think he might have flu, I'm worried.'

He promised to discuss it. Then he disappeared into his room.

F was awake, sitting blankly on the bed. 'Are you feeling a bit better?' He nodded. 'Have you still got that headache?' He nodded again. But he seemed to lack the strength to speak. He was in an even worse state than I had imagined.

I decided to put on a brave face. I said, 'I've had a look round. The scenery is lovely. We're in a commanding position. There's row after row of fruit trees. The hills opposite are also covered in trees. In the cities, you would never find anywhere like this, it's a great place to recuperate.'

'Yes, a great place . . .' I knew he had been about to ridicule me. I laughed, and from the heart. 'Let's see what happens. Always look on the bright side.'

Old Leng came in to get the bowls for the evening meal. When he saw that much of the food had not been touched, he said, 'Why are you not eating?'

'There's too much meat. He dislikes fatty food.'

F added, 'I would like a few more vegetables.'

'I'll tell them.'

The evening meal was a plate of eggs and stir-fried meat.

Again, F didn't eat much. I asked him what the matter was. He said he had a headache. I gave him an APC tablet, to stop the pain and cure the flu.

The next morning, his headache was not so bad and he ate two bowls of gruel and some pickle. Seeing his appetite, I put the leftovers in the rice pot so they could warm them up for us.

The comrade from Public Security and Director Jiang came to see us.

'I hear you're not well and not eating,' the comrade said.

'I'm fine, just a headache.'

'You want to see a doctor? We have doctors, we also have a hospital. It's really good,' said the Director. He realised he sounded as if he was showing off, and started smiling.

The comrade said, 'Leave your ideological burden to one side for now. It's not easy living in a place like this, but it's only for the time being. If there's anything you need, let us know. The surroundings are wonderful, there's no one to disturb you. You can study single-mindedly and reform your thinking. The main thing is to recognise your crimes.'

F said nothing. Then he mentioned the house in Chengdu. He said he hoped I would be allowed to return to fetch the books he needed.

'We will make appropriate arrangements. The main thing is your health. You must eat more. If there's anything you want, let us know.'

Having tried to reassure us, they left.

F still had the same miserable look. His morale had not lifted, so I took him outside to have a look. Clambering up and down the small paths, we found ourselves at the highway. People carrying wooden frames loaded with heavy objects were slowly making their way along a path, stooping forward with each stride, with an escort of PLA men. It was obvious they were prisoners. They were naked from the waist up. Their bodies, covered by sweat and sunlight, were black and shiny. When one of the soldiers shouted an order, they propped up the frames with wooden staves and took a rest. At another order, they took up the staves, shouldered their burdens, and resumed their slow march.

Deliberately adopting a light tone, I said, 'Look what good a bit of exercise has done them, that's the result of reform through labour.'

He looked at me disdainfully, and remained silent. I was afraid the sight of the prisoners would upset him, so I took him back the way we had come.

In the house, he again fell fast asleep.

He had not been in such a mood since his release from gaol, ten months earlier. He had always been optimistic and had fitted in anywhere. Apart from an occasional expression of mistrust or disappointment, he rarely thought about his own future or security. Was the sudden change due to psychological or physiological factors? His unwillingness to talk made it hard for me to know. I couldn't report to the authorities or request help – I had long ago learned my lesson in that regard.

The comrade from Public Security came, accompanied by Old Leng. Old Leng had brought a big chicken stewed in an earthenware pot. The comrade said, 'You're not eating, that's not good. I got them to stew you a chicken. You still have another two or three years to serve, you must take care of your health. We have complete responsibility for you, you can stop worrying about your ideological burden. If you need anything, ask Old Leng. If you have any requests, ask Director Jiang. They'll know what to do. You have us and the Central Committee, there's nothing you need worry about. Today I'm going back to Chengdu, if there's anything you want me to do, I'll do it if I can.'

F said, 'Could you let Mei Zhi go to Chengdu and fetch some books for me?'

'Don't worry, I'll take responsibility. You won't lose a single book, they'll be sent on later. People often go to Chengdu from here. If you want anything they can fetch it. Mei Zhi can't go. Her job is to nurse you back to health.'

I asked, 'What is this place? Can we send letters?'

'You can write to anyone – your children, your old friends, anyone. The address is Miaoxi Tea Plantation in Lushan County.'

He said a polite goodbye. We never saw him again.

We couldn't finish the chicken, and F only drank a bit of soup. I put the leftovers in the rice bowl, and found a wooden box to put the bowl in. I put the lid on as tight as possible, but the next day, when I went to get the soup out, I had a terrible fright – there was a dappled snake asleep in it. I screamed for F.

He was not scared of snakes, and told me to fetch a poker. I gave him the first thing that came to hand, a pair of fire tongs. He grabbed the snake with them. It was about a foot long. It had overeaten and could no longer crawl. Pincered around the middle, it was immobilised. F told me to fetch a brick, and smashed its head. The episode scared me. I threw the chicken and the snake into the latrine pit.

Old Leng was our sole support. He brought us three meals each day, together with the newspaper. Sometimes he sat down and we had a gossip. At first he seemed dull and inarticulate, but actually he was quite talkative. It was just that he always paused to think, which made him seem tongue-tied.

He told us about the area. The tea plantation was run by the Reform Through Labour Bureau of the provincial Department of Public Security. Several thousand prisoners were divided into teams. We were in the Team 1 area. It grew fruit trees, apples and pears and Guangdong oranges and tangerines. Some of the teams grew maize, rice and seasonal vegetables. In the hills were the tea-pickers and further off was a coal mine. The prisoners lived quite well and were self-sufficient. The tea wasn't bad, and was even marketed abroad. He promised to take us to the market.

He brought a pound of top-grade tea for us and an electric stove. (They generated electricity with diesel engines.) That made warming up the rice and boiling water easier. To get the water, you had to go to a disused paddy field and skim off the scum. The water was full of plankton. I carried it back in a tub and waited for it to clear before using it, for drinking and washing.

A few days later, Old Leng took us to the market. Initially, F didn't want to go, and said he couldn't move. Old Leng said the Plantation Headquarters could organise a vehicle. I said, 'The weather's nice today, I need to do some shopping.' He reluctantly agreed. That was the first time we left our hill to go to the head-quarters, which turned out to be a row of single-storey brick buildings and a large canteen. We climbed onto a lorry and F was given the best place, next to the driver. The road to town was all downhill, with mountains on one side and a river on the other. We crossed a bridge into the town.

That was the first time I had seen a mountain town. It was built on a stretch of plain near a stinking river. Along the road was a herd of water buffaloes eating rice straw. Dung was heaped everywhere, even in the town centre. Passers-by had to pick their way through the mess. No one complained – apparently they expected nothing better. When I asked the locals, they told me the animals belonged to the production brigade. The combina-tion of dung and rice straw produced a high-grade fertiliser. To serve the interests of our peasant brothers it was all right to disregard our townspeople's health and hygiene.

The town had only one busy street. In the centre was a circular flight of steps that seemed to be some sort of memorial. People had set up stalls around it, displaying vegetables, melons, fruits, eggs and trussed chickens. The chickens and eggs were cheap, and lots of people were buying them. We just looked – we didn't cook for ourselves.

We went into the department store (actually a general store with three separate shop fronts) and bought an aluminium wok and an enamel mug with a red sail painted on it. I had seen the Soviet film *Red Sail*, and had always liked to imagine that one day a boat with a red sail would come to take us away. F said he also hoped we could leave on a red-sailed boat.

We had our midday meal in a state-owned restaurant, with eight or nine tables. It looked full, but some people were just sitting there. We sat down with Old Leng at a half-empty table opposite a nursing mother. We had almost finished, but her food hadn't come, and the baby tried to grab ours. I fed him some meat, and the baby seemed to like it. 'Have you ordered?' I asked the mother. She didn't reply, and it dawned on me why. Seeing the baby was still hungry, I continued to feed him. To my surprise, a seven or eight-year-old boy took one of the dishes while we were still eating and walked off with it. I shouted out and wanted to run after him, but Old Leng stopped me.

In the corner of a room was a 17 or 18-year-old girl holding a container and waiting for the child. After they had emptied the leftovers into it, the child grabbed a lump of meat and ate it while returning the dish to the table.

The only other time I saw people eating leftovers was during the three years of natural disasters. But up there in the mountains it was still happening. They wore blue unlined cotton gowns and grey cloth shirts, filthy and tattered. The white kerchiefs wound round their heads had turned grey. Their trousers, made from the same sort of cloth, only reached down as far as their calves. Most had baskets on their backs. I saw no carrying poles. Many had come several miles by mountain roads to sell their produce and use the money to buy salt and other necessities.

We were too late for the lorry, so we had to walk home. We went up and down the mountain road, walking and stopping, but F didn't feel tired. Along the way were villagers' shacks, with maize and red peppers drying on wooden frames. Before we realised it, we were at the headquarters. Old Leng led us into the reception room, where we had tea.

F seemed to have cheered up. In the evening, perhaps because he had put too much effort into reading the paper, he said he had a headache. I got ready for an early night.

In the middle of the night, I heard a scratching sound. I thought another snake had come in. I waved the torch around but saw nothing. Then I heard a sound in the drawer. Inside was a mouse eating the biscuits and pastries I had bought. Luckily I discovered him in time. I put the food I had saved from the mouse in the aluminium pan. To my astonishment, the mouse managed to lift the lid. Hearing the pitter-patter, I got back up again and weighed it down with a brick. Then I finally fell asleep, exhausted.

All my life I had feared snakes and mice. Who would have thought that in that little house I would meet with both. I would have to get used to dealing with them.

19

A Serious Illness

He was always saying he had a headache, but it didn't seem serious. When his spirits were up, he sat on the level ground in front of the door taking the sun and reading the paper, and sometimes he accompanied me on a short walk. But he kept complaining about headaches. It was a bit like in 1955 after the '*Dream of the Red Chamber* question', when he developed a chronic headache. But then he was able to go to the Beijing Hospital to see a doctor and have electrotherapy and hydrotherapy. Now the only hope was that he would forget about it.

Old Leng suggested a trip up the mountain to see the tea. There were small clumps of tea bushes planted in shallow trenches along the terraces. It was long past picking season, but the neatly pruned leaves and branches were a joy to behold. I found an early flower, two white blossoms on a single stalk. It reminded me of 1942, when we were with the Dongjiang Guerrillas in Guangdong. There were tea bushes there too, with the same white flowers. F had specially plucked two little flowers on one stalk for me. This time, it was my turn to pluck them. I handed them to him, in the hope that fond memories would gladden his heart. But he looked at them indifferently, with wounded eyes. The memory remained, but not the frame of mind. After a while, he suggested going back.

He first rested and then sat down to write the Department of Public Security a letter. This is what he wrote:

Having moved from Beijing to Chengdu, my understanding is that, having completed my sentence, I will spend my remaining years in Chengdu. I therefore hope to be able to perform a small amount of labour that will benefit the people, so following instructions I took my books there. I am presently serving out my sentence. After that, the leadership will probably appoint somewhere appropriate for me to spend my remaining years (should there be any). There are only two years and eight months of my sentence left, so it is unnecessary to waste the people's money on sending me this tattered pile. Among the books are reference materials I collected so that I could contribute something to the Party. I took them with me from Beijing because I still cherished that ambition. I hope you can rent a room on my behalf in order to conserve these books. While in Beijing, Mei Zhi asked the Ministry of Public Security to be allowed to stay in Beijing near Chairman Mao and the Party Central Committee (on a reform-though-labour farm in the suburbs), since it was hard to imagine how a solitary old couple could be sent to Chengdu, where they have no one to turn to. The leadership currently tells us not to worry, since the Party is our family. Now we have no friends or kin to whom we can entrust these matters, nor any place to which we can donate them, I have no alternative other than to ask the Party, my family, for assistance.

Report on various other matters

1. On the night of the 8th, because the final section of the road was bumpy and I was unable to go to the toilet, I suffered intense pain in my cranial nerves. The doctor prescribed some medicine, but I fear no medicine can cure this malady.
2. The comrade from the Department again emphasised I should recognise my guilt and abide by the law. As I have repeatedly avowed, I submit to the court's sentence and will abide by it until completion. I have peace of mind, since it is the Party that sentenced me. As for the rest, I lack the ability to

comprehend it so I will forbear talking nonsense. As a result of this Great Cultural Revolution, everything is to be judged against new criteria, so I dare even less to engage in careless talk.

3. In Chengdu, Director X repeatedly raised the question of literary and artistic ideology. The comrade from the Department also raised the question of what I had learned from re-studying the *Talks at the Yan'an Forum on Literature and Art*. I committed numerous serious errors in regard to reaching judgments in the field of literary and artistic ideology by using the supreme principle of Mao Zedong Thought. I will carry out an investigation on the basis of the Central Committee's verdict and reform my standpoint. If it becomes possible for my remaining days to have meaning, it will be on the basis of the verdict passed by the Central Committee in its investigation of my literary practice and standpoint, my self-criticism of the errors I have committed, and the actions taken to remedy the damage I have done to the Party's influence.

After finishing the letter, he found it hard to get out of bed. He still had a headache, and he had no appetite.

Old Leng must have thought it was serious, for he informed the Plantation Headquarters. Director Jiang came in person to see F and did his best to console him. Afterwards, he suggested we call a hospital doctor.

Old Leng brought two doctors, one middle-aged and one young. The middle-aged one took F's blood pressure, asked a few questions, and concluded F had a cold and a slight fever. He told me to buy some pears and press out the juice – the fever had made his mouth dry. He prescribed various medicines. The young doctor said nothing.

If the headache was merely due to a cold, then the medicine should have led to a recovery, but it made no difference. His headache remained severe and he wanted to stay in bed. He ate some gruel I boiled for him, but he seemed weaker than I had ever seen him. His letter shows the extent of the blow to his spirit. If his physical decline continued, goodness knows where it might end.

I had lived with him for more than 30 years, and he rarely fell ill. When he did, he cried 'mother' in his local dialect and only calmed down after taking medicine. I would give him some good food, of a sort he liked, and he would recover more rapidly. Now it was different. He just lay there, asking for nothing. I began to worry.

Old Leng brought the two doctors for a further consultation. He introduced the middle-aged one as the Hospital Director. I noticed he looked constantly at the mercury, so I guessed there must be a problem with the blood pressure. I asked him about this. He said the high blood pressure was less than 200, which was not excessive, but the low blood pressure was 50, which accounted for the headaches. He prescribed Xuedeping, which he said was suitable for that particular illness.

F's spirits seemed to lift a little. He asked me to help him up, and sat on the rattan chair flicking through the last few days' newspapers. His eye fell on Chairman Mao's directive calling for cultural rather than armed struggle. He also read an article denouncing 'the power and prestige of reactionary learning' and the 'revisionist' Li Da. He put down the paper and was silent for a long time. Finally he said, 'How long will this Great Cultural Revolution continue? If there's a violent struggle, will it be like the struggle against the landlords during land reform? Isn't Li Da highly regarded by the Chairman as a Marxist? Perhaps it's because he opposed the "peak" theory.' He took his head in his hands and leaned back listlessly. After a while, he lay down again and wouldn't even eat his gruel. I went to tell Old Leng.

At midnight he awoke and said he wanted to pass a stool. I got the spittoon ready, but nothing came out, after a long wait. When I tried to help him back up, he began falling over. I cried out. He was doing his best to get up. I could hear him muttering, 'What's going on, why won't my leg do as it's told?' In the dim light, I could see him smiling, as if he found it funny. I thought, this is wrong. I said, 'Don't overexert yourself, lean on me, let me pull you up onto the bed.' I put his head on the pillow and moved his legs, so he was lying straight. He entered a shallow sleep. I sat by his side until first light.

Then I went down to alert Old Leng. I told him what had happened in the night. 'His blood pressure's not normal,' I said. 'If he has a brain haemorrhage, he could get hemiplegia and become paralysed.' Old Leng was alarmed. He blamed me, saying I should have called him, that if anything happened he would be responsible, etc., etc. I was in no mood to argue, and hurried back upstairs. What if F woke and fell out of bed?

Luckily, he was lying there peacefully. A beam of light from the window fell across his body. His eyes were sunken, making the bridge of his nose seem more prominent. He no longer had his old haughty look. The cast of his face resembled a Greek stone-carved death mask. It had a solemn and serene beauty. I had never seen him like that, I couldn't help trembling. My heart contracted. Don't leave me like this! You still have so much to do, so much to say, about the vicissitudes of your life, about the injustices you have suffered, you can't just leave us with those wrongs unrighted. Public clamour can confound right and wrong, rumours can result in killings, how many times in your case has the false been used to confound the true? In future, who will defend you? Only you can speak clearly, answer with actions, answer in writing, with blood. Live, so you can be restored to your full stature. I didn't dare express my grief by holding him in my arms, I could only sit there by his side and swallow my tears.

There I sat, not daring to move. I had no idea what was going on outside, nor even what time it was. When Old Leng and the young doctor came into the room and ordered me to get ready to go to hospital I stood up with a start. 'Go to hospital? Which hospital?' 'The local one. Hurry up and collect some things, whatever you might need, and a change of clothes.' This was the young doctor speaking. Old Leng chipped in, 'It doesn't matter if you forget something. I can fetch it for you. I'll go with you.'

I woke F and told him he was going to hospital and I was going to change his clothes. But either because he had caught cold or for some other reason, he was unable to get out of bed. Just as he was saying 'It's not good', a foul smell rushed from his body. I wiped him clean, changed his clothes, changed the sheet, and took the soiled clothes and linen to the waterhole. Old Leng and the Doctor had to wait longer than they would have wished.

They sent two strapping men to carry him on a bamboo stretcher. The young doctor tended to him from the side while Old Leng and I followed. After crossing several small mountains we reached a barracks. The stretcher-bearers asked whether we could pass through it. The young doctor used his influence to get permission, thus saving us a long detour through the mountains. They seemed to think it was dangerous, since the path was slippery.

The hospital was on level ground beside a mountain. It had originally been a small temple, and was now supplemented by several rows of single-storey dwellings. We stayed in a sickroom with two beds. It wasn't big, but it was clean and there was a table with chairs and a reading lamp. The white bed sheet was stamped with a red cross and the words Miaoxi Hospital. Just when I had got things ready for F to lie down, an old cadre entered. He was a northerner. He introduced himself as Deputy Director of the plantation. He said he lived next door and we should shout if we needed anything. It turned out we were in the cadres' sickroom.

The middle-aged doctor and the Hospital Director came to visit. After taking his blood pressure, they told me to be more attentive and not to let him fall out of bed. I sat glued to his side.

Old Leng bought me some rice tickets and wanted to take me to eat. How could I do that? But I also couldn't ask him to bring the food over for me. So I jammed the chairs against the bed to stop F falling out. At times like that I couldn't help thinking how difficult it was living so far away from one's family.

It drizzled for two days and the path was muddy and slippery. It was like an ice rink. Whichever way you trod you were in danger of falling. The more I panicked, the more I stumbled, and I almost fell flat on my face. Luckily I steadied myself with my hand, or I would have smashed the bowl. Old Leng and the others made quicker headway and kept telling me not to be afraid and to hurry up. However, my legs refused to be ordered. Luckily, a female comrade handed me a bamboo stick which I used to inch my way to the canteen. I had no appetite, and after a few mouthfuls I took the bowl and hurried back, all the while worrying he might have fallen out of bed.

He lay there safe and sound, staring at me. I asked if he wanted anything to eat. He shook his head. Later, the Hospital Director suggested I brew him up some lotus-root starch and gave me a bag of glucose. Reluctantly, he ate some of the starch. Ever since the previous afternoon, that's all he had eaten. Then he fell into a deep sleep.

Being in hospital, I was no longer quite so anxious. If things became dangerous, there would be someone on hand to save him. I too flopped onto the bed and fell asleep.

In the middle of the night, I was woken by voices. A number of people had come in, including Director Jiang, the Hospital Director, and a female doctor in a white gown. Addressing F, Director Jiang said, 'The leadership has sent a doctor from the district hospital to do a check-up.' F replied, 'I'm embarrassed to be a nuisance. I'm sorry to trouble the leadership in this way. I'm sorry you had to come here in the middle of the night.' 'That's our job.' When the doctor started her examination, F tried to sit up, but she told him to lie still while she checked his heart and lungs. F was suddenly wide awake and had the strength to speak. He hadn't been like that for days.

The doctor suggested an injection, followed by another examination the next day. She said he was suffering from a slight cerebral haemorrhage, and that if it didn't worsen he'd be all right. The main thing was to make sure he received good nursing care.

They told her I was his wife. She turned to me. 'Make sure he doesn't fall. Keep on turning him round, so he doesn't get bedsores. If he won't eat rice, make him meat broth, chicken soup, or eggdrop soup. Make sure what he eats is easy to digest. Unless complications arise, he should get better soon.'

F once again said repeatedly how grateful he was. When I took them to the door, I saw it was pouring down. They had trodden mud everywhere. I was moved by the thought that they had come in the depths of night along difficult paths. My anxiety dissipated. I could see a ray of light. F was seriously ill, but his brain was clear, and that was reason to rejoice.

The next day, while breakfasting in the canteen, I spotted the female doctor, and heard her discussing F's condition with the Hospital Director. The Director told her someone was copying the medical record. The doctor asked whether she might have a word with the middle-aged doctor. The Director replied, 'He's a prisoner, but he has a medical degree.'

Sometime after ten, the female doctor came back. She tapped F's limbs, inspected his eyes, and asked him how he felt. He said everything seemed blurred. She gave him another injection and put him on a course of Jiangyaling tablets to reduce his blood pressure and told him to stop taking the Xuedeping. She said he needn't worry as long as he ate well, that he should try to eat as much as possible, then he would recover. F thanked her, at length. She again reminded me to give him a daily rubdown and help him change his position frequently, and to make sure he didn't fall. I nodded, again and again, my eyes blurred, unable to say a word (if I had tried, I would have burst into tears).

F drifted into a half sleep, but he needed to relieve himself often, which troubled me. To fetch the pan from the latrine I had to climb a slope. Getting up was all right, since I could hold the pan in one hand and support myself with the other, but going down to the waterhole to rinse it out was not so easy, for the way was even muddier. On one occasion, I fell three times before sliding down to my destination. I decided to use castor-oil leaves to line the pan so I wouldn't have to wash it so often, but when I picked one, a voice shouted 'it's forbidden to pluck the leaves, that's next year's flowers and seeds'. A cadre on the slope opposite was watching me. The same man had gloated and guffawed earlier, when I fell over.

F's diarrhoea stopped and he became alert. One morning, he started getting out of bed. I rushed over to stop him. I said, 'You're not yet over your illness.' 'Illness? What are we doing here?' He had woken from a dream. I told him Director Jiang had brought a doctor to visit him, he had politely spoken with her, etc., etc. He was flabbergasted. 'I don't remember anything.' However, he could hardly deny he was in hospital. After chatting for a while, he became dizzy and had to lie down again.

He realised he still wasn't back to normal. His vision was blurred, and he couldn't see small things at all. Only then did he concede that he was seriously ill. When the Hospital Director came, he described his symptoms. The Director told him the nerves on his eyeball might have been damaged or debilitated.

I asked Old Leng to buy a chicken and some eggs next time he went to market, and to get me a pair of rubber boots, so I could negotiate the muddy paths.

Four or five days later, F left his sickbed and walked around within the embankment. The chicken soup and the eggs seemed to have worked. National Day came, but there were few celebrations in the hospital – there weren't even any posters. However, the prisoners got pork noodles and a day off. Their wives and children came to see them.

For the festival, there were lots more dishes than usual, and I bought one of each. They included vegetables, chicken pieces, meat balls and squid. The cadres didn't like the fishy smell and anyway it was dear, so the chef urged me to buy several portions. I ended up buying a big pot. That's how F and I spent National Day.

We sat on the embankment hoping to hear reports of the parades in Beijing and the leaders' speeches, but we were unable to hear Lin Biao's speech clearly, perhaps because of the distance. A few days later I read that Mao had reviewed one and a half million demonstrators and Lin Biao had called for the denunciation of the bourgeois reactionary line. The Hospital Director suggested F leave the hospital. He said the weather was about to clear, and he would summon a sturdy man to carry F back on his shoulders. The idea upset me. Why did they want to carry him like that? 'He weighs 150 pounds. I wouldn't be able to stop worrying.'

I had seen people being carried on back frames. Some prisoners were brought to hospital in that way. A shelf was attached to the frame and the sick person lay on it, while the carrier carried it up and down the hills. Discharged patients didn't use the shelf but sat facing forward on the frame, gripping the two main supports, like a child riding an adult.

They didn't want to stretcher him back, nor did they want him to stay in the hospital so he could get better and go back under his own steam, so they decided to send him piggy-back. I thought it was dangerous and undignified. F said, 'That's appropriate for someone of my status, what are you angry about?' However, I was unable to reconcile myself to the idea. There was a broken-down bamboo fence alongside the house. I suggested F use one of the staves as a walking-stick.

The Hospital Director said, 'It's good weather today, I'll get the man to come. He's strong, he's capable of carrying 200 pounds of farm chemicals. Don't worry, nothing can go wrong.' I said, 'Hu Feng is a man, not a thing. We can make our own way back, there's no need for a carrier.' Noticing my tone of voice, he acquiesced.

We left at midday. A cadre volunteered to escort us and found F a pair of rubber boots. The hospital prescribed F glucose and other medicines. That was a great help.

F gripped his bamboo stave, with one person in front and another behind. I was carrying things on my back. I too had a bamboo stick. We walked along a dry gully. I had not expected that underneath the dry mud the ground would still be squelchy and liable to spatter up or even trip you. The best thing was to tread in the footsteps of the person in front of you. In that way, you didn't slide. At worst you gathered a ledge of mud around your boots, so that every now and then you had to sit down and clean off several pounds of it, after which you could return to battle with a lighter pack. I learned with every fibre of my body the truth of the saying 'roads are made by people'.

It was more than an hour before we reached the stone-paved road. From there to our accommodation was much easier. Seeing large numbers of people marching by with baskets and frames on their backs made us walk faster too.

When we reached our little hilltop, I was touched by the feeling that we had arrived 'home'. However, Old Leng led us into his own quarters, which he said were on the lee side and better suited for winter conditions. The room had been prepared. I helped F to a seat. He looked as if he was about to collapse. There was still some water left in the flask, so I poured it over some glucose for him and helped him lie down. He was recovering from a serious illness, and the fact that he had walked the whole length of that muddy road was, for us, a victory.

Old Leng said he would stay upstairs, I should shout if I needed him. He also said he would take us to the First Team for a look round, and make arrangements for us to get our meals there. He would help me bring them back. He would also arrange for us to get a stove and some firewood so I could boil water, cook gruel, or make a chicken stew. He seemed to have thought of everything.

At the bottom of a slope outside our building was the main road. About half a mile along it was the First Team. You had to cross a big embankment where the prisoners lived. At the top was where the cadres lived. Old Leng took me to the kitchen, where I bought some rice tickets. I put the food in an aluminium pot and hurried back. The food was still hot and tasted good. F ate it with relish. So the two big problems of food and accommodation had achieved a satisfactory resolution.

20

Convalescing Deep in the Mountains

F was indisputably ill. His task was to get better. That was what the doctor had said, and it was also what Old Leng said, representing the organisation. So after we got back, we moved into our new room, which was better protected from the wind. We thought it an excellent place in which to recuperate. F stopped worrying and slept soundly.

Chengdu sent on some letters. Xiaofeng told us Xiaoshan had gone off with his classmates to establish revolutionary ties. He had reached Wuhan just as the 'Million Brave Troops' Combat Regiment was waging its factional wars. Sensing that Xiaoshan was reckless enough to get drawn in, his elder brother had wired Xiaofeng to order him by telegram to return to Beijing. It was not long before he returned.

Xiong Zimin wrote to say that the illness was probably just a slight wind stroke. He urged us to buy some restorative pills known as Zaizaowan, which were very effective in such cases. I think they were probably ginseng. I suggested to F that we ask Xiaofeng to send us some, but as soon as he heard the word ginseng he shook his head. 'Under no circumstances. How could I take such an expensive medicine in a place like this? They would use it to argue that my thought reform was insufficiently thorough.'

A letter from Old Nie consisted of poems, which F liked. For a while he intoned them to himself. Unfortunately, he couldn't make out quite a few of Old Nie's cursive characters, so he had to guess them. We whiled away most of the afternoon with F declaiming and guessing. But between the lines there was much that caused him to sigh. The poem about Wu He going to hospital set him thinking about his old friend, but he no longer dreamed of 'drifting back to Wuhan on the wind'. The last line of the letter read 'PS Zhou Gong once said you should go home when you're old, what a joke that's become!' This suggested to me that he did not enjoy freedom of movement. While we were in Chengdu, Big Sister Ying had written to say she would like to move to Chengdu and be my neighbour. That would not have been easy, but at the time it would at least have been possible for them to come for a holiday. Now that we lived in the remote mountains, it was out of the question. Human affairs had never been so complicated. Luckily, we could take such things in our stride.

For the time being, F could not reply. He found it hard enough to read the paper. Things rocked before his eyes, as if through fog. I tried to get him to stop reading and told him I would read out the main bits. It made very little difference, for it was always the same old tune. In my view, he should rest more and use his brain less. The good thing was that no one seemed to bother about us, and F no longer had to hand in thought reports.

Actually, I was far too naïve. They were hardly likely to leave a great criminal against the imperial order unsupervised. Not long afterwards, they set up an administrative office. Old Leng came over to introduce its head, an old cadre and public security official. He seemed to be a civilian – he lacked the warrior style. He was heavily pock-marked, even on the rims of his eyes. He was probably a country man with some education who had joined the revolution. He had richer political experience than Director X. He was polite to F, and said, 'The main thing is to get better, you can write your thought report later. If you like you can go to town to visit the market or watch a film. You can go to the restaurant for a treat. The food isn't bad, it's just the hygiene, otherwise it would be perfect.' He smiled first, and then we smiled. 'Conditions aren't good here, but we're going to build you a new house and do everything possible to make life easier for you.' He gave us the number of the post-office box and said if the Plantation Headquarters showed a film, he would let us know.

It was good there was someone to look after us, but it also implied we would be living long-term amid these steep mountains and would not be able to return to Chengdu. F mentioned the books, and said he hoped I would be allowed to go to Chengdu to fetch those he needed. 'When my eyes are better, I want to do my bit for socialism.' 'That's a good idea,' the cadre said, 'but there's no hurry.' Indicating the volume of Mao's *Selected Works* on the table, he added, 'The best thing at present would be to study Chairman Mao's works.'

The Office Head had brought some letters from Chengdu. Apart from our daughter saying all was well, there was one from Old Nie and another from Xiong Zimin. F said, 'It's odd. They were written in early October, but now it's almost December. Why weren't they passed on earlier?' After reading them, I realised why. 'It's because they don't want to excite you after your illness. It was well intentioned.'

Xiong Zimin's letter could not have been clearer. He told us his nephew had returned and talked about the public denunciation of the 'black gang' member Zhou Yang and others. He ended by saying, 'Alas, the great scholar has passed away.' He meant Li Da, Chancellor of Wuhan University.

Old Nie's letter was soberly phrased, but the bloodstains were plentiful: 'This year is the thirtieth anniversary of the death of Mr Lu Xun. They said they were going to hold a memorial, but I have heard nothing more of it. Whether they do or not has nothing to do with us, so I won't ask. A few days ago some people turned up and took away my writings, nearly a million words, and my deposit account book. I should be like the author of *Camel Xiangzi* and become a Buddha.'

This shocked us even more than the death of Li Da. After all, the author of *Camel Xiangzi* was Lao She, who committed suicide in 1966. He had hurried home from the United States to help construct socialism. His personal connections were good, and the Premier regarded him highly. Just because he was influential, should he be made to disappear from the earth? I had another look at Old Nie's letter, which mentioned some literary figures who were 'on the golden list but suffered greatly'. What about Li Da? Did he die a natural death? I couldn't help remembering that in 1954 Li Da had accompanied Xiong Zimin to our house and eaten with us. Li Da had written two short primers on Chairman Mao's *On Practice* and *On Contradiction* that received the Chairman's approval, and he had become a top-notch university chancellor. Surely this could not have been due to his comment about 'peaks'?

F said gravely, 'I can understand Lao She taking his own life. After all, "Gentlemen prefer death to humiliation." He had pride and integrity. The chastising rod Old Nie mentioned in his letter was a crude torture, who can withstand it. Even I have no wish to live.' I was shocked. He laughed. 'Don't worry, who knows how things will end up? But self-respect is all, one must not be cowardly.'

Our depressed state and F's thick beard, after days without shaving, worried Old Leng, who summoned the plantation barber to give him a haircut and a shave. F let him cut his hair but refused to be shaved. His beard was already long. He trimmed his moustache in the manner of Lu Xun, in one straight line. He said, 'A straight-line moustache is excellent. It neither rises nor falls, it extends neither to the left nor to the right, it is simply a straight line across the upper lip, it cannot attract censure. It can be trimmed with a small pair of scissors.'

'But your full beard is scarcely so obedient. If it grows any longer, it will be like Li Kui's in the *Water Margin*, and stick up at the ends. That would definitely invite trouble. People might think you want to rebel.'

'Someone of my age? Leave that to the young generals of the revolution. I just hope they don't consider me to be an antique and overthrow me.'

He ended up with a beard that grew straight down from his chin, for six inches. He looked like a kind and genial old gentleman. Sadly, I didn't take a snapshot.

Under the benevolent rule of the Office Head, we moved back into our original accommodation. Old Leng said, 'He thinks the upper room is bigger and lighter. And it's closer to the latrine.' So we ended up back on our commanding height.

F had never had so much leisure. His greatest hardship was his lack of books, but at least he was restored to health. Passing water no longer took ten minutes. His migraines also cleared up, and he recovered his eyesight and could read the paper. Even so, I was afraid he would have a relapse.

In his *Confessions*, Rousseau had talked about the illnesses of old age. Many years later, it was discovered that he died of uraemia. The word filled me with terror. I mentioned it to Old Leng, and F's experience in the prison van, when he had had to hold himself in for such a long time. I said that perhaps, as a result, he was unable to evacuate his urine fully, and retained some in his bladder. His prostate gland had become inflamed, hence his headaches and high blood pressure. Maybe he had uraemia. I wanted to alert Old Leng, so that next time we were transferred F would not be forced to hold in his water.

Old Leng took us to town to watch a film. We first ate lunch in the restaurant and then went to the cinema. If it had been looked after properly, it would have been even nicer than the cinemas in the cities, but sadly it had turned into a weed-infested wilderness, filthy and in complete disorder. The cinema could seat more than 1,000 people. The building was modern and dome-shaped. The seats were quite well designed. The audience was mostly local folk and students.

One film was about the National Day parade and another was about Chairman Mao's Red Guard receptions. It was the sort of thing you wouldn't believe unless you saw it with your own eyes. There had been lots of reports in the paper about the Chairman receiving hundreds of thousands of Red Guards, but you had to see it to believe it. An ocean of marching people, line after line, dozens at a time, filling the entire square and lapping against the podium on Tiananmen Square. It was a magnificent sight, hardly matched anywhere on earth. The marchers were shouting 'Long life! Long life! Long long life!' and other slogans we couldn't make out. A series of close-ups showed Red Guards who hadn't been able to push their way into the procession and remained on the edges, standing on tiptoe or using binoculars but even so probably unable to catch a glimpse of Chairman Mao. They looked desperately through their binoculars, their faces streaming with tears. Their devotion moved us to tears as well. In the dim light, F gave me a sideways look.

After we got back, I spoke with him about his feelings. He held Lin Biao in high regard. He said he was a great and self-effacing person who never pushed himself forward – but actually he was a schemer who followed Chairman Mao around like a shadow, a miniature attachment to the great man, who avoided appearing to commit the offence of 'the secondary superseding the primary'. He absolutely understood the Chinese etiquette of submitting respectfully to higher levels.

After watching the documentary, a wild idea occurred to me: in the past, foreigners had criticised us for the human-wave tactic, and now the hundreds of thousands of youngsters gathered around Chairman Mao, each burning with righteous indignation, would at one wave of his hand fall like a pack of wolves on his adversaries, rip them apart with their teeth, and smash them to the ground. A repeat of the Boxers, but directed against a domestic opponent.

Winter had begun, and you could feel it up there in the mountains. Our clothes and bedding no longer sufficed. But F was unwilling to wear his new woollen suit and his sole defence against the cold was his pullover and vest – hardly enough. I was about to ask for permission to go to Chengdu to fetch winter clothing when Office Head X brought along Little Li, a demobilised PLA man, to see us.

'You must be cold. Little Li has brought across your luggage. Fetch what you need.' We were delighted, but also disappointed, for it was yet more proof that we might not be returning to Chengdu. We could expect a long stay in that mountain gully.

A cold wind howled down from the heights, and I couldn't help shivering. I decided to ask for permission to fetch some clothes. Our things had been stored in a newly built house near the Plantation Headquarters. It was brick-and-tile, but the floor was raw earth. No one had ever lived there, and it was damp. The books had been tied together with string and piled up on the floor. F was upset, and he couldn't find the books he needed. We opened the suitcase and took out his cotton-padded trousers. When he had first gone to the liberated areas in the northeast, he had had a pair specially made for him. I had donated cotton-padded clothes in Shanghai during the disaster-relief campaign, and kept a pair of overalls as a souvenir. Now they came in handy. We couldn't expect anyone to sew his cotton-padded clothing for him, so I got some wadding and some unlined silk gowns and a piece of dyed cloth and started doing it myself. At home, I had only ever knitted pullovers. Now I had to learn needlework from scratch. But I had watched other people, so by mechanically copying from memory, I managed to stitch together a silk-floss wadded jacket for him. It fitted well. He said he had never worn such a luxurious jacket. But it didn't fit his status, so I dyed a length of cotton poplin dark-blue. The dye was a bit patchy, but it still served its purpose as an outer coat. I finished it in one day, and the blue overall looked more appropriate.

We were determined to live a 'peaceful' life in our mountain home. We got used to fetching food from Team 1 and walking for miles up and down the slopes. Whenever possible, I took a bit more back at midday and kept it for the evening meal. The days were shortening, and in that way I no longer had to leave the house after dark.

The walls around the square where the prisoners ate were covered with posters proclaiming 'Strive for lenient treatment in the year-end reckoning', 'Strengthen thought reform and become a new person', etc. It was approaching New Year's Day, when the prisoners would take part in the Reward and Punishment Meeting. I was afraid that Office Head X might treat F with the same lack of consideration as Director X had, and in a roundabout way I let F know this. But he remained calm. All he said was, 'Don't worry. They can say what they like, I won't lose my temper. I don't want my blood pressure to go up.'

Old Leng said, 'It will soon be New Year's Day. Do you want to choose anything to buy?' F declined, but I said, 'I would like to send the children a pound of tea. My daughter wrote that tea is hard to buy in Beijing.'

'I'll go to the Plantation Headquarters and weigh you out a pound.'

'There's no need, I've still got some here.'

Little Li and I went into town on market day and I posted a small packet. There was nothing I needed to buy, but Little Li kept saying the chickens were cheap, and I should get some for a stew. I bought a four-pound hen, and some tangerines and sweets. I invited Little Li for a meal at the restaurant. He asked if we could have some alcohol, so I ordered a couple of ounces of white spirit for him. As a result, he was much friendlier on the way back. He talked about the tea plantation and the county town, and I learned a lot from him.

I said, 'You can hardly find Lushan on the map, what is this awful place.'

'This is Liu Wenhui's old base. A couple of days ago I heard someone say he grew opium here. His troops used to fight with an opium pipe in one hand and a foreign rifle in the other. They wouldn't fight unless they smoked. Look how small the common people are. That's because they smoked so much opium, it stopped the babies growing. The land's not good here. There's not much paddy, it's all maize. They eat nothing but flatbread.'

'How do they make it?'

'It's maize cake. You bake it in the ashes. You take it out and blow on it three times and beat it three times, and then it's done. That's why the locals call it "three blows, three beats"'.

He told me it was a grim area. In the past, local people fought a lot, and used to kill each other. 'Never quarrel with a local. They're unbelievably savage.'

I thought, 'Goodness, what a place. When we first came here, our friends thought we were lucky to live on Mount Lushan in Jiangxi. No one imagined it was a poor and barren area, with yellow mud on all sides, so uncivilised that even military penal transports couldn't get here in the past.'

He told me that when Zhang Guotao advanced three times across the Snowy Mountains and the Grasslands in the 1930s, it was from this region. He said, 'There are around a dozen teams here – there's even a coal pit, in Baoxing. Teams 1 and 2 are the richest, and they eat best – on New Year's Day they kill two fat pigs.'

'Why is it called the Miaoxi Tea Plantation?'

'Miao originally meant temple. In the old days, there were lots of temples on the road from the town all the way up to Mount Jiuling. The hospital was a temple. So was the Plantation Headquarters. After Liberation, the Reform Through Labour Bureau set up a tea plantation here and requisitioned it.'

Before New Year, we were allocated several dozen pounds of coke and a small coal stove. I had used coke in Chongqing during the war against Japan, so I knew how to light it. F cut the kindling piece by piece and wanted to look for dry branches that would catch easily, but Old Leng wouldn't let him, he said it wasn't safe. Old Leng brought a basket of wood shavings. Every morning F got the stove going. It reminded him of his student days in Japan, when he had sat cross-legged enjoying the heat from a fire crock. He spoke with such passion about it that he no longer sighed at our forlornness, and merely saw it as a necessary stage.

Two days before New Year, it started to drizzle and an occasional snowflake fell. The snow melted immediately, but it was freezing in the wind. I had to put on a scarf and gloves when I went to fetch food. On my previous trip to town I had bought a bamboo basket which I padded with cotton. I wrapped the food tightly and put it in the basket, so when I got back it was still hot. I walked so quickly my whole body heated up. On New Year's Day the food was especially plentiful. They had put up a menu to order from. I bought nearly everything – four or five different sorts.

On the last day of 1966, we had chicken. F took control. He found it absolutely absorbing. He gazed at the snow-white fowl he had prepared as if at a work of art. His joy infected me. We were like an old couple newly married. I fried the giblets and we had a glass of grape wine. We spent the evening gaily drinking and eating, without a thought for anyone or anything.

Was that how things really were? I didn't dare think. And him? Perhaps he pretended he wasn't thinking about things. Each feared starting the other off. People say 'on festive occasions we think more than ever of our dear ones far away', and we could hardly not think of our children. But what could we do? It would have been nice to chatter about past New Years we had spent together, but in the end all that was left was memory and bleakness, so as if by tacit agreement we didn't mention the past or our loved ones.

New Year's Day in 1967 had little in common with a normal day: getting up in the morning, you missed the crowds of prisoners shouldering hoes or struggling forward under back frames. The road from the highway to the gully was so quiet we even felt lonely.

We got up too late to fetch breakfast. I made some chicken soup, and added two poached eggs. That was our breakfast for special days. The stove was red-hot. Not until eleven did I go to fetch the food. I saw the prisoners lining up, and looked to see what they were getting. Each had a bowl of stewed meat. When I reached the more exclusive small kitchen, I said to the cook, 'Their food's not so bad.' 'It's even better at Spring Festival. We kill at least four pigs.'

I hurried home. Walking past the square, I saw row after row of prisoners sitting on little wooden benches listening to a pep talk by their political instructor. The smell of food wafted here and there on the cold wind, and those destined to eat it could only look, while listening without enthusiasm to the lecture.

The political instructor said in a stern voice, 'Unless you improve your reform, you will let down the Government. Just a few days ago some people ran away, and others stole things. You seem to think we can't cure you. Wait and see, unless you reform, there will be no way out. You have today off. Make sure you think things over.'

To say such things at such a time really did make you think.

As I lifted my basket of food, I felt like a beggar returned from begging. What should have been a happy feeling was deflated by the experience.

I didn't tell F what I had seen. That evening, I couldn't face the cold wind, so we ate food Old Leng had brought, together with a pound of noodles and lots of pea sprouts. The food was fresh and straight off the stove. It was spicy and flavoursome, of a sort we hadn't tasted for years. F drank his wine and smacked his lips, with the same enjoyment of life we had once known in Shanghai.

21

Helping One Another in Time of Need

According to Old Wang, who had lived there for many years, winter in the mountains was not so bad. It rarely rained or snowed, so the paths remained good. Old Wang had a slight hunchback. He was an optimistic man, in his fifties. Because of his happy nature, he used to joke with the cooks, and he even risked joking and laughing with the Team Leader and the Chief Cook. We enjoyed his company. When we walked back together after buying food, he used to chat about this and that. He pressed oil in the mill. He mainly used the oil for his own cooking. When he felt happy, he would eat in the team's small kitchen. As he put it, 'What's the point of holding on to that little bit of money? I might just as well enjoy a good meal.' As well as good food he liked to buy wine in the supply cooperative and get a bit tipsy and lurch home shouldering his basket. The prisoners liked him and called out Old Man Wang when they saw him, or Master Wang. Even the cadres addressed him courteously.

I asked him, 'Did you stay on after serving your sentence?'

'I'm not a prisoner. I was never sentenced for anything.'

'So you're a worker, like the cooks. Why don't go home for Spring Festival?'

'Ha-ha, I like the food here! I'll tell you the truth, they arrested me by mistake. I had a fight with someone on the wharf. The public security people arrested me, and sent me to join a reform-through-labour team. There's always food, what more could I ask? Afterwards the Plantation Headquarters found out and said they were going to send me home. But I wasn't on the household register, so they had to bring me back. There I was, not a care in the world, with all the food and drink I needed. Isn't that the life?'

Evidently, I was less free than he was. What shocked me most was what he said about the household register. Perhaps it wouldn't be so easy after all to return to Beijing.

The Office Head and Little Li didn't come to see us, probably because they had gone back to Chengdu. There was only Old Leng, living downstairs. Each day he passed by our window quite a few times, seemingly to go to the toilet, but actually to keep an eye on us. Because of the cold, we kept our window closed, and as far as possible only went out to fetch food or water. Office Head X really was an old hand at guarding prisoners: he had moved us upstairs to keep a better watch on us.

One afternoon the sun came out, unusually for that time of the year. There was a scent of early spring in the air. Old Leng suggested we go up the mountain. F was keen too. Without even donning a scarf, we climbed the mountain road. There is a saying, 'these mountains can wear out horses.' I realised the truth of it. It wasn't really a road, more a line of depressed footholds that got easier the higher you climbed. There were thickets of bamboo and shrubs, with line after line of tea bushes in the distance, dark green and a bit monotonous. We were short of breath, so we paused for a while on a step cut into the stone. You could still see the Plantation Headquarters and Team 1, but the houses were a blur. I asked Old Leng how high Mount Lingjiu was. He said one or two thousand metres above sea level. Can you see it from here, I asked? He pointed to a wayside pavilion up ahead, and said Mount Lingjiu was not far from there. I could see two or three peaks between us and it. I didn't want to go any further, but F did, and kept asking whether there was a temple. Old Leng said, 'There used to be a big temple with lots of murals, but it was demolished.' We stood up and continued the climb. Old Leng told us we were near Baoxing County, where there were thick bamboo forests and pandas. I looked down. It was an endless sea of bamboo. I thought how easy it would be to lose one's footing, and perhaps fall to one's death. I asked him what the path was like. He said we would have to follow tracks to get to the next mountain. If you shouted, there was an echo. It seemed unlikely we would make it to Mount Lingjiu.

A wind rose up from the valley. At first it seemed to come from a long way off, but then it began to howl and shook the branches. I said, let's hurry down. It was as if the wind was angry with us, it pursued us relentlessly. It caught us by the throat and neck and even seemed to lick down into our stomachs. I realised why the locals bound straw ropes round their waists when they entered the mountains and tied up their trouser legs — it was to keep out the blasts of cold wind from the valley.

The wind chased us away like stray dogs. I don't know how many ridges we crossed until it subsided. We weren't far from Team 1. Only then did we pause for breath and slacken our pace.

The first thing I did on getting back was to wipe away the sweat. F merely made himself a cup of tea. That evening, I got a headache and my whole body ached. I took an aspirin and sweated copiously. After that, I felt more relaxed.

The next morning, my head ached and I had a bad cough. I was worried I had pneumonia, so I took another aspirin and some penicillin. I soon used up the penicillin, and the only cough medicine I had was liquorice root. I asked Old Leng if he could go to town to buy me some penicillin and cough syrup. He said I should go to hospital for a check-up, and see a doctor in Team 1. I thought, I'm not a prisoner, why should I consult a prisoner doctor? So I said that if it got worse I would go to town and see a doctor of traditional medicine.

The cough was worst at night and first thing in the morning. F got very worried. He wouldn't let me get out of bed, saying that if the cold air and fog blew onto me it would freeze me to the marrow. He made me stay in bed until he had the stove going. I was moved by his love for me, but he was already over 60 and had only just got over his own illness. I tried to dissuade him. 'Don't light the stove, wait for the sun to come up and then do it, there are no regulations about when we have to get out of bed.' He smiled. 'The air is wonderful in the morning. I haven't enjoyed the benefits of nature for ten years. Let me get up and light the fire, and do something for you.'

I drank some hot water and had a hot breakfast, and my body warmed up. There we were, two old people without support – as the saying goes, 'people in desperate situations help each other out'. By the look of it, he was physically stronger than me. He didn't even get a cough. I was also not delicate – I rarely fell ill, and if I was ever poorly, I normally looked after myself. But this time it was different. I wasn't getting better, and I was short of breath. What if I contracted chronic bronchitis? I rummaged through my medicine bag again and found some ephedrine. That was Xiaoshan's idea, she used it for her asthma. I was like someone who had discovered a rare treasure. I took a tablet then and another that evening, before going to bed. The cough subsided, and by the morning my breathing was back to normal.

After New Year, Office Head X came to see us together with Little Li and Old Leng. He was carrying a newspaper, and I guessed the reason for his call. A few days earlier, we had seen Yao Wenyuan's article 'Criticise the Counter-Revolutionary Double-Dealer Zhou Yang'. The article had infuriated F. He could ignore arrogance, but the despotic tone of a man bent on hacking down everything with a broad axe made him burn with anger. He started underlining it in blue, so forcefully that he broke the lead. I said, 'What's it got to do with you?' 'He insists on coupling me with Zhou Yang. He wants to hack down the two of us with one swipe.'

By the time I got to read it, it was thick with blue underlining, and the occasional red. It made me angry too, but I persuaded him to look on it as a blast of evil wind and ignore it.

Now, Office Head X had come to discuss it with him.

'I suppose you've read Comrade Yao Wenyuan's article. Tell us what you think.'

'I don't think anything. Lots of it does not accord with the facts, it would be inappropriate for me to say why.'

'Tell us what you think. After all, Yao Wenyuan represents the Central Committee.'

Raising his head – and his voice – he said, 'In my view, what he says does not represent the Central Committee. It's not fair, so it can't accord with the Party's spirit of seeking truth from the facts. I'm not interested in his assessment of Zhou Yang, but I can't accept his conflating of Zhou Yang and me, as 'jackals of the same lair'. One of the crimes I was sentenced for was precisely opposing Zhou Yang. The passage he quotes saying Zhou Yang applied my literary viewpoint has nothing to do with me.'

He wasn't answering Office Head X's question, but was advancing a theoretical defence, made on the assumption that justice was on his side. Luckily the Office Head was a cultivated man, so instead of shutting him up he said in a measured way, 'As a result of this Great Cultural Revolution and Yao Wenyuan's article you will have to review your literary standpoint and develop new opinions, there's got to be some progress.'

'I can't simply give the rudder a flick to suit the new fashion. I've not changed my position, I want to serve my sentence and never again talk about art and literature. Unless the Central Committee orders me to explain my literary theory, I will not write a single character or say a single word.'

Office Head X picked up his newspaper and stalked off.

The conversation had annoyed F. Although they had gone, he had not yet simmered down:

'They harass me at every step. In Chengdu, they wanted me to say where I stood, but I couldn't please them. Now they use Yao Wenyuan to attack me. Even if they sentence me to another 14 years, I still won't bow my head to a man like him, wrapped in his tiger skin.' He sighed. 'Each generation is worse than the last. Literary thought? That's not literary thought, it's pure rubbish. Who would have imagined that Yao Pengzi's son would end up criticising Zhou Yang. We should not allow ourselves to be intimidated.'

After he had calmed down, he excused his failure to write a thought report by saying that his eyes were failing.

I too felt depressed, so I wrote the character for mountain on a piece of paper. Then I turned it round and wrote it again and again. Then I wrote a poem:

> Mountain mountain mountain mountain,
> layer after layer,
> big mountains and small mountains
> weighing down upon your shoulders,
> you try to avoid them,
> your legs tremble,
> don't bend your knees,
> don't fall down . . .

He read it and laughed. 'You're no good at poetry, stick to children's verses. Personally, I lack the urge to write. It's the same with Old Nie's poems, I can't compose anything in reply and I'm not even interested in reading them. I've become insensitive.'

'There's no greater sorrow than the death of the heart. You can't carry on being passive and negative.'

Little Li brought an order from Office Head X. He said a new year had begun, and it was time to write a summary. He also said if you're not well, write less. That was an order. F couldn't put it off with an excuse. He had to say where he stood:

FOUR MONTHS LIVING IN THE MOUNTAINS

Here is a brief report on the situation since arriving at the plantation. As I said in my letter to the Department of Public Security, on the night of September 8, on the way here, I had an attack of neuralgia that worsened after my arrival. By the afternoon of the 18th, I was unconscious. [. . .] I entirely support the editorials and theses on the Great Cultural Revolution published in *Red Flag* and *People's Daily*. I believe they are a concerted exposition and flexible application of Mao Zedong Thought.

16 January 1967, Miaoxi Tea Plantation, Sichuan

Perhaps as a 'reward', Old Leng took us to watch a film. On the square in front of the Plantation Headquarters was a projector and rows of chairs. We sat about four metres from the screen. That was the optimal distance – seats of honour. Along the side sat cadres, together with lots of local children who had got there early enough to grab a seat. The cadres chased away the bigger children, but some seven or eight year olds were not prepared to move. They were dressed in rags. They followed the film attentively, but kept on looking round and scratching themselves. A cadre said, 'You're covered in lice, you can't even sit still.'

The film was *Little Soldier Zhang Ga*. We were deeply moved by Little Ga's heroic and resourceful actions in the face of the enemy. F said it was a great film. He added, 'Did you see those children? You probably only noticed them scratching lice. But did you see how they swarmed round the projector and watched it going round and how the film was changed? They're so full of curiosity. Perhaps they will become actors, technicians, scientists. You're a children's writer. You should pay attention to these things. Don't just think about the lice.'

What he said thrilled me. I didn't feel it was directed against me. He was not at all as passive as he claimed. He was still concerned about literature, and about our future.

The next day, Old Leng invited us for a walk along the highway. These vehicular roads were cut into the side of the mountain. From the top, you could see layer after layer of hills and mountains. It was not the tea-picking season, so there were few vehicles and even fewer people. We walked up to the foot of a towering peak thickly covered in clumps of trees with small red berries. I broke off a branch. The berries were like holly, or like the carved landscapes made of coral beads that you can find in antique shops. Old Leng told me they were called water branches. They were edible and you could buy a small glass of them in Chengdu for a couple of cents. Children loved them. I tasted them. They were both tart and sweet. Hearing a chirping sound, I looked up and saw a gaudy bird hopping along a branch. I guessed it was a woodpecker.

At home, F stuck the branch in an empty wine bottle. It added a note of happiness to the room.

We went to town to buy fish, a chicken, and some pastries for Spring Festival. There were only the two of us, but I wanted to make the best of it. F went out of his way to help me.

Old Leng told me there was beef on sale, for the first time in months. A cow had fallen to its death the day before and the small kitchen had been allotted a few dozen pounds of meat. A big bowl cost ten cents. Little Li said, 'That's cheap, I bought two bowls.' I also bought two bowls. They just about filled the pot, which I balanced all the way home.

At the carpenter's work shed, a young prisoner was sitting on a pile of wood with his hands bound. He looked less than 20. He had a dull expression. Such a cold day and everyone off to eat, why was he there? The carpenter said, 'People like to go home for family reunion at this time of the year. They run away to see their wives. Not a bad idea. But two or three days later they get caught and brought back.'

The idea that he had 'gone home for family reunion' robbed me of my peace of mind. I told F. For a while he didn't say a word. Then he sighed and said:

'How many years have I dreamt of spending Spring Festival with you and the children? But there was no way I could escape. You can't grow wings. There's no point in being sad. As long as the two of us are together, that's a family. With you I have every-thing.' He cocked his eye at me, and it seemed to flash with the same passion as on the eve of Spring Festival 30 years ago.

Up in the tranquil mountains there were no firecrackers to create a festive mood, no gaily dressed merrymakers, no women and small children to embellish the awakening of spring. But we let the stove glow red and sat opposite one another to celebrate this rare holiday in one another's company. F drank several glasses of wine and became excited. We forgot where we were. Gazing at his big flushed face, I felt Spring Festival was not so disappointing after all. The stove's glow, the wine and food, that flushed face, those tiny berries . . . we were no more lacking than a family of aristocrats. Apart from that, we were united in the determination to spend those lonely times together and await the true spring.

22

Learning How to Plant Tomatoes

The fruit trees were beginning to bud and new leaves to form. They no longer sprawled out like frightful demons but were like green-hatted children dancing to the baton of the spring wind, nodding and waving to us, as if to say 'spring has come, we have awoken!'

Office Head X came to tell us that the new house was finished, and we should move at once. Old Leng and Little Li helped. The house was on a hill to the right of the Plantation Headquarters, but first you had to go up and down a slope for about half a mile. It was on a newly cleared piece of ground levelled out of the side of the mountain, the back wall was mountain. We lived in the two rooms off the side entrance. The main entrance gave onto a compound with lots of rooms, which was partitioned off from us. Between the two entrances they had built rooms for Old Leng and the guards. One room was connected to ours by a door.

Inside, some prisoners were moving in our things, so we showed them where to put them. The job was completed in a day. There was a kitchen with a one-ring gas stove and a big wok, but no windows and no other utensils. From the kitchen, you had to pass through a yard to reach the room. I suggested putting a small stove outside the front door and they agreed, but they said we would have to buy the coke ourselves and maybe it would be unavailable, so I gave up the idea. I warmed up some gruel and pickled vegetables left over from breakfast. It couldn't have tasted better. The door into the compound was closed, so there were just the two of us. It was like being at home.

But that was wishful thinking. We had just finished sorting out the rooms – a bedroom and a study, with the books neatly arranged in the bookcase – when a newly arrived cadre, Director X, ordered the land in the courtyard to be turned over. He told Little Li to put a hoe and a night-soil pail outside our door. He shouted, 'Zhang Guangren, you have to take part in manual labour. You have to turn this land over and plant vegetables.' F waved his hand disapprovingly and sighed. 'Come on,' he said, 'I have to do manual labour. It doesn't matter. It's not that I can't do it, it's just that they never let me.' But inwardly, he was far from happy.

He received a letter from Old Nie telling us to burn his letters and poems. I got the letters out. Looking at his minuscule hand-writing, I was loath to put them to the flames. F read the poems one last time. Grieving, he laid them on the table without a word, and went off to dig the soil outside the door. Secretly, I separated the sheets and wrapped the chopsticks in them. In that way, we could take them with us wherever we went.

Office Head X came to 'pay a visit', accompanied by a new secretary. The secretary had delicate features and looked like a student.

After a few pleasantries, Secretary X stood up and glanced through the books. 'There are quite a few poisonous weeds here.' Office Head X chimed in, 'The best thing to do with poisonous weeds is destroy them.'

'I kept them to use as criticism materials,' F responded.

'We have people for that.'

'Didn't Chairman Mao say poisonous weeds can be used as fertiliser?' F was resisting.

'According to the newspaper, the Three-Family Village black gang is a poisonous weed, and so is anything by capitalist road-ers, black writers, and Soviet revisionists. I suggest you check. Hand over those you find.'

The two left.

I said, 'That's an order, we had better check.' I sorted out some books to hand over as poisonous weeds.

Two or three days later, we received another letter from Old Nie. It was short and to the point: we should burn his poems and stop writing to him. Living as we did deep in the mountains, we were at a loss to understand what was happening. What was going on? What had happened to Old Nie? Things looked bad. F told me to burn the poems immediately, so I unwrapped the chopsticks one by one. That was the first time we had ever burned a friend's poems. F comforted me: 'Don't worry, he probably knows them off by heart. After all, he wrote them with his heart's blood.' However, I secretly hid a few in the pocket of a pair of trousers I didn't normally wear. Even if they searched the house, they would never think of rummaging through those old clothes.

For a few days, we were sad in the way only those can be who have destroyed something dear to them. Xiong Zimin was also no longer corresponding with us. It seemed everything was revolution. We couldn't imagine what was happening.

F said, 'Last year Old Nie's bank accounts and manuscripts were confiscated, but it didn't seem to concern him, he still used to copy me his poems.'

F devoted himself heart and soul to digging up the courtyard. It was only a few dozen square metres, but all the hoe seemed to bring up was stones and broken bricks. My job was to sift them out with a winnowing scoop and dump them down the slope outside the door. F got blisters on his hands, and I was told I didn't have to open the door to tip the stones out. I got the message: I wasn't allowed to leave the house.

I was surprised when things suddenly got very noisy next door. There seemed to be some new arrivals. They stopped us going out – even the building workers stopped working for two days. We took the opportunity to rest.

Our life as lonely 'kings' of the mountain had come to an end. Under the 'administrative correction' system, there were not only specially assigned individuals but 'special regulations'. F was ordered to take part in manual labour and was reminded again and again that he had to write a thought report. The idea of doing so upset him. 'I don't want any more of that nonsense. I'm hardly likely to be so stupid as to write what I think. I've promised to behave myself. But they still want me to write a report.' He wrote one, hoping to put an end to it, but got no reply.

As for me, I could go to the Plantation Headquarters to fetch letters and to the canteen to buy food, but if I wanted to go to town, someone had to go with me. I didn't mind, but F did. He said, 'You're free, and you're still a state cadre. What are you afraid of? Don't be so compliant. The more you do as they say, the more they'll cheat you.' But what did he know of what they were saying on the big-character posters? I didn't dare tell him, lest he get upset or frightened.

Luckily I didn't want to go to town, and I didn't even have time to go to the Plantation Headquarters. That was because I received a letter from my daughter saying she had given birth to a boy and wanted me to send some baby clothes. I had already knitted a pullover and a warmer, and now I sorted out some left-over cloth and put together a few bits and pieces. That gave us something to concentrate on. Although F couldn't sew, he did his best to help me for the sake of our new grandchild. He wound the wool and did other odd jobs, saying it was the least he could do. In that way, he forgot how unhappy he was.

However, the good times didn't last. Office Head X and Secretary X came to ask about his study and proposed he read Chairman Mao's 'Three Old Pieces', preferably every day. F said he would start immediately. F also said he couldn't abandon his manual labour. He told them he would soon have turned over the soil, that he'd brought tomato seeds with him from Chengdu, that they had already sprouted, and needed replanting. So he could both reform his thinking and harvest the fruits of his labour. He said turning over the soil would not take long. Just as I was thinking how well it was all going, Office Head X said, 'Our comrades aren't happy about the way you are being treated. They think your reform is unimpressive, and so is your manual labour. They say your income should be cut by half, from now on you'll get 25 yuan.' 'No problem. Otherwise I'll be a burden. Actually, a bowl of prison food is enough, why give me money anyway?' 'If you need money, submit a request. We're revolutionary humanists.' Secretary X added a word of warning: 'Start studying tomorrow morning.'

Every morning we read aloud from the 'Three Old Pieces'. He read a few sentences and then stopped, and then I read some and discussed it with him. I said, 'People are listening. If you're not conscientious, they might not even give you the 25 yuan. Who knows where they might send us?' He shook his head, and laughed bitterly.

But he was very enthusiastic about the digging. In just a few days, we removed two wheelbarrows of rubble and stones. It appeared immediately you started raking. There was no way you could plough deeply unless it was removed. Office Head X brought some cadres to turn the soil on the slope above the houses. It was loamy and turned easily. F seemed competitive and didn't want to fall behind. By the time he had finished, his hands were oozing pus.

I washed them and rubbed in some ointment. His feet were red and swollen and very itchy, so I boiled a bowl of wild pepper water and bathed them in it.

Secretary X said F had done a good job of turning the soil, and he praised his thought report. He said it was linked to reality and combined learning with practice.

Half smiling, F said, 'That's because of what I learned from Chairman Mao's "Three Old Pieces". They instil a spirit of fearlessness – to fear neither hardship nor death.'

I said, 'Look at his hands, they're covered in blisters.'

'Would you like me to fetch a hygiene official?'

'The lightly wounded should never leave the firing line. It's just a light wound, I washed it for him. It's fine as long as it doesn't flare up.'

He was happy to hear me say that, and returned to his room.

F whispered to me, 'See, all they want is superficial stuff. But if you tell them what you're really thinking, you end up in big trouble.'

He was ordered to write some so-called external investigation materials. Secretary X brought a form to check up on his past acquaintances, senior cadres who had not been labelled 'Hu Feng elements', and some questions about things he had published in *July* magazine. Do you have a connection with this person? Has he or she done anything (bad)? In short, they wanted dirt.

F wrote much more than they wanted. He wrote about his connection to this or that person and what he had published of theirs, and then he reviewed it.

He asked me to copy it so he could keep the original. 'This is the truth. If they come back for more, I'll just copy it out again.'

'That won't satisfy them. You're not producing materials, you're writing essays.'

'If they don't like it that's their business. I can't just write what they tell me.'

I was surprised F knew how to be a peasant. If I hadn't seen it with my own eyes, I wouldn't have believed it. The vegetable garden at his family home was tiny. His eldest brother's wife and his nephew's wife had tended it. None of the males ever did anything.

'When I was a boy I used to watch my mother and my brother's wife dig the vegetable garden and I even helped them plant the seedlings. That's why I haven't made a mess of it. If they think I'm just some stinking intellectual who can't tell his leeks from his wheat seedlings, they will have to think again.'

We got out the tomato seeds and planted them in the little beds F had dug.

I had grown up in the city and had never seen with my own eyes how grain and vegetables grow until the war against Japan, when we moved to a village near Chongqing. However, it was not so easy to get land to grow vegetables. We were renting a house from a landlord. The family of Guo Fuguan, who was sharing the house with us, asked the landlord for a vegetable garden. Seeing them eat their own fresh beans, spinach and pea shoots, we decided to ask the landlord for a patch of land. He pointed to an overgrown slope next to a bamboo grove. 'Clear that land and plant some vegetables, you'll have more than you can eat.' I borrowed a hoe and took my young son with me to reclaim it. We worked all day, but the bit we cleared was smaller than a table top. When the landlord's hired hand passed by, he laughed and said I was wasting my time, the soil was full of bamboo roots and the slope never got the sun. The landlord had cheated us, because he knew we were amateurs. After that, I returned to the city and never had another chance to grow vegetables. Now I could observe the entire process: turning over the soil, creating tiny beds, and planting the tomato seedlings.

F used two thumb-sized sticks to make holes an inch deep to put the seedlings in. Then we firmed up the soil with our hands. It took a whole morning to plant more than 100. F was wilting. When he stood up, he reeled backwards, and I rushed to support him. He was in his sixties and not used to manual labour, so it was not surprising that he felt dizzy after squatting down.

While he was taking his midday nap, I planted the rest of the seeds. But would they live?

The next job was to water the roots. Secretary X told us to use liquid manure. Neither of us was capable of carrying water buckets on a pole. While living in his village, I had tried once, for fun, and with only half a bucket, but I tilted over and spilt it, and my shoulder hurt the entire night. I didn't dare try to carry a pail of night soil, so we ended up carrying one between us. The people on the slope stopped to look. They probably thought it a strange sight.

Very soon, the crop was more than a foot high. I remember in Beijing when Lu Mei had told us to plant tomatoes and said he would look after them. He talked about the Single Whip and Two Dragons Playing Ball, mainly to do with pruning. So we inserted a bamboo pole alongside each plant, propped it up, and waited to bring the crop in.

Each plant started sprouting branches and leaves that danced in the wind and grew big and strong. Cluster after cluster of little yellow flowers opened and formed into tiny tomatoes. I happily watched and counted, willing them to ripen. But they started turning black. We were studying the matter when Office Head X arrived. We showed him. He said, 'Ours are the same. It's a disease, there's nothing you can do about it.' He got out a magnifying glass so I could have a look. The black bits were mildew. Ours were apparently less blighted than theirs. They had used rice straw to tie the branches, and where they were tied they had gone black. We had used cloth, and the stalks looked as if they could be saved.

We went to the supply cooperative in the Plantation Headquarters to buy some pesticide. They had none, but we did take back some 'news'. Our Office Head had been caricatured in a cartoon on the propaganda blackboard. I recognised him immediately, because his face was covered with pock-marks. His crime was protecting 'capitalist roaders' or 'reptiles' belonging to the 'February Adverse Current'. Across Capital Construction Team Square hung a banner of the Rebel Command. We didn't know the details, but Liu, head of the Construction Team, no longer came to see us, and next door had quietened down a lot. One day when we were climbing the slope to see how their tomatoes were getting on, we noticed the houses had acquired dark blue curtains, all of them drawn. Director X was waiting for us at the back door. He told us off, and said we should stop running about.

Things seemed to be going from bad to worse. I knew from the posters that the Great Cultural Revolution was becoming ever more complex. However, we could no longer read *Sichuan Daily*, and our sole occupation (and pleasure) was trimming the tomatoes. Nearly every day we cut away new patches of blight, which I threw away as far as I could. New branches and flowers started growing, and these turned into fruit.

Office Head X brought Secretary X to see us. Office Head X talked animatedly with F about how he had followed the Field Army into Guizhou and Sichuan, and how he had later gone to Tibet. He talked about a soldier who had violated discipline because he didn't understand local customs and was punished by military law. He said we had to do that to gain the national minorities' trust, the reason we had defeated the enemy was because the PLA had observed discipline. He told F, 'If you have any ideological problems, ask Secretary X.'

F took out a winnowing scoop full of tomatoes and asked me to give it to the office, because theirs had all died. He wrote a report in praise of thought reform, for enabling an intellectual like him to learn how to grow tomatoes. Our hard labour – pruning the branches, fetching more than 100 pails of liquid manure, and lavishing endless care and attention on them – had borne fruit.

F said, 'I don't know why they class labour as a punishment. During my ten years of solitary confinement I couldn't imagine even in my wildest dreams that I would one day be allowed to kiss the earth and participate in labour. What's so terrible about it? Truly terrible would be to exclude me from it so all I could do would be to think my so-called thoughts. No sky to see, no people to hear – how can you have thoughts under such circumstances? However much you think, you can't jump free of the circle of the past. Mountain gullies, manual labour? No problem.' I said, 'No, I don't fear manual labour either. And it means we're not parasites, people who have never dirtied their hands. I hope they let you stay here permanently working the land.'

23

Taken Away Yet Again

Summer in our little courtyard was a lively time. The Sichuan high mallow I had brought with us looked like a row of pretty girls: its multicoloured flowers were their ceremonial dresses — when the wind blew, they danced. The short-stemmed cock's combs that stood under them with their little red and yellow hats were a gift from Director X. The maize was no longer in flower and had reached the milk stage. The peas and beans had flowered long ago and we were eating them. In the midst of the harvest, we sat on the step sipping tea and admiring everything. F's feeling of contentment brought joy to me, for he knew nothing of the 'beating, smashing, and looting' that was going on in the outside world.

When we had first moved here, it was one big building site. In the distance, on level ground, they were building a dining room and a place for showing films. We were also told that they were going to build a small road leading off the big road so vehicles could drive right down to our door. Later they built houses in a gully even further away, which they said was in preparation for war.

One morning, going through the back door to empty the rubbish, I saw Office Head X and Little Li climbing up from the distant gully carrying some things they had apparently collected from the residents. They looked awkward, so I didn't greet them but simply turned round and left. Some people like us must have been living down below and perhaps they'd just been sent away.

What about us? I could only observe these things to myself, and formulate conjectures. I didn't dare reveal this to F.

F hoped he would be able to study, starting with the Chairman's works. We arranged the room and stuck up two big photos of the Chairman and Vice-Chairman Lin Biao, as well as some of Lu Xun's poems in the Chairman's calligraphy, which Xiaofeng had sent us. So we had on our wall elements of both revolution and classical elegance. F read the poems out loud: 'When thoughts spread wide to fill the whole of space, amid the silence comes the crash of thunder.' It seemed as if he was hearing the thunder.

Office Head X and Secretary X came for a talk. Rather than thunder, it was a blast of cold air. Office Head X said, 'We've read your study plan. It's got to relate to yourself, you've got to investigate your own past anti-Party utterances and deeds. If you manage to study Chairman Mao's works in that way, we will be happy.' Secretary X said, 'Make sure you study and perform manual labour conscientiously, we've shown you enough leni- ence. Don't go running around all over the place. If you need anything, ask. We'll do our best to consider it. Your wife [point- ing at me] must also stop running around, especially in town. If she wants to buy anything, she can ask.'

With that they left, coldly.

F wrote out the following study plan:

Initial plans for re-studying Mao Zedong Thought in my remain- ing years

First method:

Every day I study important documents, editorials and articles in the press, as I have done for more than a year now.

i) This concerns the process of the struggle of Mao Zedong Thought against non-Mao Zedong Thought and especially anti-Mao Zedong Thought. Given my circumstances, this study is to some extent of the nature of 'learning through practice'.

ii) Nearly all of them cite Mao Zedong's quotations. I put the emphasis on linking those quotations to the text as a whole and strive to study them more deeply.

iii) Whenever possible I look up relevant quotations and study them simultaneously, to strengthen my comprehension and judgment of those documents and accumulate an understanding of Mao Zedong Thought.

Second method:

I initially selected the following articles and used them as a focal point for making an initial breakthrough.

i) *Three Old Pieces.*
I hope to strengthen my understanding of the spiritual quality of the revolutionary successors nurtured by Mao Zedong Thought (the young revolutionary generals), and to put an end to my own selfish interests.

ii) *Report on the Investigation of the Peasant Movement in Hunan.*

iii) *Let the Whole Party Unite in Order to Realise the Struggle for the New Tasks.*
   On the Correct Handling of Contradictions Among the People.

I hope to strengthen my understanding of basic issues in the process of revolutionary development.

iv) *On Practice.*
   On Contradiction.

I hope to grasp dialectical materialism a little better and to eliminate my muddled ways of thinking.

Third method:

Read the four volumes of *Mao Zedong's Selected Works* and after that the separate works (I read them too hastily and casually in the past, and most of what I learned has disappeared).

Goal of study:

Read it through, to experience in an all-sided way the spiritual force of Mao Zedong Thought, as well as the spiritual force formed by the historical mainstream of the struggle for the liberation of humanity over the last 40 years. To keep the ancestral country in mind, to keep the entire world in view, to confront the present leading directly to the future – by means of study I wish to experience to some extent the heart of the Chinese of the Mao Zedong era, so I can cure my own spiritual narrow-mindedness and backwardness.

Programme of study:

1. Read it through relatively quickly, to gain a general understanding. Not link it to other circumstances, not consult reference materials. Should take a year (four articles or chapters a week).
2. Study some works in detail, link them to other circumstances, and consult reference materials. Some will be merely reviewed. Roughly two years.
3. Re-read everything comprehensively. Roughly half a year. This is the method I used in the past, in my view it is comparatively effective. I believe one cannot expect to succeed quickly with true study.

The timetable is a general estimate. It also depends on our health. If my wife's health is good and she remains strong, it might take a little less time, or otherwise a little more (my eyesight is poor, so I usually ask her to read aloud for me). One must also take into account the actual revolutionary situation, like the Great Cultural Revolution. Nearly every day brings important news, and every few days an important document appears. It is more than we can deal with, and it may mean the schedule will be extended somewhat.

Later, I heard that the supply cooperative had slaughtered a pig. As I was taking my liver and giblets down the slippery slope, I saw Office Head X climbing in the opposite direction, also clutching a bamboo stick and a cotton bag. He had tied several layers of rice straw round his shoes. He stopped to remove a thick layer of clay from them. We could hardly avoid speaking with one another.

I said, 'This road's really hard to walk on.'

'Look at the clay that stuck to me. It must weigh several pounds. You bought some meat?'

'Some pork giblets.' At the end of the exchange, I hurried off. It was obvious what was going on.

I told F Office Head X might be returning to Chengdu and that it looked like things were about to change. He wasn't surprised, and he even said it was a good development. After all, he was honestly accepting reform and was bound to gain the understanding of the Central Committee, which would let him return to Chengdu. Such was his obstinacy and self-confidence.

Even Secretary X and Old X, who used to help us buy things, were no longer to be seen, and we hadn't seen Old Leng for ages. Only Little Li remained, as well as Director X and a newcomer we hadn't been introduced to. It also meant we hadn't heard them reading out 'Three Old Pieces' and the *Quotations*, so we too decided to stop.

We were waiting for the maize to ripen, and from time to time we plucked tomatoes. We were living a free and easy life. F concentrated on reading Lu Xun, and tried to persuade me to read it too. 'Read carefully, this is your chance, make sure you study well.' Sadly, the thoughts in my brain were a lot more complicated than his and I knew a lot more than he did about the outside world, so I was unable to settle down to reading. Thinking back on it later, it seemed a pity.

Every month or two, we received a letter from our daughter. Our little grandson was babbling his first words. She sent a photo that F put in his wallet. It became the only thing that could bring us happiness. We couldn't even read the newspaper – *Sichuan Daily* had ceased publishing. We had no radio either – we were deaf as well as blind. But no one was telling F to write thought reports, a lucky respite in the midst of disaster.

The apples and pears had been harvested, and people no longer climbed up and down the mountain. Everything seemed bleaker. An autumn wind blew up, and the apple trees shed their leaves and the remaining apples. Some children gathering greenfeed for the pigs scrambled for them, creating a brief burst of excitement. But in the late-night silence, you could hear no human voices, only the screeching of owls. It was hard not to be frightened.

F had to get up every night to pass water, and I would wait for him to return to bed. In the summer, I got up to kill mosquitoes. To distinguish our room from the cadres', we had no insect screen. I bought some cotton gauze to stick in the windows, but the mosquitoes found a way in. When F was outside the net passing water, they followed him back in. Even when the autumn winds started up, they continued to bother us.

One night, we heard a crowd of people shouting and careering down the mountain. We thought a prisoner must be trying to escape. F asked nervously whether I had closed the outside door. I wanted to check, but he held me back. 'The wall's not high enough, people could jump in. Bolt the door to the room and lock the windows.' The shouting grew more distant until everything became quiet again.

The next day Little Li told me a thief had tried to steal some chickens. The coops were built on open land, but in the past there'd been lots of people about and no one had ever dared to try to break into them. Now, however, the thief's chance had come. Not content with two, he went for a third, whereupon a cock came running out flapping his wings and making a big noise, thus sparking off the chase. They got all the chickens back, but they had had their necks wrung – one had been abandoned on the slope, the other by the side of the road. All the thief got for his night's work was a handful of feathers.

The incident showed that the power of the 'Office' was on the wane. We had been waiting for a long time for a new Office Head to talk with F. Once Director X came for a quick look. When he saw the maize, he said, 'Why don't you eat some, why don't you cut some off for yourselves?' F said, 'We have to hand it over.' 'No need, we planted some up there too.' So we started eating corn planted with our own hands. We had irrigated it, picked it, and cooked it with our own hands, how could it not delight us?

There was no longer anyone next door to buy food for us, so I had to think up ways of getting to the Plantation Headquarters to make my purchases. Once, I stole into town. I saw a 'monster and demon' parade and big-character posters in which different factions mercilessly assailed each other. I didn't dare say a word to anyone, least of all F.

The harvest had been gathered in and the maize and tomato stalks had been pulled up, but Director X hadn't come to tell us what to plant next. We were puzzled and a bit bored, but it wouldn't have been good to ask. Our feelings about labour and production were probably the result of transformations in our thinking.

I told Little Li I would like to buy some asparagus and other seedlings, and he brought a packet of spinach seeds. I had no idea how to plant them, and I had never seen that sort of barbed and rhombus-shaped seeds before. I asked F, but he didn't know either. However, he carefully turned over the soil so it was flat and smooth, like a row of patties. We scattered the seeds and waited for them to sprout.

F squatted down almost daily to watch, but there was no sign of life. Later, a few green leaves struggled into sight, but it was hard to believe they were spinach seedlings. Secretary X said he wanted to see if our spinach had come out. F was embarrassed. He said, 'I've never grown spinach before. Only a few have come out. Should we buy some more seeds and re-sow them?'

'More of yours have come out than ours. We'll give you some of our seeds.'

So they didn't know how to grow spinach either.

On my way to the Plantation Headquarters, I passed by a vegetable plot full of neat rows of young spinach plants. A man was tending them. I asked:

'How do you sow the seeds?'

He advised me to mix them with plant ash and not to scatter them but to sow them directly, because they were light and had thorns and corners. If you scattered them, they stayed on the surface and the birds ate them.

I did as instructed, and lots sprouted. We had finally managed to plant spinach. We checked every day for weeds and watched the young plants grow. When they were a couple of inches high, we fed them liquid manure. They shot up, and we looked forward to cooking them with noodles.

Director X came to sit with us for a while. He had a silk quilt and a suitcase full of clothes with him. F thought it strange and said later, 'Is he showing off how rich he is?'

'I don't think that's the intention.' I didn't dare say what I actually thought, and I hoped I was wrong.

Could the changes be coming to a head? There were numerous signs to suggest so. One day, Director X took out two bottles of brandy and tried to sell them to us, saying they were cut-price, just four yuan each. Later he gave us one, but still he tried to sell me the other. He also gave us some cured meat, saying it might not be easy to buy in future.

They collected quite a few five-star bottles and put them in the corner of the wall that linked up with our place, together with an

assortment of cigarettes. All this set us thinking: highly privi-
leged people must have lived next door, and now Director X was
clearing up after them.

One afternoon at the start of November, several new cadres
emerged, accompanied by Director X. He said, 'This is Zhang
Guangren,' and then left. The new cadres fetched themselves
some cane chairs and sat down. F didn't have a chair and was left
standing, so I brought one for him. The cadre seated in the
middle, an ashen-faced man, gave me a supercilious look and
asked F, 'How have you been recently?' 'Nothing special.'
'Nothing special? You think you don't have problems?' He said
no more. Another man said, 'We've come to take you away. Get
ready.' 'Am I going for interrogation? Will I be allowed to
return?' 'All I know is you're going. I don't know when you'll
return. It would be best to take bedding and other things. We're
doing this for your safety, for your convenience.' 'Don't say any
more to him, tell him to hurry up and get his things ready,' said
the ashen-faced man.

I got a change of clothing ready and a thin quilt, and started
tying it in a bundle. The ashen-faced man said, 'That's not
enough. You'll need a thick quilt.' The more polite one said, 'It
might be a while, it's best to take a bit more.'

While I was in the bedroom re-stitching a thick quilt, F came
over. He whispered, 'Don't worry about them. Things will soon
be cleared up. I'll be back in a few days, or they'll come to fetch
you.' I smiled. I didn't want to say what I was thinking. I also
hoped things would be as F said, so I put aside the grey cotton I
was holding and exchanged it for a red-silk quilt cover, even
though the grey one would have been more appropriate for prison
use. F too smiled, to show he understood. I knew instinctively
what he meant: 'I am not a prisoner, with all my red heart I am for
the Party.'

One of the men came in. He seemed to think it odd I had chosen
a red-silk quilt cover, but he ignored it and said fiercely, 'You'll
need a second quilt.' I got out a red blanket and the grey material,

together with some pillows and other things, and tied them in a big bundle.

I put a jar of tea and some biscuits and sweets in the bag F was holding. He asked, 'Can I take books?' Yes, he could take Mao's *Selected Works*. I secretly slipped him a purse and whispered that it contained a deposit receipt for 200 yuan. If they let him go, he should use it to get back to Beijing. We were both so naïve.

Dressed in his woollen suit, F looked every inch a senior cadre. A young man, seeing him dressed like that, went over to help him lift his bedroll. I accompanied them down the slope, but then I was stopped. Director X and Little Li told me I would see him again before long. I watched them board a jeep. It set off followed by a big lorry, on which two PLA men sat. So he was under escort. This journey was not what F imagined. The future boded ill.

24

Hoping

Now he was gone, only I remained. Luckily, I had never been spoiled, and the noises you heard at night on that isolated mountain failed to terrify me. Fortified by his optimism and self-confidence, I believed he would soon return. Every day I expected him to come towards me along the road I could see from our home.

New Year's Day arrived – it was 1968 – and I constantly re-warmed the food I had made for him, until it was practically ruined. Keep hoping – it will soon be Spring Festival. But all I could hear was the cold wind rattling our windows, rather than the sound of his laughter. Every day I waited up for him, in case he arrived at midnight, like on the first occasion. But all I heard was the wind whistling in the electric wires, rather than the roar of an approaching vehicle. I wanted to cry out, 'Where are you? When will you come back?'

I realised the situation was worse than he thought. I asked Director X for news. His reply was the same as that in the past of the Ministry of Public Security: 'He's fine, no need to send him anything.' 'When will he come back?' 'I don't know. Sometime.' Would I have to wait another ten years?

From my point of view, the cleverest thing would be to believe that he would soon return, safe and sound. I consoled myself by thinking, aren't I now free? Didn't that mean there were no problems? Whenever the market was on, I went to town. Not to buy anything, because I needed to watch my spending now I no longer had F's 25 yuan, but to read the posters and find out whether there was any hope of an end to the Cultural Revolution. I squeezed in among the crowds to watch the leaders being pilloried.

One day I was watching some 'small reptiles' being denounced. Their faces had been daubed black and their backs were painted with crabs and prawns. They were lined up on a long bench. People were jumping up onto the stage to denounce them. Without realising it, I found myself moving with the crowd. I watched them with their dunce's hats being escorted away by a combat team wearing red armbands. I reached a big gateway. I realised that it was not a good idea and that I should return as quickly as I could, but I was spotted by a cadre from Plantation Headquarters.

The next day, the Political Instructor of the PLA unit paid me a visit. He told me to stay at home and reform my thought. He said, 'You even go to the Rebel Headquarters, do you realise what that might lead to? You once wore a hat. If anything happens, we won't be able to do anything.' Even though it sounded like a rebuke, he continued to look polite. He then asked about my family, and he seemed rather sympathetic. He took a look at the room and said, 'It's not very practical having you live here, but don't worry, we live up above, we constantly send out patrols at nights. We aim to keep you safe.'

After that, I no longer dared go out on expeditions. A few days later, Secretary X asked me if I had anything to take to F. I had no time to go shopping, so I gave him a pound of tea I had. I thought, F likes tea, and it will raise his spirits.

During the day, I stood by the door watching the vehicles and people coming and going, and at night I read until late. I also took notes, so I would have something to hand in. I whiled away the days and imagined to myself that I was doing something for him. I even had the feeling he was standing there with a smile on his face, signifying his approval.

A few days later, the wife and three children of a Party Secretary who had been criticised and suspended from office moved into the three rooms next to the gate. The eldest daughter was mentally deficient, a disabled child who could neither speak nor walk and who had a children's nurse to look after her. F and I had seen the wife earlier, in the Plantation Headquarters. She asked whether F was feeling better. Now she was also in trouble, so she was kind and genial towards me. Having such a neighbour, and hearing the cries of the eldest daughter, gave me the feeling I was once again living among people.

The nurse was in her early fifties, a local woman. I learned a lot from her about conditions in this remote mountain town. Her life represented in miniature women's passage from the misery of old China to Liberation. She said, 'If it wasn't for Liberation, where would my family be? My old man would have kept on smoking opium and would have starved to death. After Liberation, he got land, he got a house, and then youngest son came along. I don't know how to thank the Communist Party for its loving kindness.' She worked loyally and devotedly for the Party Secretary's family. If anyone criticised her for not having a stable political position, she answered, 'I just do as the Party says. I don't care what people say, I refuse to listen.'

The Party Secretary's second child was an eight-year-old boy and the smallest was a five-year-old girl, who was a bit spoiled. The children often came to play in my house. When they saw the things, especially the books, they were amazed. I realised they knew next to nothing about the outside world. The boy often went with his father to the production teams, and had got used to people fawning on him. He talked with me about the limestone cave that supplied the plantation with drinking water, with a mixture of magic and terror that suggested to me he was quite a storyteller. But I didn't dare tell him any of my own stories, especially not fairy stories. I was afraid things might change and they would say I was spreading bourgeois ideology and trying to win over the second generation. I just told them about Tiananmen (I didn't even dare tell them about the Imperial Palace) and the Zoo, of which I had a colour photo. They had never seen anything but cats, dogs, cattle and goats, and were delighted when I told them about lions, tigers, giraffes, kangaroos and ostriches. They didn't even want to go up to the Plantation Headquarters when the nurse called them. The nurse told me they were often bullied by other children, and chased to the back of the queue. That gave me a fellow-feeling with them. Their mother was transferred to a team a long way off, and the children and the nurse were left at home, so I became their temporary support. I wanted to get out my copy of *Andersen's Fairy Tales* and read it to them, but I didn't dare.

One day, the children were playing with me when suddenly the little girl shouted 'Daddy, Daddy!' A middle-aged man came up the slope, a leader in the Plantation Headquarters. He nodded at me, smiled politely, and entered the house. The eldest daughter started crying. They hadn't seen their father for a long time.

Previously, we had never seen this person, and the Plantation Head had always dealt with us. The last time I had seen the Plantation Head, he was wan and thin, and he hurried past me holding a file of papers, perhaps to hand it over to the Rebels.

In early June, a crowd of Red Guards turned up. I gasped. What did they want of me? They included quite a few middle-aged cadres and workers. Their Political Instructor pointed me out, as if to verify my status. Then he left.

The mob crowded in. A middle-aged man said:

'We're from the Sichuan Provincial People's Security Team. You seem to be very comfortable!' He glared.

I didn't know what to do or say. All I could do was look back wide-eyed.

'She's a calm one! Search the place!' That was a Red Guard speaking.

'Drag her out and show her what for.'

The middle-aged man waved his hand and said, 'Search!'

'Find the evidence, she's a crafty one . . .'

Chairs went flying as the invaders rummaged through the drawers. They searched the books one by one. But they lacked patience and soon lost interest. However, other Red Guards searching the inside room called me in and pointed to a trunk.

'Open it, hand over your secret documents!'

I tried to unlock it, but the key wouldn't work. With so many eyes pinned on me, I started sweating. They thought it contained secrets. I fetched a pair of pliers and broke it open. I then flopped down on the bed. A big crowd swarmed round the trunk grabbing things and holding them up, and then throwing them on the floor. It was old clothes.

I was summoned out again. A teenager, evidently the boss, pointed at me and said:

'Hand over the reactionary materials you've been writing.'

'We haven't written any reactionary materials.'

'You wrote the 300,000-word memo, didn't you! What more have you written?'

'Nothing. Didn't you just search us?'

'You dare resist?'

He flicked through the *Famous Selected Poems of the Tang and Song Dynasties* that our daughter had often read and pointed at a poem by Li Houzhu that had been underlined:

'What does "how much hate" refer to? I suppose you hate us. Isn't that reactionary?'

I didn't answer, which he took for agreement. He rummaged through the drawer and took out two song sheets:

'So you're still hiding away song sheets. Songs to whitewash the capitalist-roaders. You're hoping they'll be restored?'

I was lost for words. Only later did I realise it was songs from the films *Raging Tide* and *Prairie Fire*. The children must have kept them. All I could do was answer in all honesty: 'I really didn't know they were against the law.'

'Don't think you'll get away with it. This time the capitalist-roaders won't protect you. We've already trampled them underfoot. They'll never rise again. Be more honest. You're facing imminent catastrophe and still you don't repent.' He sneered and said:

'Hu Feng is already in prison. If you don't confess, you'll be there too.'

In prison! The news went bang! in my head, but I immediately calmed down – the real nightmare would have been if he had not been in prison. A great thinker of the past once said the law punished criminals but also protected them. Now I was even more convinced of the truth of that. They thought they had fired a piece of heavy artillery and I would be smashed to the ground. They must have been surprised when I simply stared back.

Then came another bombshell – they demanded I hand over my valuables and bank book. Lots of little eyes fixed on me, especially the female Rebels from the tea plantation. They expected me to refuse and start blubbering, but I handed over everything, without exception. They got very excited, jostling and pushing.

The female Rebels fought one another for a glimpse of three gold rings I handed over. One was a present from F, which he had had made for me for 20 yuan when we were fleeing calamity during the war against Japan – he had thought we might lose touch in the turmoil and perhaps die; another was from a classmate, engraved with the words 'My dear friend' in English; the last one was from my mother. I didn't care about the rings, but I was scared they would start asking questions about the English inscription. Thankfully, they were more interested in trying it on, and then they made haste to take it off again, as if bitten by a snake. 'Get it off, it's a feudal yoke!' I watched calmly. They asked no questions and started looking at some old photos in my bag. They studied them with great interest and kept finding fault – they described my tight-fitting chipao gown as bizarre and monstrous.

The middle-aged one, who had kept largely quiet, said:

'Is that all? If you don't hand it over and it disappears, we can't be responsible.'

I thought, will you really take responsibility? It seemed to me that once I had handed it over it could no longer be considered my property.

A Red Guard called me over. Pointing at a novel I was writing, he said:

'What reactionary article are you writing? Will you confess?'

'I'm writing about workers' families. I want to describe their outstanding qualities, so we can learn from them.'

'Don't try to make yourself sound good. I bet you're showing us in a bad light. You're not qualified to write about us.'

'That's not true. I've not even finished yet.'

Luckily, they hadn't the slightest interest in reading what I had written. They said as if joking, 'The handwriting's not bad. Don't forget, you're not allowed to write about us, we're the leading class.' They turned to examine the valuables and the old photos on the table.

The one who looked like a worker came rushing over. He seemed to have discovered an important secret. He started waving some pieces of paper in my face:

'This is a secret code. Explain it! Don't think you can conceal the truth!'

I panicked. But then I saw it was pages from an old calendar.

' "Another year goes by, when will I be set free? Alas!" What's that about? Are you waiting for the KMT to liberate you? What's the code? Confess, tell the truth!'

'That's May 17, 1955, the anniversary of our arrest. We had been locked up for a long time. I hoped we would soon be set free. I hoped the Party would liberate us.'

He took out another sheet with some Arabic numerals on it.

'What's this code? How are you going to argue your way out of this?'

It was page numbers I'd jotted down after reading Mao's *Selected Works* (you weren't allowed to scribble on the book). I explained to him, 'If you don't believe me, you can check.' He stalked out.

The middle-aged one, who hadn't said much, came in. The Political Instructor stood at the door gesticulating at the Red

Guards, who put down what they had in their hands and swarmed out.

The middle-aged one called me over to the table. Pointing at the things I had handed over, he said, 'We'll look after these, I can give you a receipt.'

He took out a piece of lined paper, but the one who looked like a worker grabbed it and said, 'I'll write it.'

The middle-aged one shook his head when he saw the terrible handwriting. He grabbed the pen and made a detailed list and wrote Sichuan Provincial People's Security Team at the bottom, together with his own name and the date. Except for an official stamp, it met all the requirements of a receipt. I was grateful. He did his job conscientiously and knew the legal procedures.

He wrapped my things in a handkerchief and handed me the receipt, telling me to keep it somewhere safe. Then he left, together with the little bundle and the crowd of people.

It was past 12, and I was hungry. I cooked enough rice for several meals, for who could say when I would next get the chance? They had sent some relatives of people working for the Plantation Headquarters to keep watch on me and stop me leaving the house. In those few hours, I seemed to have been smitten by a severe illness. I had lost my strength, and was mentally drained. I wanted only to sleep. However, it was not easy with all those eyes fixed on me. The female generals sat there twittering.

One of the women told me to get up. They ordered me to stand on the embankment. I was surrounded on all sides by Red Guards and others who had come to search the house. It seemed they had come along for the fun, since they were strangers to me.

A Red Guard reprimanded me: 'You continue to resist. You remain resolutely counter-revolutionary. You are inviting destruction. Confess your crimes!'

I recited a speech I had long since worked out: 'I was wrong to pursue the anti-factional struggle. It led to opposing the Party leadership. My crime deserves a thousand deaths. With all my heart I accept the criticism and guidance of the revolutionary masses.'

Two Red Guards came over as if to grab me. I thought I was going to be beaten or made to stand in the airplane position, bent forward with my hands stretched out behind my back. But I thought, let them do what they want, and resolved to stay calm.

The middle-aged man said solemnly:

'You're a counter-revolutionary and you've worn a hat. You responded badly to reform. You did not draw a class line with Hu Feng and you maintained a reactionary position. Our People's Security Team has decided to make you participate in manual labour, to strengthen your thought reform. You will go to work in Miaoxi Hospital.'

He called over a young woman. Pointing at me, he told her:

'Her manual labour will be under your supervision.'

To me, he said, 'You may not resist. Obey the revolutionary masses in everything. Write a monthly thought report and deliver it to the Military Control Commission.'

I nodded.

Manual labour! I wasn't scared. When had I ever been divorced from manual labour? I had not forgotten the principle of conduct known in the old society as 'resigning oneself to adversity'. I prepared to engage conscientiously in manual labour.

I was escorted home to put my things in order. I thought it would be all right to take a change of clothes and then come back to fetch some more things when the opportunity arose. So I packed just a small bundle. However, the Political Instructor told me to take a suitcase and some bedding and summer clothes. While sorting out the clothes I discovered a small diary I had left on the bed and some letters in the form of diary entries that I had intended to show F, so I stuffed them in the pile of clothes. When I went to the toilet I found a pile of paper on the floor – it was F's 'Songs in Memory of Spring'. I secretly put it in the wardrobe.

I lifted the basket onto my back and put a small bedroll and suitcase on top. That was the first time I had carried a back basket. No one tried to help me, nor even to show me how to do it. Luckily, I had studied how people loaded up the baskets. I put the suitcase at the bottom and the bedroll on top and tied them together with a length of string. Then I got them up onto the washstand so they were easier to shoulder. At first I swayed from side to side, but I thought of how F always told me to 'keep going, be brave' and managed to steady myself, and I started off without a hitch. In that way, off I went to undergo reform through labour.

Part Three

Behind High Walls

25

Escorted by Snowflakes

After F was taken away in 1967, my communications with him were cut. No one told me where he was. I was kept at Miaoxi. At first I washed bandages for the hospital as part of labour reform. When my fingers began to fester, they let me switch to needle-work. After three months, the Political Instructor sent me 'home'. The two rooms I had shared with F had been sealed off with paper strips. Arrangements were made for me to stay in a small room next to the latrine. I was told to clear a patch of soil and grow my own food. Each month, the Plantation Headquarters allocated me a grain quota and a meat ration. I was guarded by a leader of the Rebel Command whose family occupied two big compounds and kept several dozen chickens. I used to watch them pecking at the ground and fighting each other. It broke the monotony.

A succession of guards followed, until in the winter of 1969 the Plantation Headquarters told me I was to be moved elsewhere. I asked the ex-Secretary's wife, who had by then been integrated into the Revolutionary Committee, what I should do. I only had a few yuan left, compared with 300 yuan two years earlier (during my three months at the hospital, I didn't get any pay and had to buy my own food), and if I was sent elsewhere I wouldn't have enough to eat. She told me I would have to wait for the leadership to investigate and decide. So my departure was delayed. In August 1970 I was sent to Women's Team 2, where I got 21 yuan a month. I joined the Women's Reform Through Labour Brigade up in the mountains.

I did manual labour for more than two years. One day, as we were cutting vegetables and preparing to kill a pig, I was suddenly summoned back. Something had happened. I lifted the basket onto my back and went down to the headquarters.

One of the cooks in the small kitchen started shouting, 'Hurry up and give me some vegetables, we have guests.' I ignored him, but he continued shouting.

A jeep was parked within the embankment. I went into the office. Some people I had never seen before invited me to be seated and asked me how I was and whether I had received any letters from home.

'We want to transfer you to where Hu Feng is. After all, he's over 70.'

I nodded.

'He's old, so you should be with him. We believe in revolutionary humanism. Get your things and you can leave.'

One asked, 'What are your views?'

What views could I have? Could I tell them how anxious I was about F and how much I wanted to be with him? I just said, quietly, 'I have no views. Where is he?'

'We'll make appropriate arrangements.'

The correctional officer added politely, 'Go home and get ready.'

They had told me not to worry, but how could I not worry? How was F? Where did they intend to send me? Obviously they weren't going to restore my freedom. They were simply going to change my location. The most comforting thought was that he was still alive and they wanted me to look after him. In a daze, I left the office.

When I got back to my accommodation, I climbed up into the loft. The room was built for a couple of dozen, but now there was just me in it. I sat down on my makeshift bed by the window staring at my suitcase and my bedding. I was confused and perturbed. I had no idea how I was going to sort my things out. I would have to take everything, including some very old and even broken things. Who could say whether I would ever need them again? Maybe I would end up destitute. I had to take everything into consideration. I had heard about a prisoner who thought she was going to be processed for release, so she had given away all her things, but it turned out she was being sent to engage in intro-spection and a few months later they increased her sentence and sent her back. She no longer had even a rice bowl, and the people she had given her things to ignored her. That was a warning. It was no good being optimistic, I had to prepare for the worst. I was drifting on a choppy sea. Would I manage to draw close to shore? I was again to follow my beloved into the rushing water and towering waves. I was sad, elated, alarmed, and fearful – all sorts of emotions flooded in. I was not in the mood for packing. All I wanted was to cry my heart out.

People were already trickling in from work. Some who had heard the news came over for a word. I gave brief and equivocal answers. Some said they envied me, 'You've been through so much suffering, now you can leave.' Others said, 'After they let you go they're bound to restore you to your job and let you be a cadre.' I forced a smile.

The Political Instructor came to tell me there was no rush. They would send someone to take me to the Plantation Headquarters first thing next morning. That meant I would have to stay another night.

I went for my evening meal. The canteen workers smiled and gave me an extra spoonful. They said, 'Make sure you remember us.' I couldn't eat a thing, I was so distressed.

Most of the team had already returned, and there was a great clamour in the sleeping area. They swarmed round congratulat-ing me. We had been living together for two or three years, and even though people were never particularly friendly to me, today I felt close to all of them. Perhaps that was why I couldn't eat. There were more than 20 of them. Each had a history of hardship. Each had her own reason for committing her offence. Cruel fate had robbed some of their human feelings. But each one was just an ordinary woman, someone's wife, someone's mother. From my long contact with them, I knew they were not bereft of goodness and decency. Unfortunately, the policy was not to release people who had completed their sentences, so although they had homes, they were unable to return to them. Today, they learned I was to leave. Naturally, they thought I would be reunited with my family. I could understand why they were congratulating me and I was grateful, but in fact my future was even more uncertain than theirs.

That night, I twisted this way and that and was unable to sleep. I could hear my companions talking in their sleep, making it even harder for me to drift off. Granny Zhou was shouting her son's name, and mumbling things. She was over 70, and desperate to see her son again. I had written lots of letters home for her. How could I console her the next morning?

I had just dropped off to sleep when the wake-up whistle sounded. Bringing back my four ounces of rice, I saw Granny Zhou standing in the doorway. She was usually the first to go to work. I said, 'Do you want me to write a letter?' 'No, I stayed behind to say goodbye. I knew you would probably get out early, you're different from us. You're a cadre, aren't you?' I didn't know what to say. I gave her half my rice. 'Mother Zhou, you know that straw mattress you made for me? Why don't you keep it!'

Chen from the pig-rearing team came over. She was about to give birth. I had promised to sort out some old clothes so she could use them to make nappies, which I then started doing. Some men arrived to fetch my luggage. Each took an item, leaving behind a pile of things that I packed into a tea basket. Without waiting to see if everything was in order, they set off. It was not an unpleasant task. The luggage was light, and if they got to the Plantation Headquarters in good time they could do some shopping. I originally intended to ask Zhan, a member of my team, to help me, so we could have a chat on the way and I could console her (like me, she was from another province; she had five children, but her relatives had disowned her). She couldn't bear to part, and escorted me all the way to the road. It started to snow. Lots of people on their way to work nodded and smiled at me. Mrs Huang came hurrying over and squeezed my hand. 'I made sure to get here in time. Your life will improve from now on, don't forget us.' 'Please take care of yourself, things might turn out well for you too. You should ask whether you can go home to visit your family and see your mother.' She nodded, and then left. She had married a mid-ranking official in the KMT who had gone to Taiwan. The way she shook my hand showed she still knew how to behave like a woman of rank.

The snow got heavier as I walked down the mountain. The bamboo forest and the grass were covered by snow – not pure white like in the north, but white speckled with green, with bright red berries sticking out here and there. The air was so fresh I didn't feel at all cold. I immersed myself in it, drunk on the rare beauty of the mountains.

By the time I reached the Plantation Headquarters, the beauty had dissolved and the snow had stopped. Arrangements were made for me to stay in the guest house. I sat there, staring blankly ahead, thinking back on the night F and I had first arrived in these high mountains. The scenes were as if from a previous life. F, where are you now?

The door opened and the Party Secretary's wife brought in a cadre, Secretary X, who had come to fetch me. He greeted me politely. I asked when we would leave, and he said the sooner the better. He was kind enough to tell me that 'Zhang Guangren is in good health.' The Party Secretary's wife took me to the canteen to buy some food, and told the kitchen staff I needn't queue. The two cooks stuck their heads out of the hatch, saw me, and nodded. We were old acquaintances.

Three days later, it was New Year. Seven years (1966 to 1973) had passed since my arrival at the Miaoxi Tea Plantation. I went to the canteen to buy some food for the holiday, but I didn't enjoy it. I thought, right now the team would be sharing out chilli chicken, stewed meat, and deep-fried vegetarian balls, happily eating and joking. And there was I, with no one to turn to. The time dragged. The Party Secretary's wife told me sternly not to go out without permission, so I had to stay indoors and read the sole copy of *Sichuan Daily* or simply sit there staring at the wall.

Another week passed. The Party Secretary's wife called me over and said she was going to sort through Hu Feng's clothes. She wanted to confiscate them, together with his books. There had been no mention of confiscating Hu Feng's property in the 1965 judgment. Obviously it was not easy to ask questions, but I kept my wits about me and did my best to claim as many as possible as my own. I argued that many of the books belonged to me, for example, Lu Xun's *Collected Works*. Also, I pointed out that I needed to study the Marxist-Leninist books, and that some of the classics by foreign-language authors had my name on them. They reluctantly agreed. As for the clothes, Hu Feng could keep only the old ones. I tried to get as many as possible. It was sad, because F didn't have many possessions. The only thing that could count as new was a Western suit I had made for him after Liberation. There were lots of odds and ends I didn't want, but I wasn't allowed to leave them behind, so I had to carry them.

I heard the Party Secretary's wife say there would be a meeting and the guest house needed rooms, so they were even more eager to send me away. However, no one came to pick me up, until finally the Plantation Headquarters provided a vehicle.

Early one morning, all the things (apart from the books) were loaded onto a lorry. The Party Secretary's wife, wearing a brand-new Public Security uniform, sat alongside the driver. A family insisted on getting a lift, but there was no room. They began quarrelling. One said, 'If a prisoner can sit there, why can't we?' They blocked the vehicle and wouldn't let it go. The man was a brigade-level cadre and just as unreasonable as his family. He said his wife had to get back to her village. The Party Secretary's wife was unable to exert her authority. The row delayed us for several hours, until finally they let the wife and her sucking child on board, leaving the others behind.

The lorry sped down the mountain. Unfortunately there was no time to see Director Jiang and other old acquaintances who had received us in the middle of the night all those years ago. I wasn't qualified to say goodbye, but in my heart I took my leave of those mountains and rivers.

When we reached Chengdu, the sky was black. We went to the guest house of the Department of Public Security.

While we were eating in the canteen, the woman with the child turned up. 'Just you? Where's the baby?' asked the Party Secretary's wife. 'He's sleeping, so I thought I would come and get something to eat.' 'You see how inconvenient it is, one woman and a baby? I said you should have waited. If you had waited two days, you could all have come. Wouldn't that have been better?' She didn't dare answer. She simply lowered her head and ate. I ordered a meat dish and a vegetable dish, but I couldn't finish it. I poked the leftovers into her bowl, saying, 'You have a baby, you should eat a bit more.' She smiled gratefully. It made me feel better.

When we left the next morning, it was drizzling. Apart from two unarmed PLA men, a young man had joined us, who was the relative of a cadre in the Department of Public Security. The woman stayed behind in the guest house. When we reached the suburbs of Chengdu, a fog descended and you could see barely more than a few yards. The driver turned his main-beam yellow lamps on and made slow progress. Before long, it started showering sleet, and the driver had to get out and put tyre chains on. I sat in the lorry getting drenched, looking out onto the deserted road.

Just before it got dark, we reached Nanchong. The young man jumped down, happy to have arrived. The rest of us waited for the ferry. By the time we had crossed the river, it was nine. We drove into No. 1 Prison. I was surprised, thinking we had reached our destination. However, the driver told us to get a good night's sleep, because the next morning we would be hurrying on our way. Hurry on our way? But where to?

We waited in the reception room for a long time before the Prison Secretary was called out from his home and let us in. He knew we hadn't eaten, so he arranged food for us. The driver and the PLA men went off, leaving me and the Party Secretary's wife. The Prison Secretary took us to a guest room. I couldn't stop thinking about the next day's early start, so I didn't fall asleep until one. At five, the driver woke us.

I didn't see a single prisoner. Only when the Prison Secretary was escorting us out did I notice we were walking on a concrete path surrounded by flower beds. The Prison Secretary seemed to be a friend of the Party Secretary's wife. They had a good chat. He made a special point of turning to me and asking, 'Did you sleep well? Did you have enough to eat?' I couldn't help but feel grateful. 'I slept very well. Thank you, you have been very hospitable.' 'It goes without saying.'

That should have been the final day, but the sleet was still falling and the road was icy. It was market day and there were lots of people about. At midday, we had a bowl of noodles at a roadside restaurant. In the late afternoon we reached the Qujiang River crossing, where we had to queue for a boat. After more driving, we entered the gates of Dazhu County's No. 3 Prison. The Party Secretary's wife and the two PLA men got off and left me. We drove up a side road and stopped at a small gate.

We entered a compound with four single-storey houses, probably offices. I hadn't eaten, so a cadre brought me a bowl of rice and a plate of mutton and cabbage. It was cold and tasteless. I poked at it for a bit and then put it aside. For a long time I was left alone. Finally, the Party Secretary's wife came in, accompanied by a female cadre. When she saw the food on the table, she apologised: 'I forgot to call you over to eat with us.' She also said, 'I'm going back to Miaoxi tomorrow. Is there anything I can do for you?' 'No, there isn't.' 'Don't worry about anything. We'll deal with the books you left.' She said goodbye.

The female cadre stayed behind with me. She asked me about

my family, my studies, my experiences over the last few years, and so on. It seemed to me like a polite form of interrogation, so I held nothing back.

I was taken to my accommodation. It was a small courtyard with three rooms, cut off by a wall five or six metres high. My room had windows on two sides so the light was good, but there were thick iron bars across them. When you closed the door, it became a prison cell. I was going to have to get used to living behind bars.

Our things had been brought in. We occupied the middle room, where there was a double bed. On one side was the kitchen.

I was exhausted, so I spread out the bedding and prepared to sleep. The cadre handed me a night-soil pail and a thermos flask. He didn't close the door onto the courtyard – seemingly, I was not yet considered a prisoner. Only then did I realise how cold and hungry I was. I drank a cup of hot water and began to feel warmer.

Lying on the bed, my lids drooped and my eyes hurt, but they wouldn't close. When I put out the light, the bars on the window looked like fangs. The four walls pressed down on me and scared me. Where was my beloved? I had come all this way but still I couldn't see him. Why wouldn't they say anything? Was he alive? The more I thought, the more I worried.

26

Is It Really Him?

I woke at daybreak. I thought I was dreaming. I lifted my head and saw the barred window. Only then did the events of the previous evening come back to me.

I heard voices outside and jumped out of bed. In front of the door was a pail of hot water and some rice and mutton, just like the evening before. I forced myself to eat a bit. The food was much worse than in the work brigade. I didn't dare go out for a walk, I just sat on my bed and looked vacantly at the barred window.

The cadre who had come to Miaoxi summoned me. I followed him to the office. Some people were warming themselves round a stove. One looked like F from the back, especially in his black overcoat, which resembled the one I had made for him. All I could hear was someone saying, 'We're taking your age into consideration, you need someone to look after you. The two of you can live together. The Government is giving you special consideration. Make sure you strengthen your ideological reform.'

The black overcoat turned round. It was him! It was really him! But there was nothing left of his old demeanour, I could hardly recognise him. I stood there in the door, looking stupid. The comrade in charge said to him, 'Go on, go together with her.' He stood up, stooped. He seemed shorter even than I. His bag was lying on the floor. He stared around, confused, and the cadres looked embarrassed. I pulled myself together and carried his bag back to the compound. Not until quite a while later did he follow the cadres in. Again, they gave him his instructions. He just listened, his arms hanging by his side, in a respectful gesture of attention. After they had left, he continued to stand there on the steps, his arms still stretched downwards. He had always been so erect, so dignified and courageous, my beloved husband, indomitable and irrepressible. How could he have changed so much? I couldn't believe the person in front of me was him.

'How are you? Why don't you sit down?' He seemed to wake from a deep dream. 'You really came. This is a terrible mess. You shouldn't have come, I didn't ask you to come. What a mess . . .'

I stared at him wide-eyed.

Suddenly he grabbed my hands. 'I've been given a life sentence, I'll die soon. I've let you down.' He got down on his knees. 'Do you know what crime they say I've committed? A monstrous crime! Every conceivable crime is heaped on my shoulders, it's too much for me to bear! Now you've arrived, I'm in an even bigger mess. I've got you into so much trouble.'

He spoke in snatches. It scared me and aroused an enormous sorrow in me. Such a healthy person, and now reduced to this state. I lowered my head and wept.

A cadre called F out. All my pent-up anguish and dread gushed out, as if a sluice gate had been thrown open. The tears flowed freely, to my enormous relief.

I have no idea when they returned. I heard the cadre say, 'We haven't got your rations yet, just these noodles. Zhang Guangren, don't frighten her again.'

'Uh, uh,' he replied, his arms dutifully hanging down until the cadre left.

I quickly dried away my tears and pulled him towards a chair. I started getting ready to cook, for it was midday. I poached some eggs with noodles and made him the first meal since our years of separation. I thought he would be happy, but he just held his bowl and looked at it, not daring to use his chopsticks. I told him to eat it while it was hot, but he said timidly, 'That's not what I eat. If I eat that, they'll denounce me.' 'Be brave, eat it. If they denounce you, I'll take responsibility.' 'Really? You'll take responsibility?' I nodded vigorously, whereupon he started eating just like in the old days, emptying the entire bowl.

I got the room ready. He sat to one side, not even looking, like a block of wood. I told him to help, but he waved his hand, as if listening to something. Finally, I told him to take a nap. While he was undressing, I noticed that his clothes had turned to rags: the sleeves of his cotton-padded jacket were burned, the sleeves of his woollen suit were badly frayed, and the sleeves of his pullover had disappeared completely. Perhaps because of the cold, he had worked his hands up his sleeves and had shrunk back inside his collar. His eyes, which in the past had sparkled, drooped. He looked like a temple beggar. My heart leapt.

While he slept, I rummaged through the clothes I had salvaged for him from Miaoxi. I wanted him to look neat, to dress warmly, and to live like a human being. Again, the tears welled.

In the afternoon, I had boiled some water and was washing his head when the Prison Director arrived. F wouldn't even let me dry him. He jumped to his feet and stood there respectfully, his arms by his side. To our surprise, the Prison Director adopted a friendly tone: 'Sit down, dry your hair.' I got a hat and put it on him, but he snatched it off, as if burned. The Prison Director again spoke, 'Put it on, don't catch cold.' He turned to me. 'Is everything sorted out? If you need anything, raise it with Secretary Y.' Addressing the cadre who had brought our grain and oil rations, he said, 'From now on pay more attention to their daily needs.'

As soon as he had gone, F took the hat back off. He said prisoners aren't allowed to wear cadres' hats, you have to cut off the brim, also you weren't allowed to wear cadres' uniforms with four pockets, you had to cut those off too. I said, 'But doesn't your woollen suit have pockets?' 'You don't know how much I suffered because of that. My cellmates wouldn't stop denouncing me, they even . . .' He didn't finish the sentence.

It was clear he must have gone through some very unusual experiences. I did my best to comfort him: 'Now we're together. You're not a prisoner for me. There's no need to be afraid.'

By the evening, I was at my wits' end. He sat there on the bed, unwilling to sleep, and then he got agitated and said someone would come to get him. 'Look,' he said, 'they haven't closed the door.' 'They didn't last night either, you don't have to worry.' 'Are you sure? Did they really not close it last night?' Only then did he lie down. At first he didn't dare take off his clothes. He kept insisting someone would come for him at midnight.

At midnight, he sat up. I woke with a start, and I grabbed hold of him and wouldn't let him get out of bed. His eyes were blank, his mouth was crooked, and he was trembling. I was worried he might fall, so I held on to him and stroked his big forehead. I pulled his head towards my bosom, as if pacifying a child. Gradually he calmed down. But then he was wide awake again, and he said, 'Is it really you? I'm not dreaming? This is terrible!' 'From now I'll always be with you, you have nothing to fear.' 'If that was true, it would be wonderful.'

His behaviour saddened and puzzled me. It made me think of Dostoevsky. When we met at Qincheng after ten years apart, he was calm and firm, but now, after just five years, he was broken, mentally and physically. I would restore him.

Next morning, when I opened my eyes, he was up and dressed, sitting there at the door. I had no choice but to get up too, although I had intended sleeping longer.

I again poached two eggs, with a few spoonfuls of honey. At first he shook his head, but then he started to eat with relish. After he had finished he poured in some boiled water to rinse the bowl and gulped that down too. I could understand. Sugar had been difficult to buy for years, and he probably hadn't tasted it all that time, even though he had a sweet tooth. But he still told me off: 'If anyone else finds out, they'll hold a struggle meeting.' I ignored him.

We established a rule: he could say what he liked and I would do what I liked. I did my best to make him sleep and eat well, and he did what he was told. Even so, there was endless trouble.

When I unrolled his bedding, I had a big shock. When he left Miaoxi, I had sewn on some red silk quilt facing. Both the underside and the facing had been reduced to a fishnet. Even the cotton wadding had big holes in it that he had covered with bits of rag. Even the grey cloth-wrapper had been put to use as underside and facing. It broke my heart to see how he had pulled the quilt to pieces and torn big holes in it.

I found some bits of blue cloth and re-did the quilt. Only then did he calm down. He put down his bedding and rose every day before daylight and sat on it. When I summoned him for breakfast he rolled it up and put it in the corner. If I asked why, he said he had been told to return to the big cell. On weekdays, he ate breakfast and then sat at the desk, racking his brains for a whole day and sometimes for two or three days. Then he started writing confessions. After he had finished, he handed them to the office.

I got fed up, and on one occasion I snatched the confession from his hand and read it. 'What's all this about revelations? This is superstition, it belongs to the past, not the present. You've done all your confessing and received your sentence. Who inspired you to write this rubbish and confess things that never happened? You sit in your room from dawn to dusk, how could you find the time to go out and spread poison, causing the people in the town to fall ill?'

'What do you know? I'm suspected of being a top criminal, I'm capable of any crime you care to mention. If I told you, you would drop dead of fright, your husband is wicked beyond redemption, the biggest criminal . . .'

But what crime? In what way was he wicked beyond redemption? I had to find out. Slowly he explained.

'It was the eve of Spring Festival in 1970. I was in Chengdu. Old Leng came to tell me I was about to be moved. They handcuffed me. I was escorted by two PLA men. I could see out through the crack between the window and the frame. We were driving along mountain roads. I thought maybe they were taking me to Xiaogu in Xi'an, so I was surprised when we stopped at Sichuan No. 1 Provincial Prison in Nanchong. From there, they sent me to the detention centre. It was already dark and there were lots of men in a big cell. They crowded round me, asking where I had come from, what my case was ... endless questions.

'A young man said, "Not long ago there was an old man with a white beard here, he said he could make sure everyone in the country had enough to eat. They tortured him. Even the Rebels said they had never seen anyone less afraid of dying." A man who looked like a worker came up to me. His hand was bandaged. He said they had broken his bones.

'They were just saying that, it was meant for me to hear.

'A PLA man brought me some supper, a bowl of rice with the chopsticks stuck in it, no meat or vegetables. The next day, they told me to get back in the vehicle, without breakfast. At noon they stopped somewhere and ate. Old Leng came over and said, "You didn't eat breakfast, I'll give you some extra rice." Finally I got some food.

'That afternoon we arrived here. The first night they put me in a little room in front of this courtyard and gave me some rice and cabbage. When I asked for water, the administrator said, "Wait a while, the issue of drinking water will be sorted out."

'They took me to the big cell. Two cadres from Chengdu read out my sentence. I had committed two crimes. During the reform period I had written reactionary poems, and I had written reactionary poems on a picture of the Chairman. My sentence was increased to life, with no right of appeal. They showed me the judgment. I said, "I won't appeal, even if you tell me to." Then they put me in the big cell.'

'They changed the verdict? For those two crimes?'

'That's what they said. But in 1969, when I had served my 14 years, I told Old Leng, "They should let me go now." He pretended to be surprised and said, "What? You've served your sentence? We didn't know. You should write a report." So I wrote a report. I said I had served my sentence and asked to be released. I said I still had a bit of money left so I could stay in a hostel and then make arrangements once Mei Zhi arrived. Not long afterwards, someone told me I could write a report to the Central Committee and they would pass it on. I said, "That is for you to do, not me." '

'You must be mad, everything was in chaos in 1969. What do you think would have happened if you had gone out and told the Red Guard Rebels?'

Then I asked, 'Why did you start writing poems again?'

'In Chengdu they put me in a big courtyard. I had my own room and a small latrine. There were lots of rooms in the courtyard. They pushed a food cart round three times a day. Things weren't too bad, but I got depressed. You could hear people's voices, you could even hear the loudspeakers on the street, but you were alone all day, completely by yourself. It was like in Qincheng, when I used to recite poems to get out of my depression. This time, they hadn't taken away my pen and ink, but they wouldn't give me paper. I started writing poems in the corners and margins of newspapers, but Old Leng took them away. He even found the ones I had cut out and stuffed into the soles of my shoes. One day, I wrote a poem on the blank bit on a picture of the Chairman, and they confiscated it. It was a conspiracy. It was so they could increase my sentence. Someone was out to frame me.'

He was starting to panic, so I tried to change the subject, but he wouldn't stop. 'Listen!' Someone coughed outside the back window. 'That's a hint. It means I should confess as soon as possible that I've been spreading poison so people get the flu and cough.'

'But you've been here all the time, you haven't been anywhere.'

'Do you think that bothers them? They think I can do magic. They think I can be in two different places at the same time.'

There was no way I could talk him round.

Spring Festival was just a few days off. Secretary Y sent us some fresh meat and lard, and asked me if I wanted to buy anything. I said I would like to buy a chicken.

When F saw the meat, he said:

'Do you want to get me into trouble? They'll organise a public denunciation of me, they'll hang all that meat on me, how could I carry such a weight?'

'If they're going to denounce anyone they can denounce me. I bought the chicken. As for the meat, we didn't ask for it.'

'You're wrong, send it back.'

I sent it back, and told the cadre.

Secretary H arrived, and gave him a telling off. He didn't dare reply, so the meat stayed.

At Spring Festival, we were in our little prison, but there was a holiday atmosphere. We had more food and Secretary Y even brought some glutinous-rice dumplings, which F loved. He calmed down and was even happy. He temporarily forgot his terror.

The hot food warmed up my entire body and even my heart. We were both in better spirits, and felt like having a chat. I asked him how he had spent the holiday over the past few years, but instead he said:

'Tell me about you! You've never told me anything about you. Do you think I'm not interested? Do you think I don't want to know? I kept on thinking about you, and about the children, all I could do was talk about it in the poems.'

'During the three years I was by myself, I was desolate whenever a holiday came round. In 1970 I joined the Labour Brigade and I was back among people. Nearly all of us were lonely and helpless, so it didn't hurt quite so much to think of you and the children. The brigade did what it could to improve our lives. There were four dishes at New Year and even chilli chicken.'

'You had chicken? This is the first time I've eaten chicken in seven years. In Chengdu, we had noodles at Spring Festival. But I was the last to be served, and by then the bowl was empty. The man bringing the food round scraped together some sticky bits, but they were cold. They brought me hot water to pour over it. It was disgusting. Even my heart seemed to ice over. Last year I was ill, so at Spring Festival they put me in a cell together with some criminals who had not yet been sentenced (I don't believe for one moment that they were criminals). They gave us lots of food and even a bottle of wine. I didn't dare eat, I was worried they would use it against me. They would pile one offence on another.

'In the big cell, they put me in the Third Brigade. The correctional cadre took me to my accommodation, a big room with rows of bunks along both sides and a gangway in the middle, about a foot wide. I didn't realise until night time that 60 or 70 people used those bunks, sleeping head to foot. Everyone had just over a foot of space. The first night I kicked somebody's head by mistake. Luckily, I slept next to the note-taker (the team leader). Next to him was a wooden plank, also just over a foot wide, where they kept newspapers and study materials, so he had a bit more room. I too had a few more inches. Only then did I grasp the full meaning of the phrase "inch of gold", money couldn't buy it.

'I rejoiced at having finally put behind me my life of solitary confinement. I chatted with people with no thought for the consequences. Our note-taker was originally from Yan'an. Later he led the Sichuan Bureau of Civil Aviation, but he was arrested for stealing aviation fuel. They discovered he had a blood debt, so he was sent to prison. We talked about No. 50, Zhou Enlai's former residence. He even knew about Qiao Guanhua and Gong Peng's love affair. I saw him as someone you could talk to. I fell into the usual trap, a fondness for observing and trying to understand people. It all went into their report. It became one of my crimes in the end-of-year general reckoning. Then there were my "reactionary" poems, and the tens of thousands of characters I wrote explaining them. That was also a crime. After that, I didn't like to talk any more, I just sat there on the steps of the glue room sorting out the hemp. I no longer read the newspaper. If they read it out loud, I dozed.

'National Day was coming up. They were going to hold a reward-and-punishment rally. Some people had cursed me for not studying hard enough and resisting reform. At work they pushed me and said, "Old man, get out the way!" They hit me hard in the back or hit my head. They chattered behind my back, as if preparing to expose some crime I had committed. That was when I heard a revelation: I was no longer Hu Feng the author but a "KMT spy", a "traitor", a "murderer". I was scared they would make me stand in the "airplane position" or beat me to death. I wasn't worried about dying, that would have been fine, but I was afraid I wouldn't die and would have to suffer. The best thing would be an early death. One day when I was washing vegetables in the kitchen I found a brick and bashed my head with it, in the hope that it would split open and I would die. But I didn't, my head's too thick.'

He showed me the scar.

'They sent me to the clinic. I thought they were going to shoot me. I confessed repeatedly, but it was impossible. I knew they wouldn't let me die yet, they even made you come, because they still hadn't worked out what punishment would cause me to die with the greatest suffering.'

He seemed intoxicated with his own terrible imaginings. I couldn't bear to listen, so I stopped him. 'It's all in your head, you're losing your mind.' For a while, there was nothing I could do to bring him round. Finally I realised the cause of his illness. His cranial nerves were as thick as a hemp rope, but the burden was too great and had been going on for too long, so they had undergone a qualitative change. However thick, even they have their snapping point.

The prison authorities called me to the office. They said, 'We're being lenient towards him, we've ignored some of the things he's said and done. We still want to give him a way out.

That's where you have to help.' Finally, they asked me to write a thought report. I wrote down some of my thoughts and asked whether it would be possible for him to be released for medical treatment, so he could go to hospital and be cured. They gave no clear answer, other than to say, 'We want to cure him, but he refuses to see a doctor or take medicine.'

His condition remained unstable. The Secretary brought some balls of hemp for us to twine into smaller balls, called 'fish eggs' (used for weaving burlap). F enjoyed this for a while and seemed to calm down, but he quickly became demoralised. He said his weaving was no good and they would say he was trying to sabotage things and adding to his crime. He only calmed down when I swapped my fish eggs for his.

Our room faced west and at midday the heat was unbearable. Throughout the summer we sat in an alley outside the door, where it was shady. I simultaneously read the newspaper and wove fish eggs, six in three hours. Old women in the region could tend a fire while chatting among themselves and at the same time do their weaving and earn a yuan a day. I probably earned about 40 or 50 cents. In the autumn, they stopped giving us the work.

One very hot day, F asked me to make him a two-pound cotton-padded jacket and a pair of cotton-padded shoes with thick front and back soles. He continued writing those terrible confessions. He also wrote supplementary confessions explaining that he hadn't put poison in anything. He told me, 'If I admit to putting poison in things, they'll ask me who made me do it, who bought it for me, that sort of thing, and a lot of innocent people will be implicated. I can only account for my own criminal behaviour, no one helped me.' This endless confessing suggested to me he was not beyond hope: his thinking was not yet completely confused, the terrors he was imagining were the result of external influences. If external circumstances changed, he might get better.

Secretary H had told me I could go shopping if I wanted, since I wasn't a prisoner. But only once a month at most, and accompanied by a female cadre.

At the New China Bookshop I bought *Battle Chronicles of Hongnan* and *Golden Road*. I talked with F about them. I said, 'Isn't that admirable, to put the Chairman's Quotations in a novel? Who would have thought! The subject matter of *Golden Road* is more or less the same as *The Sun Shines Bright*, which I read a long time ago. It's just that the characters have been enhanced. My impression is that this one is general rather than representative.' He got curious, and had a look. He put down *Battle Chronicles of Hongnan* after just a few pages, and only read the opening paragraphs of *Golden Road*. He said, 'Gao Daquan is completely different from everybody else, as soon as he appears on the scene you know everything about his entire life, it's even in his name, "Tall, Big, Complete"! When he reaches the highway, there's someone in the ditch digging out the soil. He looks up and thinks, how tall! The backdrop is the highway, bathed in sunlight, how big! With novels like that, you know what happens even before you read them.'

How come I hadn't noticed that? Even though I had read it very conscientiously from beginning to end, I had shown none of his acuity.

We sat together in the little courtyard between the high walls, looking up at the strip of sky. That's how I discussed the novels with him, in the moonlight. He said:

'We'll never see anything like Lu Ling's novels again. I wonder how he is? Destroying him was a crime against the new literature. Every time I think of him my heart aches. All the things he was going to write.'

It was too dark to see his face, but I heard him sob. I took his hand and squeezed it.

'Don't think about it, it will all pass, everything will get better.'

I was happy, because at that moment he came back to me. He still hankered after his literature, he could still appreciate literary creation, he was still full of feeling and fond thoughts for his friends. He hadn't destroyed that pure faith because of his own imagined horrors. I knew he knew that some day in the future he

27

Terror and Confusion

I wrote our daughter a letter. I had already been told that I could correspond with the outside world, but with F in such a state, it was too much to write about such things to one's child, so I kept putting it off. Even though F never asked about his children, he often introduced his elder son into his imaginary terrors. On one occasion, he said to me, with an air of mystery, 'Xiaogu's here. Perhaps they're torturing him, he's being tortured for me.' I asked him why. 'When he goes to college they have to check back for three generations. His father is an active counter-revolutionary, a landlord, a special agent, a poisoner, a murderer, someone who's committed all sorts of other crimes, how could he not get implicated? They brought him here, I saw him at one of the rallies.' His words triggered my maternal instinct and I cried. I knew that when the students made revolution and engaged in armed struggle, things could not have been easy for elder son, but I didn't believe they would drag him off to prison. To put F and myself at ease, and to do so with facts, I wrote a letter to our daughter.

She wrote back to say that elder brother had restored his organisational ties and was a lecturer, while younger brother was in the countryside and had become very fit. As for her, she had added another boy to her family. This was wonderful news. F read it but said nothing. The letter had a good effect on him.

During the hot evenings, we were sometimes told to go to the square to see a film. F told me to take a stool, but the Secretary said there was no need. It was a long way from our courtyard to the square. I saw the prisoners for the first time. They had shaven heads and wore deep-blue jackets and trousers. When they saw the Secretary with us, they stood to one side, their arms hanging respectfully. We were led to the front, where chairs had been set out for cadres and their families.

Line after line of prisoners came in, carrying small stools, and went to their places. The name of the film – *Tunnel Warfare* – appeared on the screen. They showed the same films over and over again, but no one objected, since this was class education. As for us, at least we could get out of the courtyard for a while.

Before my arrival, he would never have gone to watch a film. He said it might give him 'ideas': 'After we watched *Taking Tiger Hill by Strategy*, they suspected me of having been a local bandit. I was apparently also involved in the fire at Jiapigou. I confessed everything and took complete responsibility. But it wasn't true. It cost me a lot of worry. After that, I stopped going to films.'

I asked him about his life during the years of our most recent separation. He told me he had lived in a big cell below the square, behind the prison office. He showed me when we went past. It was some 20 or 30 square metres, with high windows. Round the walls was a plank covered by a bamboo mat. The gangway was wide enough for one person. They put a pail out at night. If you were unlucky, you ended up sleeping next to it.

'It wasn't so bad, I slept next to the note-taker. He was no. 1, I was no. 2. We had a bit more room than the others. They put me to work in the glue room. There was a stove for boiling glue. My job was to sort the hemp, people used to envy me. In winter you could get hot water and if the rice was cold you could heat it up on the stove.

'I was in the team for old and weak people. We got 24 pounds of food. As you know, I've always been a big eater. It didn't take me long to eat my couple of ounces. The military changed my ration to 36 pounds, which was grade two. That annoyed some of the older prisoners.

'We were four to a team. We used to supervise each other. When you went to the latrine someone had to stand by you. I had an inflamed prostate and piles, so I was always going to the toilet. They hated having to accompany me and suffer the stench.

'The person on duty had to fetch the food. The note-taker served it out. It was mainly vegetables, fried or boiled. Sometimes we got meat steamed in the bowl, or fermented soybeans, I can't tell you how delicious that was. I used to eat half and keep the rest to heat up for my second meal, so I could enjoy it twice. Occasionally they gave us steamed buns or cornmeal bread steamed in the bowl. That was my favourite. It was better than any other bread or biscuit in the world. I even used to like the buffalo-skin soup.'

At this point, he started grumbling. After my arrival the prison authorities gave us three pounds of pork fat and six pounds of meat a month, which was enough for both of us. So I used my own living expenses to buy fruit and cakes and some of his favourite food. Needless to say, I didn't buy buffalo-skin soup, which upset him. Even if I'd made him some, he probably wouldn't have said he liked it.

He continued:

'One day, it was my turn to fetch the food. There were eight or nine bowls in the basin, it must have weighed 20 pounds. My piles were bleeding, so my arms and legs were weak. I staggered and ended up on my knees, breaking several bowls. The other prisoners gathered round shouting that I was a fool and a good-for-nothing. Luckily, the correctional officer decided not to punish me.

'In the mornings, everyone took turns to fetch hot water for washing. I couldn't lift it, so I used cold water instead. Throughout the winter I washed my face in cold water, but I couldn't bring myself to brush my teeth with it. They turned black and some fell out.

'Here they're very particular about hygiene. In the summer, old and weak prisoners like me were allowed to bathe in the big pond once every three or four days. Men doing manual labour were allowed to go by themselves to the kitchen and take water to the latrines to wash with. In the winter, you took turns to bathe, two or three times a month. You bathed in batches. The last batch had to endure a mud soup. I always shaved my head first and then soaked for as long as possible. That was one of my greatest pleasures.

'In Chengdu, I could only take a shower in the summer. I used to get bitten by mosquitoes and bedbugs and I had to get up two or three times a night. I tried to paste over the gaps between the bed planks with rice grains stuck to bits of paper. Some hope! I kept asking Old Leng to help, but it was more than a year before he sprayed it with insecticide. In the big cell, there were no bedbugs, and the Secretary gave us a coil of mosquito-repellent. So at first I thought swapping my single cell in Chengdu for this big cell was a good thing. Later, I realised I had ended up on death row.

'One day, the note-taker told me that the military wanted to see me. I thought it was because they had settled my case. I left a note under my pillow telling them not to inform my family after my death and to scatter my ashes in the vegetable garden. But instead, the army handed me your letter. What you said was right, of course. You told me to accept reform and strive for leniency. But as you know, I'm innocent. I had been seriously ill, my piles were bleeding, I found it hard to pass water. All that tormented me, to the point where I confessed, even though I had no idea what they were talking about.'

I couldn't bear to listen. All I could do was whisper, 'You can stop being frightened, it's all over. I'm here now, I'll protect you whatever happens.'

'You? Protect me? Aren't you also in this cage?' he said with a scornful laugh. His laughter, and his question, sent a cold shiver through me.

What he had said wasn't made up. I found records of it in drafts of his confessions on scraps of straw paper and in his notebook, where he had written from the depths of his soul. Unfortunately, I could only sneak an occasional look. Even so, it helped me to understand the complexity and perils of his situation, and the causes of his phobia.

I did my best to avoid talking directly with him about it. Instead, I tried to create a relaxed and comfortable existence for him. That was why the Government had transferred me there, to be by his side. His mind was normalising. On the surface, he seemed much better, but I knew there was no way of completely excising the terror.

He was visiting the latrine three or four times a day. He was usually unable to pass a stool. I suggested he take some medicine. 'That's not allowed!' 'Why?' But he said no more.

Later, he began to get blood on his hands when he went to the latrine, and I discovered blood round the pit. He told me it spurted out when he squatted down.

I told the Secretary and asked him to get a doctor. The Secretary knew about the blood, but he said F would not take medicine and even tipped it away when no one was looking. I said, 'I'll talk him round. Losing all that blood can't be good for him. Don't let him know I reported this.'

The Secretary called him to the office. He told me he had seen a doctor. 'It's strange, how did they know I was passing blood? He said the medicine would cure my constipation and act as a blood tonic.' He said it as if he didn't really believe it.

Every day the Secretary brought him a big bottle of ready-made decoction. A few days later, he announced happily, 'I passed a big stool, now I feel a lot better.' I found no more blood round the pit, though there was still some in the stool.

I was just celebrating the cure when he got diarrhoea. He said it was because of the medicine, and he suspected they had done it on purpose. After that, he refused to take any more medicine. Whatever I said he wouldn't listen, and the Secretary couldn't force him.

His constipation returned, and he bled again and his face turned yellow. He started wearing his thick cotton-padded jacket earlier than everyone else. The only thing I could do was trick him by spreading more lard than usual on his bread. Whenever I got the chance to go shopping, I bought as many eggs and pastries as I could, to improve his nutrition. The town had only one big street. Lots of things were only available if you had a residence booklet, which didn't include me.

He seemed a lot calmer. In the mornings, he even helped me get the fire going. He stopped sitting by his bed waiting to be called back to the big cell. He believed we could live together, and help each other. After he had started looking after the fire, he asked me to prepare some firewood on the preceding night, with each stick exactly the same length and walnut-sized lumps of coal. He got up just after six, and I deliberately stayed in bed. Once the fire had got going, he would call me. When I began my day's work, he sat by his desk, deeply absorbed in thought; or not thinking about anything, for by that time he was rarely forced to work on his confessions. Sometimes he read books I had brought for him, or listened to me read the paper (that was a job the Secretary gave me).

One morning, he said, 'Just now I almost couldn't move. I got dizzy and my eyes blurred over. I had to squat on the step.' My heart jumped. I thought perhaps he was hungry, so I said, 'Tomorrow you mustn't get up so early. I'll get up and stir you an egg in water. You won't eat meat. You're lacking in vital energy.' He never dared accept the six pounds of pork and thought it would cause problems, that they would start denouncing him. He knew meat was rationed and a prisoner was only allowed to eat five or six slices a week. So how come suddenly he received six pounds? I was in a quandary. We couldn't refuse it, for it had been sanctioned from above. I racked my brains for ways of persuading him. I asked them to buy lean meat and stewed it and then slipped it into the noodles or dried it into flakes and mixed them in with his gruel. If he noticed, he told me off. He said I was causing him trouble.

In the end, it led to advanced anaemia. One morning, a day or two after he told me about feeling dizzy, he got up and went to light the stove. Suddenly, I heard him say 'What's happening, that's bad . . .' I heard a fall. I jumped out of bed and found him lying stiffly in the well of the stair. I cradled his head. He stared at me blankly. I shouted but he didn't respond. I tried to pull him upright but couldn't. His pupils were dilated. Shocked to the core, I bent over him holding his head and shouting, 'Wake up, you can't go just like that!' Not a sound came back, and his pupils didn't move. I rushed to the office. Not a soul was to be found. I ran to the long alley that led to the prison. All I could hear within the high walls that enclosed me was my echo. I didn't dare go any further and ran back, thinking the main thing was to watch over him. His legs were moving. Joyously I embraced him, shouting 'Wake up, wake up!' He opened his eyes, looked at me in surprise, and said, 'Where am I? Where have I been sleeping?' 'You fell over, it doesn't matter.' I tried to pull him up, but couldn't. He said, 'I'll do it, don't worry.' He struggled into a sitting position so it was easier for me to pull him up. I dragged him towards the stairs and he was able to go up them on his hands and knees. I pulled him towards the bed. It was as if a stone had fallen from my heart. Although it had all happened very quickly, I had been through a life-and-death struggle. I sat there weakly. But then he started shouting, 'My trousers are wet through.' I asked him whether he had hurt himself in the fall. 'It's not that.' He had soiled himself. I wiped him clean and changed his clothes. He was happy, however, because he was no longer constipated. I didn't know whether to laugh or cry. Luckily he had been wearing a thick padded jacket, so his chest and limbs were unharmed by the fall. Every cloud has a silver lining.

Administrator X came in and asked, 'Why is he still sleeping, is he ill?' I told him what had happened. 'I went to the office, but there was no one there. I didn't dare go any further.' Without a word, he left.

28

A Turn for the Better in Our Lives

The illness was frightening, but it returned a degree of lucidity to his mind. A new desire to live had replaced the terror and the eagerness to be executed. Now he could read books or newspapers with me, in all calmness. I rejoiced.

Thinking back on his panic and unease, I had bouts of anxiety. I skimmed through some drafts of his confessions, and recalled what he had said about his days in the big cell. Only then did I really begin to understand the progress of his illness.

Not long after my arrival, the Director of the Military Control Commission came to inspect our little courtyard. He asked Hu Feng about his studies and urged him to study well. However, he gave me an unmistakable directive: 'We've brought you here to help Hu Feng. If he recognises his guilt and submits to the law, he will have a future.' I thought, you've been helping him all these years and haven't managed to get him to acknowledge his criminal behaviour, and now you want me to help him. How am I supposed to do that?

This is what F wrote on a loose sheet of paper, three months after my arrival, for submission to the Government:

Although informally judgment has already been pronounced against me, what will be the rest of my punishment and my final destruction? As long as it is in the slightest way possible, I will endeavour to confess as quickly as I can so as to alleviate the unimaginable suffering and shorten its extent. Even so, apart from phrase-mongering (I'm not even any good at that), I have not the slightest idea how I can confess to 'facts' that are not facts. Regarding my previous experience: all my life I have been a patriot. Regarding the political crimes and common crimes attributed to me, the common crimes are fabricated, either accidentally or to shift the blame. There is no way I can confess, nor can I try to cover things up. I am aware this does not remotely correspond to the judgment of the People's Government. Apart from accepting in advance the unimaginable final verdict and obliteration, there is no way I can express the sincerity of my wish to submit to the law. That is why I have repeatedly stressed my sincerity, but failed to win approval.

Disregarding universal condemnation, I here set out the facts:

(1) The punishment the People's Government ordered in my case is a rarely seen if not unique victory in the history of the punishment of crime. However, it is an 'empty' victory, not a 'real' victory, because I did not commit those crimes; if the facts about the original course of history and relationships are changed because of me, that would be a 'monstrous lie' on an unprecedented scale.

(2) My tragedy (especially the tragedy of those innocent people who were victimised because of me) cannot be described in words. If only the exploiting class elements in the age of the great Mao Zedong could learn from it. If only it could push forward the date of the liberation of Taiwan, so it returns to the bosom of the socialist motherland. Otherwise, the human and material resources the People's Government has expended on my case for 20 years will have exacted a political price that will fail to achieve any commensurate meaning and the people will have in vain pardoned the reactionary forces that framed me.

(3) I am a criminal 'held in contempt by all'. However, I did not really cause the great Chinese nation and the whole of humanity to lose face, since none of the 'crimes' were committed by me. I am a fool. I have become a scapegoat for domestic and foreign reactionaries and the bearer of responsibility for non-existent 'crimes'.

(4) Precisely because I do not have the slightest connection with domestic or foreign reactionaries (and even less so with their system of secret agents), they have framed me. Otherwise, I would already have become a leader of the reactionaries in the 1930s, or I would have 'laid down the burden' (immediately become a Buddha), or been obliterated.

Such is my 'definitive judgment' on myself. In its final summing up, the People's Government should agree with my opinion.

Perhaps by pouring out my heart I have increased my offence, but only now, having arrived at this final point, have I more or less truly understood how hard it is to imagine the price paid for 'being responsible for history'. Only now do I realise how unimaginably terrifying is the role idealism can play in the practice and passion of materialism.

I implore you to take measures within the next few days to help me directly (rather than educate me).

I thought it useful to provide these extracts, because the writing and the analysis are relatively clear and one can grasp from it the nature of the obsessive pressure from which he was unable to free himself and his self-induced sense of terror. I don't know how the cadres could have helped him. The fantasies he created were beyond most people's imagining. The cadres intimated I should help rescue him from the abyss of suffering, but that was easier said than done. And should I fail, I would be destroyed together with him.

Before his illness, we often argued about these confessions. I tried to persuade him not to write at such length, but my words had little effect. Once he fell ill, his physical health weakened to the point where he slept peacefully and stopped having nightmares, and the hallucinations stopped. I took the opportunity to study the *Report to the Communist Party's Tenth Party Congress* with him, a task the prison authorities had given me. I was also told to write some topical articles. If he had written them, they would have been better, but he might have made unnecessary digressions. Moreover, I was well-versed in writing thought reports from my time in the labour brigade.

In studying the Tenth Congress, we concentrated on Premier Zhou's discussion of the line of the Ninth Congress. One point I found hard to grasp: hadn't the Party Constitution issued by the Ninth Congress specified Lin Biao as the successor? How had he become a renegade? In his *Report to the Ninth Congress* hadn't he opposed continuous revolution under the dictatorship of the proletariat?

F said, 'Maybe he only urged an increase in production, not proletarian revolution. The documents say he had been at it "not just for a dozen or so years but for decades". Wasn't there a process in his development and exposure, and also in our recognition of it?'

'But did he really destroy himself on the Mongolian border?'

For a while, he was quiet. Then he said, 'Burn those cuttings.'

While sorting out his things, I had found a scrapbook in which he had pasted quotations from Marx and Engels and Chairman Mao. There was also a pile of loose cuttings with quotations from Lin Biao. I had asked him to let me burn them, but he was adamant I should not. He had said, 'Do you know for a fact that Lin Biao did these things? It's not possible. It's a false front. They must have sent him there to do secret work. If it turns out when he returns that I've burned his quotations, that could be a big crime.' Seeing how scared he was, I had dropped the subject. Now I was delighted that he agreed of his own accord to burn the quotations.

From then on, he stopped talking about his dreadful fantasies. It might also have had something to do with the fact that the names of some important people we hadn't heard about for ages started appearing in the newspaper. Some literary people we knew even attended state banquets. That made him feel things had changed. He could study quietly. The two of us jointly studied the volume of Marx and Engels' *Selected Works* I had brought with me. We read *The Communist Manifesto*, *Theses on Feuerbach*, and so on.

After his illness, the administrators showed great concern for him. Section Chief X brought 30 tangerines. It was winter and they were no longer in season. They were something truly precious.

At first, F wouldn't eat them. He said they weren't appropriate to his status. Since when did criminals eat fruit? When accounts were settled, there would be hell to pay. I didn't make a big speech. I simply peeled one and handed it to him. And he ate it. He ended up eating all 30.

His colour returned to normal. His piles stopped bleeding and he stopped being constipated. We seemed like a normal family. In the mornings, I read the paper out loud and he quietly listened. After the midday meal, he took a nap, for two or three hours, while I read or did housework. I also used the time to write to the children. Whenever I wrote, he stared at me suspiciously. So he would trust me, I showed him all my letters, even simple notes requesting permission to go shopping. He often opposed even such requests, for fear of getting implicated. He would say, 'You've not been sentenced, but I have, and they can increase it.' So I was especially careful, until at last he accepted that I hadn't been sent to keep an eye on him. I realised that after he was moved from the big cell to the small cell, he had again become paranoid, because he thought his cellmates had been assigned to collect evidence of his crimes. So his imagination ran riot. He lost his appetite, couldn't sleep, and ended up getting even more poorly.

Just before New Year, I made several requests to go shopping, but no female comrade was sent to accompany me. I found out later they were busy preparing the annual report. They also made F write one. I read it, and it seemed to me his stabilisation was purely on the surface, and underneath he was still full of fear. My optimism had been premature.

His report was seven or eight thousand characters long. His analysis was lucid and managed to focus on the issues. It was well adapted to the needs of the time. It was just that in the end he returned to the formulations he had repeated again and again in the confessions written after my arrival. However, the style was less impetuous. I still can't forget his declaration to the Government: 'I implore you to conclude this stage within the next few days, and hand me over for immediate sentence no matter how cruel.'

My heart sank. So that was the result of a year's work! Luckily, the administrator didn't make me write a summary, or I would have had to criticise my own incompetence. But what help had I received? My sole consolation was that F had made physical progress and had aspirations, unlike in the past, when all he had done was sit there imagining his own execution. Now he more or less believed in the difference between 'illusion' and 'reality'.

29

A New Beginning

In February 1972, Administrator X (a woman) took me shopping. It was two or three months since I had last been out, and there were things I needed to buy.

It was busy in town, and the department store and the food store were full, not only of people but of things to buy. There was wool – pure wool, although it was from Nyingchi in Tibet, and a bit coarse. I bought enough to make F a pullover for when spring came. I also bought some ox-tongue cake, because I knew F liked it, and some candied fritter (which I hadn't seen for ages). The administrator pointed out a small bag of sweet dumplings made of glutinous rice flour, which he was bound to like. I was especially pleased to come across three or four volumes of *One Hundred Thousand Whys* in the bookshop.* Even though they weren't as nicely printed as the Eight Model Works, they were a refreshing change, and provided scientific knowledge as well as class struggle.† It was like eating a plate of vegetables after a diet of nothing but meat and fish.

We ate our New Year's Eve dinner in an atmosphere of peace. He didn't grumble about the sumptuous food and behaved like a normal person. Not much was said, but we were each at ease, delighting in one another's company.

It had been our custom for years to gather as a family at New Year to chat and hear the children sing. Now neither of us could

---

* *One Hundred Thousand Whys* was a popular science series.
† The Eight Model Works were based on Mao's instructions on drama and literature.

think of anything to talk about. He sat without a word, and I didn't dare open my mouth either. Then he decided to have an early night.

I thought, I must tell the children what has happened over the past year. I had only written two or three times since my arrival, never more than a few lines. There was never any good news, so I just reported that we were safe and sound and left it at that. What should I say now? Tell them father had made great progress? Of course that was true, compared with when I first arrived. He no longer stooped, and he no longer stood there shivering, his nose dripping and his hands thrust deep inside his sleeves. He was an old man who ate well, dressed well, and lived a normal life. But as soon as I thought of the word 'normal', I no longer dared continue writing. I went over and watched him sleeping tranquilly, his lips slightly quivering, a faint smile on his face. Was he dreaming of Spring Festival with his children? That for such a long time he had not been jolted awake by nightmares was a big improvement, but he still used to mope during the day, so I could never relax. Finally, I wrote this, 'Father has been ill, but he's a bit better now. His health is a lot better than it was.'

You couldn't say Spring Festival made us happy, but nor did it make us sad. Our life was confined behind four high walls. The tiny courtyard was two metres across and five or six metres long. A wall five metres high blocked the sun. The yard was full of moss. You couldn't walk around in it, you didn't even dare step in it. The only place you could move about was on the step outside the door, little more than two feet wide. F sat on a chair by the table. I used to watch him slowly nod off. However, as long as my beloved charge didn't cause me intolerable grief, I was happy. The weather was warming up. The small west-facing room was no longer assailed by cold winds, and the afternoon sun dispensed warmth. Sometimes we read *One Hundred Thousand Whys* together, which he preferred to the newspaper. He was astonished that our country had built the Nanjing Bridge with its own resources, and he thought the Longmen Planing Machine was amazing. But I noticed he was forlorn. He sighed and asked, when will I be able to see the Nanjing Bridge, when will I be able to walk across it? I said, 'The day will come. As soon as you get out of gaol, we'll go to Nanjing to see the bridge.' 'That will never happen!'

My empty promises and empty encouragement had no effect, so I stopped talking about a visit and instead we concentrated on studying the bridge pier, which took up as much space as a dozen basketball pitches. In that way we could discuss relatively safely and without becoming too excited.

Pretty soon, he tired of reading that sort of book. He usually sat alone, his head lowered, but sometimes he looked up in alarm, and then looked down again, and fell into a deep sleep.

I decided to ask the administrators to arrange some manual labour for us, even if it was only winding balls of string. I also said it would help if F could be allowed to take walks in the deserted courtyard in front of where we lived, which was separated from us by a wall. The courtyard was three times as big as ours, and in the mornings it caught the sun. There were tangerine trees with green leaves, unlike the two in our own courtyard, which had withered and were covered in white spots (caused by a beetle). Because of the sun, the trees in the big courtyard weren't infested and were a beautiful dark green colour. Whenever I felt depressed, I went there for a solitary walk, which is why the idea occurred to me.

In an official reply, Administrator H said:

'There's no need, we're about to make arrangements. When the new house is built, you'll have work, and somewhere to stroll.'

'You're building us a new house?' It was as if I had been stung by a bee. My whole body was in pain. So we really would be locked up here forever.

'You're going to lock us up here until we die, we'll never get out of prison.'

'Aren't you pleased that we want to improve your accommodation?'

What other way was there of looking at it? But I didn't tell F.

Just before Spring Festival, things began to change. On my visits to the assembly hall to watch films, I was accompanied by a woman in her thirties and her four children (they didn't ask F to go). The children were all girls. The two big ones were seven or eight and the small ones were one or two, and seemed to be twins. The family didn't look or sound like local people. Since they were together with me, it was not difficult to guess their status. Watching the four children cluster round their mother, I both envied and sympathised with her. I couldn't guess how they managed to live under such circumstances.

One night, a commotion started up in the alley behind our house, with lots of yelling and cursing. The voice making it was a vigorous tenor, apparently a middle-aged male. He shouted, 'You're all counter-revolutionaries, you're all KMT reactionaries!' 'You're running dogs of the imperialists!' 'You're fake Marxists, you're swindlers!' To judge by his accent, he was a Hakka. I guessed he was a returned overseas Chinese, and the family was his. No wonder the children had black faces and big eyes. Two even had curly hair. You could tell from the insults he hurled about that he was not only an intellectual but a revolutionary intellectual. He had come back to China to join the revolution, and now he was suspected of being a foreign agent.

I turned round to look at F, who was quietly lying there, wide awake. I said someone was quarrelling. He said, 'Just ignore it, it's always happening.' It didn't appear to have disturbed him, thank goodness.

The man seemed to be jumping up and down with anger as he shouted out his curses. I could hear his wife trying to calm him down. Some cadres arrived and tried to stop him. I heard one of them ask, 'Did you bring the rope?' They were going to tie him up! I stood on the kitchen table and through the iron bars I could see shadows moving around, but I couldn't see the man, who was loudly resisting. I worried someone might notice me, so I got down. I heard Section Chief X order him to go to the office. Not long afterwards, he was brought back, seemingly docile.

I couldn't sleep for ages. I kept on thinking that next door to us was someone who, like F, was feeling unbearably wronged, torturing himself, and losing his mind. I also kept on thinking of his young wife and children. Like me, they were cut off behind these four high walls. I felt boundless sympathy for them. Immediately my own suffering diminished, as if suffering always seeks out a companion. I slept well.

One day at around noon, not long after learning that we were to be moved from the small courtyard, a quarrel again started up outside our back window. This time it was between the young mother and an administrator. She couldn't contain her emotions. She said something about having asked to leave, but they wouldn't let her. She wept as she spoke. The official answered in a soft voice and sent her back through the door.

Shortly after that, we moved. We had lived there for more than a year. They were our hardest, most painful days. Could it get worse? While I was preparing things, that thought was foremost in my mind. However, I also looked forward to escaping the four walls that bore down on me. The only thing I would miss was a pair of swallows nesting on a roof beam in the neighbouring courtyard. They had come to build their nest at the same time the year before. That was when I was grieving because of F. I used to steal out when no one was around and hide in the courtyard and cry. How I had envied them flying back and forth together and building a happy and harmonious family. Later, I saw the chicks had hatched, and I watched the parents fly off with them to who knows where. I used to pace around under the empty nest, willing them to return. Now they had come back. Was it the parents or the babies? Sadly, I couldn't talk with them, or who knows what wonderful stories they could have chirped to me! 'You can fly wherever you like, while I've spent an entire year locked up behind these four high walls. Now I'm leaving, never to return, and never to see you again!' I stood beneath the beam, whispering goodbye.

Some prisoners came to help us move. We were ordered to stay in the kitchen until they had finished. Administrator H led us to the new accommodation. It was behind an iron gate at the end of the alley. F told me he had once stayed in a cell behind the second gate. Now he was in a panic, fearing he was about to be sent back.

The thick wooden gate swung open. It was covered in tinplate with three automatic locks. No wonder all the administrators had huge bunches of keys jangling at their waists. I too was now locked up behind a big door from which there was no exit. In the past, I could always go to the office if I needed to find someone, but now no one would have the slightest idea whether we were dead or alive.

Behind the gate was a big courtyard rank with weeds. In the middle was a T-shaped concrete area and a row of four houses facing south. Beneath the steps outside the buildings was a stretch of concrete lit by the sun where we could take a stroll. In the middle was a concrete table and four square concrete blocks where we could rest, or keep cool on hot days. They had put some thought into it.

A high wall surrounded the courtyard. One end abutted onto the neighbouring courtyard and the other onto the street. There was also a prison factory. You could hear factory sounds, and if you looked up you could see kites being flown by the children in the next courtyard. There were no swallows, but you could hear birdsong and the chirrup of insects. Here we could have our own house. We wouldn't have to hide away in the sunless alley. We were receiving better treatment. Our job was to clear the wasteland.

30

'Chopping Down to No Avail, Disentangling into Disarray'

Our lives had changed for the better. We had moved from a courtyard no bigger than the palm of your hand to one with four houses occupying a big strip of land. I could have my own room, what luxury! I had forgotten what it was like to have your own work room. Either side of the T-shaped concrete was a slightly smaller untended area, which was where we would do our manual labour. In the past, we had talked about it, and decided there was nothing to fear – what was fearful was to live in isolation, only able to see a tiny bit of sky through the barred window. Such was the life F had lived in his lonely and isolated cell, how hard it must have been to bear. Now he had land and me as his Man Friday, to stand by his side. As long as he kept his paranoid imaginings at bay and stopped telling those terrible stories that caused me so much grief, I would feel immeasurably consoled and elated.

F and I each had a bright, clean area of our own for reading and writing. I put his ink slab, brushes, fountain pens and other things on his table, together with Mao's *Selected Works* and some books by Marx and Lenin. I hoped he would be able to concentrate on his studies and have a new beginning.

An official gave us instructions: 'First pull out the weeds and plant vegetables. Both of you should do manual labour to the best of your abilities.' To me, he added, 'You've grown vegetables before. We won't set quotas, but we expect you to work conscientiously.'

They brought us hoes and wooden pails. First, we pulled up the weeds. They were two foot high, but they grew on stones, so they weren't hard to uproot. F stopped after a short while and sat down on one of the concrete blocks staring into the blue sky. All at once, he shouted, 'Swallows, a pair of swallows!' Sure enough, two swallows were flying round the courtyard – perhaps our old friends. I waved at them, but we lacked a common language so I was unable to translate my welcome into words. After that, they kept flying down to peck at the insects among the weeds, making our lives more interesting.

One day, Administrator H saw F sitting there not working. He said, 'Zhang Guangren, why have you stopped weeding? You temper yourself through manual labour. The sooner you clear this land, the sooner you can plant vegetables and maize.' The comment was also meant for my ears.

I speeded up my weeding and digging, but F still seemed to lack drive. I got him to start working as soon as I heard the key turn in the lock, to avoid a lecture. On that point, at least, he complied. When the weeds had been cleared, Administrator H praised F and said he was making progress. F said to me, 'It's a pretence, they won't allow me to stay here permanently.' He was still dejected and distrustful.

I did the hoeing and F helped pick up stones and bits of tile. It wasn't proper soil. In the past it had been a rubbish tip, so there was no way the two of us could clear it by ourselves. Administrator H sent help, and finally the ground was cleared. We planted celtuce, aubergine and kidney beans. Between the two strips we planted maize and made holes for pumpkins. Come summer, we wouldn't need to worry about vegetables.

F showed no interest, from start to finish. Apart from asking him to help plant seedlings and carry the manure pail, I never bothered him. He spent most of the time reading Marx and Engels and Kawakami Hajime's translation of *Capital*, as well as the Chinese translation. He said he had never properly read *Capital*, let alone studied it.

When I was serving the last bit of my own sentence and no longer under interrogation, I had asked to be allowed to do some studying. I read all three volumes of *Capital* (which our daughter had sent me), though I couldn't claim to have understood it all. Now I wanted F to read it, so we could discuss it together.

I started reading *The Condition of the Working Class in England*, which Engels had written as a young man. I was fascinated, and F also found it interesting. He said, 'My Japanese has become rusty, I can't read Kawakami Hajime any more. Why don't I read your book?' So we sat together side by side, reading and discussing. We immersed ourselves in studying the maturation and suffering of the nineteenth-century working class, and we forgot that the world had already entered the dynamic age of the dictatorship of the proletariat. We congratulated ourselves on getting a good grasp of the issues, and F became less anxious.

After that, we read Marx and Engels's *The Holy Family*. According to the introduction, 'By this time, Marx and Engels had completed the transition from idealism to materialism, from revolutionary democratism to communism. The works in this volume reflect the process of the further formation of their revolutionary materialist world view . . . Marx and Engels criticise to deadly effect the Young Hegelians' subjectivism.'

I said, 'Perhaps we'll pick up some ideas about how to get back on the right path.'

He reacted by snapping the book shut.

'I'm not reading any more. Our problem is not that we fail to understand Marxist-Leninist theory. Who has ever discussed theory with us? It's facts they want. That's what you have to explain. They always ask me about counter-revolutionary facts. Where can I find them? It was not until I arrived here that I understood from the revelations . . .'

It was as if a deadly virus had spread throughout his inner being. The light-heartedness of the previous month vanished like mist and smoke.

He resumed his old habit of writing self-condemnatory reports on the basis of his 'revelations'. He criticised his beloved and intoxicating poetry from the higher plane of principle and the two-line struggle. As for the classical *bianti* poems he had written in prison, he linked them time and again to his ideological examination.

Racking his brains for ways to denounce himself quickly led to a return of his old illness. I couldn't bear to see the poison invade his mind and muddle his brain. An idea occurred to me. 'Didn't you once tell me that some people sent the Party a history of their lives from the age of eight? You never handed in an autobiography to the Organisation. You should start one now, and tell the Party about your life. Isn't that better than letting people tell lies about you?'

He listened half-heartedly, silent and expressionless.

The next day, however, he started writing. He began with his birth, and went on to describe his schooling, his experiences, and the places he'd lived. I read it and thought it was insufficiently detailed and wouldn't be approved. So he re-wrote it, adding specific content. Writing in this way, one step after the other, was good for him, because it gave him the chance to examine his life. He couldn't help having positive thoughts about it.

'Throughout my life I've never once committed a crime, I've never done a bad thing.'

I helped him analyse it. The result was, he had not only never committed a crime, but he had braved numerous dangers in pursuit of progress and revolution. He started to believe he was a good man rather than a heinous criminal.

My first achievement was that he stopped seeing himself as an offender against the nation during his years in Japan. In Qincheng Prison he had been repeatedly interrogated about his time in Japan, and they had done a lot of research. But they found no evidence, and in the end the charge did not stand up. During the period of his derangement, he fabricated stories about himself. Although he retracted them, he never dared cast off the label 'offender against the nation', which he himself had manufactured. Now, on the basis of what he had written about his years in Japan, I analysed it for him as follows: 'The facts as you describe them don't make you an offender against the nation. They show that you upheld national honour: you took part in the Anti-War League, which opposed the Japanese imperialist invasion, and you went back and forth between Japan and China to convene the Far Eastern Anti-War Congress; you organised the publication of *Rising Culture*, which proclaimed the anti-Japanese resistance, and you secretly joined the Japanese Communist Party; the Japanese Government deported you because you were a member of the anti-Japanese resistance. What's "bad" about that? What is it you "can't tell people about"? In what way are you an "offender against the nation"?' He agreed, and removed the label from his report to the authorities.

However, he was still not ready to drop the term 'convict awaiting execution'. I tried to convince him. 'You haven't been sentenced to death, and you haven't committed a capital crime. Your 300,000-word memo was a challenge to the literary leadership and a proclamation of reactionary artistic thinking. You didn't rob anyone. You didn't kill anyone or set fire to anything. You didn't hit anyone. A quarrel is a quarrel, but it's a verbal battle, you can't be put to death because of it.'

'Don't say any more. People are intent on driving me into a death-trap. They're collecting material all over the place and raising it to the higher plane of political principle and the two-line struggle. There are so many traitors and KMT spies about. Who wouldn't want to gain merit on the basis of my case? They will attribute some unimaginable crime to me in accordance with the needs of the authorities. I'm asking them to sentence me on the basis of the materials that have come to light, but they won't, they say there's no need, they don't have enough materials to send me off to be shot.'

He was suffering but clearheaded – unlike after my arrival, when he was longing for death and doing his best to prove his own guilt. And there was something in what he said. They had changed his sentence to life on the basis of a few poems, so why shouldn't they change it to death on some other charge?

My other achievement was that what he wrote about his childhood helped me too understand things better. We had shared each other's lives for 40 years, but I had never heard him talk about his youth. Now, it was as if we had reverted to our childhood, innocent, pure, and filled with happiness. Counter-revolution, Cultural Revolution – it was as if they had vanished from the universe. His descriptions took us back to the vast countryside, the lakes and the pine forests, an idyllic life in which we cut hay, collected firewood and grazed water buffaloes. These beautiful memories put us in good spirits for quite a few days.

Summer came, and the vegetables and maize grew tall and strong and ripened. We would soon enjoy fresh kidney beans, aubergines, tomatoes and hot peppers. Section Head X brought us four fig tree saplings. 'Plant them! Then you'll have fruit to eat.' I was doubtful. Would they bear fruit? Two survived, and produced lots of red-mouthed figs. F loved them. He said they were soft and sweet, like bananas.

I was able to go shopping most months. However, by the time the female cadre came to fetch me, it was usually gone nine, and the fresh vegetables were already sold out. All I managed to get was some confectionary, or occasionally a bit of fruit. The market was brisker than the previous year, and the shops were full of products you could never get in the past. The locals seemed more animated and happy.

We too were in a far better state of mind. From time to time we saw old comrades' names in the newspaper, and some had been restored to their posts. Was the Cultural Revolution being wound up? Was a return to normality underway? Were we moving into a stage of reconstruction? There was a general recognition that Deng Xiaoping had taken charge of the State Council, and the horrible articles by Zhang Chunqiao, Yao Wenyuan and the leftists rarely appeared. It was as if a mild breeze blew over us, moistening our souls baked dry in the scorching heat of the political hurricane. F put his heart and soul into writing his autobiography, and his health improved.

One summer evening, just before nightfall, we were sitting on the concrete seats enjoying the cool. Although the walls were high, the courtyard was big enough for the wind to blow through it. We sat opposite each other, without uttering a word. We could hear the neighbours' children shouting and singing, and we forgot we were a pair of criminals.

The houses faced south, so it was not as hot and muggy as the west-facing courtyard. I was able to read indoors, and help F copy materials. Sometimes he started with a rough draft and asked me to copy it out after we had checked it, so I was able to keep the first draft. I thought, if we manage to get out of here and want to write about our experiences, these materials will be invaluable.

First thing every morning, I inspected the vegetables and caught or sprayed the insects. The most important job was spreading night soil. For that, I needed F's help, to carry it up from the latrine to the vegetable patch, where I added water and applied the mixture with a spoon. The night soil had been tipped in by prisoners at the entrance to the alley. The two of us didn't provide enough for so much land.

We began the harvest. First we cut several hundred pounds of spring celtuce. Each stem was a foot high and as thick as my arm. Then we harvested the aubergine. Because of the poor soil and aridity, they were not a great success. I put my main effort into the tomatoes. I watered them every day, so they made a big harvest. F ate them as fruit. By the time he woke up from his midday nap, the tomatoes I had cut early the same morning had cooled off in the water. Peaches were among his favourites, if I managed to buy any. I liked pears, especially the crispy sort. The nearby county of Linshui was famous for its pears, but sadly my shopping trips were infrequent.

According to the newspaper, Premier Zhou had gone to hospital, which alarmed us. Sometimes at a film show we saw the Premier receiving foreign guests in hospital. F said, 'Look how thin he is!' 'But he seems to be alert and in good spirits. It can't be anything serious.' Each of us fervently hoped for his speedy recovery.

That autumn, F seemed anxious, as if he wanted to give a full account of his life before the year was up. He worked at a hectic pace, and I did my best to keep up with the copying. Even though he still thought the Government was continuing to investigate his criminal acts, he gave a dispassionate account of himself, except for a few sentences at the end of each section, for example 'Apart from this, I went nowhere, and I did no bad things,' 'Anything of that sort is the result of framing by people with ulterior motives,' and so on. The writing was methodical and the recollections were accurate and exhaustive. This was his personal summing up, and he put great effort into it. He explained various criminal acts that he had written about during his mental breakdown. He asked the Government to investigate and review the circumstances, because the materials he had provided were unreliable.

In accordance with the then prevailing method, he did his best to link everything concerning himself to the higher plane of principle and the two-line struggle, as well as negating and denouncing himself. I had my own view of this and told him so, but he replied, 'That's what they want, you have to negate yourself and call yourself names.'

After New Year, he started again on a self-criticism to do with his use of revolutionary funds in Chongqing during the war against Japan. Premier Zhou had given him money to register a periodical. The periodical didn't appear and the money stayed in the bank, but he withdrew the interest to buy a ticket to go home to his village. In his self-criticism he said he had failed to return the original sum to the Premier, and by complying with KMT regulations that required the handing over of a cash deposit he had caused the sum to depreciate. By taking the interest he had made corrupt use of public funds, which was why he was requesting disciplinary action (actually, by the time *Hope* was wound up, we had handed over sums equivalent to dozens of times the original value).

On the whole it wasn't too bad, he didn't think up any additional imaginary crimes. But it was clear that he was still agitated. He had spent 19 years behind bars, and soon it would be 20.

31

Hope, Distant Hope

F spent the whole of 1974 completing an autobiographical confession, which he rounded off with a self-condemnation and admission of guilt in summary form. His state of mind had progressed to one of hope – that he would be treated leniently and freed.

He waited and waited, but no reply came. All he got was a casual comment from the correctional officer: 'We didn't ask you to write that. Why did you write it?' F speculated on what to do. 'It's because I didn't write to the point, they think I'm hiding something.' He asked me if he should rewrite it, write about the people he knew, so they could get to the bottom of it. I thought it would be better for him to have something to do than to indulge in flights of fantasy. It could hardly be to his disadvantage. So after New Year, he resumed writing.

Many of the people he talked about I also knew, and it seemed to me that what he wrote was in accordance with the facts. Unfortunately it was supposed to be a confession, and every now and then he added some doubts and frame-ups he had thought up himself. Fortunately, he always pointed out that they were his invention. If he'd had the chance to polish up the characters he described, it would have been a good memoir and a unique piece of reportage. However, he was unable to keep a rein on his imagination and he mixed fact and fiction, so the outcome was chaotic. Even so, I thought highly of those materials, which would come in useful in future. I urged him to retain the drafts, but he didn't want to. However, I made a few furtive copies. So apart from planting vegetables and looking after the house, I always had something to keep me occupied.

What I most feared was idleness, for then my thoughts gravitated towards my loved ones. Loneliness can slither into your heart like a snake. Only then did I truly understand how F must have suffered in his lonely cell all those years. When they transferred him to the big cell for three years he ended up losing control of himself. Who could blame him? All I wanted was to focus his thinking, and steer him towards work that would not harm him physically or mentally. Writing the confessions at least allowed him to work in peace.

After he had handed in two batches, a cadre said, 'The newspapers are studying the Criticise Lin Biao, Criticise Confucius movement. Why don't you write about what you've learned from it?' He wrote 'What I have learned from the Criticise Lin Biao, Criticise Confucius movement'. Here are two excerpts:

> The article puts us on a par with [Lin Biao's] anti-Party clique with its intention of launching a big coup. That left me baffled. I'm just an ignorant petty-bourgeois intellectual. In 1927, in the red-hot fire of revolution, I failed because of the influence of Confucian and Mencian conservative thinking to join the guerrilla war. I lacked ambition and I became a feeble-minded person of mediocre ability. I muddled my way through life. Later I managed to secure the status of a progressive writer, but politically I never aspired to power. As for Confucianism, apart from once uttering the phrase 'cherishing love for humanity' in the forties, I have never mentioned it – not in articles, not in letters, not in conversation. I had no personal ambition whatsoever. Compared with Lin Biao and the others, I was not worth noticing. As for the reactionary Confucian references I used in my prison poems, they were intended as praise for the revolution, the Communist Party and Chairman Mao. I did it to console and affirm myself. Naturally it was a towering crime. But there was no ambition. Apart from the Government, no one read it. It had

no social impact. Apart from thought crime, I've never engaged in any sort of criminal activity.

I quote this passage because some articles tied F to Lin Biao. I was worried it would bring his paranoia back and he would have a relapse. Fortunately that didn't happen.

Not long afterwards, we were told to move to another place for a few days, because they wanted to do a deep plough of the court-yard, something that was beyond our own physical ability. We moved to the next courtyard, which had three east-facing houses. They looked as if they had not been lived in for a long time. I cleaned the house and fetched the bedding and cooking utensils. When I had created a semblance of order, F came across. He carried a cloth bag with his written materials and a chamber pot – his two essential belongings.

There was a workshop in one of the courtyards. It seemed as if there were lots of little courtyards, but not many families living in them. I had only seen one – the family behind the back window. The two big children took their schoolbags to school, while the little girls no longer used nursing bottles and could walk by themselves.

On the morning of the third day, when I was getting the gruel ready, I heard a crash in the vicinity of the latrine. F had fallen over, and was struggling to get back to his feet. I almost slipped myself on the surface, which was wet with urine. I helped him up, but his left foot hurt and he couldn't put any weight on it. I dragged him step by step to the house. His left leg was red and swollen, and too painful to massage. The doctor said he had sprained a ligament, and gave him a bottle of Yunnan Baiyao capsules. It hurt so much he couldn't sleep. I had to prop his leg up with a pillow. This relieved the pain a little. A few days later, he got out of bed, but still he couldn't walk. All he could do was read. He said the newspapers had started to have a bit more content. There were fewer of those long articles by the Mass

Criticism and Repudiation Group and there was even some world news. Sometimes we heard about things from the administrator that were not in the news. F's morale rose even further.

By the time he could get up and walk about with the help of a stick, the deep ploughing had been finished and we were able to move back to our original accommodation.

They had dug out three feet of soil, sifted out the bricks, and replaced the sifted earth. There was now a layer of soil in which you could grow crops. They planted some aubergine for us, and I planted some chilli and kidney-bean plants and dug holes for pumpkins. Later I planted tomatoes, maize, aubergines, etc.

I had lots of chances to go shopping. Each time I sensed a slightly different mood. There were more books in the bookshop, and I was able to buy new volumes of *One Hundred Thousand Whys* and even a copy of the *New China Small Dictionary*, unobtainable for years. I could even buy white sugar in the grocery store.

Since moving here, F had not fallen ill, except for occasional bouts of depression. Now he put his energy into writing supplementary confessions, in which he invested much hope. The hope was tenuous, but I shared it.

The vegetables thrived, but the weather was against me. A big storm blew over the maize and tore some out at the root, so it didn't flower or pollinate. There was a drought, so the leaves wilted. Each morning I took a bowl of water to give some extra sustenance to the tomatoes, chilli and long beans, which were beginning to flower. Some of the leaves were crawling with black aphids. Again, I had to spray them. Only the pumpkins looked after themselves – as long as I mucked them enough, they grew. After they started flowering, I pollinated them, and very soon there were pumpkin vines everywhere.

We handed over more than 1,000 pounds of aubergines and kidney beans. F said, 'Who would have thought you could grow such wonderful vegetables on a pile of rubble?' The administrator praised our efforts. He said most of the state vegetables had died because of the drought, whereas ours had prospered. He told me to keep some chillies for drying in the sun. I wasn't very interested in that, but I did dry lots of long beans. I thought it might be nice to send some to Beijing, and I imagined giving them in person to my family, so they could taste the fruit of our labour. I didn't tell F this.

In August and September, the press launched a wave of criticism of *Water Margin*, and published Chairman Mao's critical comments: 'The merit of the book *Water Margin* lies in the portrayal of capitulation. It serves as teaching material by negative example to help all the people recognise capitulationists.' '*Water Margin* is against corrupt officials only, but not against the emperor. It excludes Zhao Kai from the 108 people. Song Jiang pushes capitulationism, practises revisionism, changes Zhao's Justice Hall to Loyalty Hall, and accepts the offer of amnesty and enlistment.'

What was going on?

The administrator told F to write about it. F said, 'I've never written anything about *Water Margin*. I always accepted Mr Lu Xun's view: "Because the rebels didn't directly oppose the Emperor, the moment the imperial forces arrive they give in and are pacified. Then they help the Court attack other brigands, rebels who didn't want to accord with 'the way of Heaven'. They end up slaves." Chairman Mao points out that Song Jiang is a capitulationist revisionist, that's really worth studying.' F started writing an article criticising his own past views and explaining his present views.

He wrote, 'After Liberation, many people said *Water Margin* was a great work, that it was alone in praising peasant risings, and that Shi Naian was a great realist. I, on the other hand, saw it as a novel that praised feudalism and didn't praise peasant risings but opposed them. The peasants and farm labourers in the book were Li Kui, the Xie brothers and the three Ruan brothers. Most of the rest were basic cadre elements of the feudal system. The leading group included landlords and even feudal aristocrats. Its main theme is loyalty to the monarchy. It is the biggest distortion of historical reality under feudal rule.'

Not long after that, I bought the complete *Water Margin* on one of my shopping trips. I had never read the *Sequel* to *Water Margin* before, and I discussed it with F. 'After the War of Resistance, when we were living in the Anti-Japanese Writers' Association building, Xiaogu found a copy of the *Sequel* and read it. He said to me, "Song Jiang is really bad, he's a real traitor, he used tricks to poison Li Kui to death." Then he burst out crying. He also said, "I can't bear to read any more. Li Kui was so loyal to him." Do you remember?'

'Yes. We even laughed at him.'

He took the book and started reading it. After he had finished, he was troubled and sat there brooding for a whole day. 'My previous effort was highly unsatisfactory. I missed the main point. We shouldn't criticise *Water Margin*, we should criticise Song Jiang. Song Jiang was the capitulationist and revisionist, Song Jiang was the one who gave in and enlisted, but I didn't criticise him. I even praised him in my old poems. I'll be in deep trouble if they find out.'

He hurriedly wrote a supplement to his self-criticism regarding *Water Margin*. 'In one of my poems I said, "Song Jiang pledged to obey military orders", to match the line below, "Li Chuang's political principles are new". The lines about "King Chuang not taxing the grain" and "Killing a person is like killing my father, raping a woman is like raping my mother" are clear-cut programmatic political slogans, but I couldn't find any suitable materials, so I used the popular story about uniting for justice in the Liangshan marshes. To interpret "military orders" as Song Jiang acting on behalf of Heaven would be completely reactionary. If I had not read Chairman Mao's instructions, there is no way I could have made this progress in my understanding.'

I said, 'This isn't so serious.'

'You don't understand the current comments on *Water Margin*. They mean something, but we don't know what.'

The administrator called him in for a talk, and Political Commissar X personally spoke with him. That was the first time that had happened, and I could see he was happy. The Political Commissar told him, 'You've made progress over the past two years. We didn't ask you to write these confessions, but it's good that you have. Don't lose confidence in the Party's policy, you have a future. Yes, you should have the label 'national traitor' removed. We must seek truth from the facts. But it's not true that you've been condemned to death, we don't want you to die.' F said, 'The Political Commissar wants me to believe in the Government's policy of giving people a way out. He said the Government is not concerned about things that happened in the thirties, all that belongs to the past. He said I must transform my thinking and assume responsibility for my crimes. In the past, I missed the "opportunity", he hopes I won't miss this last opportunity.'

32

A Bolt from the Blue

On the morning of 9 January 1976, while we were eating breakfast, the radio started broadcasting a dirge. We listened intently. 'Premier Zhou Enlai's heart ceased beating at 9:57 on the 8th.' F sat in the courtyard completely motionless, the cold wind blowing onto him. I called him to lunch, but he didn't hear me. He was disoriented and immensely tired. The Premier's death was an enormous blow to him, for the Premier had always been his spiritual pillar.

For several days, he was incommunicative and moody. He wrote notes on slips of paper. He wanted to write poetry to express his grief, but managed to produce only a few fragments. That made him even more depressed. Every day he waited for the newspaper. The reports of mourning from all over the country moved him. 'Such a politician is rare in the world, let alone in China. I fear there's no one to succeed him. Who will head the family?' He seemed to have a premonition that something big was about to happen.

He wrote a two-page admission of guilt to the Premier, full of apologies and self-remonstrations. The paper was smudged with tears. Administrator X came to see me and took away the unfinished text.

When the administrator brought the newspaper, he often exchanged a few words with F. He told him how the Premier's body had been sent to Babaoshan for cremation. F said he would like to see the memorial ceremony on television: 'I am not qualified to participate in a memorial service for the Premier, but may I watch the live transmission?' They let us watch the TV broadcast, including the memorial service held that morning, and we quietly wept.

There were reports of comets and meteorites that in the old days would have been taken as presaging a terrible disaster. We knew it was a natural phenomenon and the newspapers offered a scientific explanation, but we couldn't help seeing it as an omen.

F sat there staring into space. In his year-end summary report, he analysed and interpreted things that had happened in the past and criticised the poems he had written in prison. Finally, he accepted the Government's suggestion that he admit his guilt.

He was then ordered to write about his feelings for the Premier, and in greater detail, since what he had previously written was not sufficiently comprehensive. Again he wrote 'An admission of guilt to the Premier'.

A few days later, the administrator brought some forms for him to fill in. In addition to the names and addresses of relatives and people with whom he had social ties, he was told to provide their work details and mailing addresses. He did his best, but it was difficult, so he added a note saying he didn't know all the details, having spent 20 years in isolation. He also said that his relatives in the village and his children should not be held responsible for his criminal acts.

I asked him if he had filled out such forms in the past, and he said he didn't think so. So, was this routine, or were there special reasons for it? Was it to put a quick end to his case, or was there some other plan? He wasn't thinking of unfavourable outcomes, but he seemed disturbed. I wanted to ask the administrator what was going on but didn't dare. F said that no one would tell us anyway, and it was best to keep quiet.

He returned to criticising the 'reactionary ideology of Confucian loyalty to the emperor' that he had expressed in his poetry, mainly the poems confiscated in Chengdu, for which he no longer had the manuscripts. Even so, he could still clearly recall fragments.

> My writing often offends against 'grammar'. Grammar is a funda-mental law of human thinking, it is the basis of the materialist way of thought. It is a tool that reflects reality. However, because the exploiting class live in a world divorced from practice (production and any form of physical labour and work entailing political, social and other responsibility), they have not devel-oped a sense of responsibility as to what is important and unim-portant. The poison of reactionary romanticism exaggerates subjective arbitrariness in writing. Only in recent years did I become aware of the absolute importance of ideological crimes, which violate the truthful reflection of the reality of the rules of language. My failure to develop a minimum sense of responsibil-ity towards language and my violation of the rules of language are a root cause of the tragedy of my life.

His thinking was still lucid, but he went too far. He said most of the characters in his poetry were fictitious, and he requested the Government to deal with his 'reactionary poetry' as abnormal psychological activity.

He calmed down for a while. However, the newspapers carried important news day after day. We couldn't make out what was going on, but we sensed turmoil. Each day the administrator left immediately after handing me the newspaper.

Later, we read about the appointment of Hua Guofeng as First Vice-Chairman of the Central Committee and Premier of the State Council and the cancelling of Deng Xiaoping's posts, as well as reports of 'a counter-revolutionary political incident in Tiananmen Square'. All we could see was a black mist and dark-ness. An article mentioned a Right-deviationist wind aimed at reversing the verdict: 'The bourgeoisie is within the Communist Party.' According to the announcement, this was initiated by Chairman Mao.

The correctional officer told F to write a thought report on this movement, especially his view of Deng. He wrote:

Chairman Mao raised the issue of the 'bourgeoisie within the Communist Party'. His directive demonstrates that the Communist Party is a powerful force. There are no longer any hostile forces of the bourgeoisie that would dare to attack the Communist Party. In terms of the correlation of social and political capacity, the bourgeoisie in China has been eliminated. The recent rebellious political incident in Tiananmen Square was destroyed in the blink of an eye. The problem of Deng Xiaoping, while serious, is a problem of inner-party ideological struggle. I explained in previous confessions how I came into contact with Deng Xiaoping in 1951. He met leading members of the land reform group. I participated, but did not speak personally. I had a favourable impression of his attitude and manner. At dinner, I toasted him, and he exchanged polite words with me. I heard him give a report on land reform, and gained a favourable impression of its content and the simplicity of his demeanour. He quoted Lunacharski's *Don Quixote Delivered* in his report, so it seemed to me that he both rigorously upheld the dictatorship of the proletariat and understood literature and art. In Shanghai, I sent him a couple of my books, including a brief review of *Don Quixote Delivered*. I also had a personal motive – to make a good impression on him.

Later, he wrote some criticisms:

Because my mental disorder has intensified, this confession must have committed even more serious errors. However, I must do all I can to draw out the lessons of this incident, to stay calm, to overcome my difficulties in learning, to raise my awareness, to transform my thinking, and to take the final step.

His mental disorder intensified, as he himself said, and he sat there distracted. On April 29, he handed in his 'Extremely Urgent

Report': 'My mental disorder and psychological frenzy and my psychological delusions are so serious that I cannot describe their extreme terror, in all sincerity I make this request.'

On May 1, he wrote a 'Confession of a particularly serious thought crime'. A supplementary note read:

> Over the past two days, my mental disorder and psychological frenzy reached even more indescribable heights. Every few minutes I am under the terrifying illusion of committing or re-committing crimes. Some of the crimes I imagined myself committing were greater than any in the past, immeasurably greater.

The administrator advised him to take a sleeping pill, but it had no effect. I told him that fantasising was not the same as committing a crime, and that sometimes I also imagined things. I wanted to bite a certain person, for example, but that was a fantasy, not a crime. The administrator also tried to talk him round. But F insisted that there were people using precision instruments to record his ideas, and in future they would count as real crimes. I was unable to convince him. This went on for a month. He was immersed in his illusions and refused to read newspapers or watch TV, saying it would make him even more likely to commit crimes.

One night, he woke me up with a push: 'There's someone speaking to me through the air. The Central Committee has sent a special investigation team.' He started to reply in solemn whispers to the imaginary voice. Occasionally he paused, as if trying to remember something, and then he started up again.

He spoke clearly, and my memory of what he said is unequivocal. I was familiar with the past events he talked about, but if you'd asked me to recall them independently I would have been unable to do so – who he met, what they talked about, and so on. It was like he was in a film. I couldn't believe his subconscious could store so many memories, and that those memories would so overburden his brain. I tried to interrupt him, but he hid in the latrine, talking to himself.

The prison authorities said I should let him speak, but make sure he didn't fall ill. Once the thick gate clanked shut, it was just the two of us. I felt claustrophobic. I wanted him to eat and sleep regularly, but it was impossible. Everything was disrupted, but I still had to get up on time to do the cooking and weeding.

One night, when I had just dozed off, he woke me. 'I'm calling your name, I need to talk. Explain your question. I've already got their guarantee. I told them you have no political problems, it's entirely due to my involvement.' I looked into his deep sunken eyes, which emitted a strange light. 'Why can't I hear it?' 'Don't blame me, I was only trying to save you. They've gone, they won't talk with you any more.' 'If I can't hear them, they don't exist.' He became angry, and pushed me: 'You don't understand electronics. You don't know how far they've developed. You interrupted my conversation, damn you!' I thought it best to get up and go into the next room.

I had always slept in the same bed as him, comforted him when he woke from nightmares, and talked with him when he couldn't sleep, but that night I had to sleep separately. He, on the other hand, seemed happy. He was now free, and could weave his dialogue at will.

His illness got worse. He said, 'Members of the investigation team told me they had met with resistance. They asked me if I had offended anyone. It seemed to me I had offended lots of people. What can we do, if people sink their teeth into us and won't let go?' He told me to get ready, for the Premier was coming to look at the case and was waiting in the prison. I said, 'The Premier is dead.' 'That's not true, he's alive.' He sat there thinking, and very soon seemed to have forgotten about it.

He tossed and turned until past midnight, and went out to sit in front of the house, his thin face turned despairingly towards the sky. I slipped over and stroked his big head. 'If I believed in spirits, I would shake peachwood divining sticks forever, until the demons that possess you go far away and never return.'

He didn't try to argue back. 'What can I do? Maybe I really am possessed by demons. You don't know how many wrongs have been heaped on me.'

I thought he had calmed down, but a couple of days later I realised that at night the spirits still came to him. I cooked rice, and he said he wanted noodles. I cooked noodles, but he wouldn't eat them. At one point, he ate two eggs I had poached with the noodles. From then on, I always added eggs, regardless of what I cooked. He ate practically nothing else. I asked the administrator to buy some pastries for him, but he threw them on the ground and told me he had been warned by a message transmitted by air that they were toxic.

His airborne 'conversations' were held in whispers, to stop me hearing. Secretly, I listened from the window. If he found out, he flew into a rage and said I was spying on him.

I kept asking the administrator to let me take him to a doctor and even said I would pay the hospital fees. During my two years working for the brigade I had saved more than 200 yuan, which I guessed would be enough. But they said, 'There's "fire" in his heart, when the 'fire' has passed, he'll be all right.' All I could do was wait until the 'fire' had gone out.

Late one autumn night, he woke me and dragged me out from under the mosquito net, a kitchen knife in his hand. 'Where's my long poem? Where have you hidden it? I'm looking for that old peasant who gathers herbs for the elixir of life. Lin Biao has started fighting with Chairman Mao, and Chairman Mao is seriously injured. I want the peasant to save him.' He was in such earnest and spoke with such ferocity that I thought I might die, but he was simply being loyal. I remembered I had put the poem in the top of the trunk. I told him, and he turned round to look, but at the same time he bolted me in, waving the knife. 'If I can't find it, you're in trouble.'

This was the first time his illness had turned dangerous. If he killed me, he would never have survived. What to do?

After a while, he told me he had found the poem. He didn't open the door until it got light. I then pressed the bell, which the prison had installed for us not long before. He seemed to have quietened down. He tugged at me. 'Don't tell the administrator.' 'How can I not? This could be a matter of life and death. Of course I must report it.'

The administrator arrived and I told him what had happened. He reprimanded F. I said I hoped they would not leave me unprotected in the same room as a sick person. What if no one heard the shouting? Secretly, I was hoping they would send him to hospital.

They decided to leave him locked up inside the house, and move the bolt to the inside so I could escape if he threatened me. Later, he said he needed to use the latrine, so they let him out. I could shut myself in at night and he was free to wander around the courtyard, until daybreak. Sometimes I watched him from the window. Naturally, I found it impossible to have a good night's sleep. I had to get up early as usual and make him breakfast. By then, however, he was fast asleep. Sometimes he left notes, saying things like 'You can get XX to testify', 'XX can verify this', etc. He didn't eat the breakfast I left for him. At midday he forced down a bowl of gruel, after which he again fell asleep.

He didn't like me to enter his room. Once, when I went in to fetch his bowl, he was lying there awake, his big eyes fixed on me. On his table was a fruit knife Lu Xun had given him. It gave me a fright. When I was at the end of my tether, I thought of dying with him. Death was what he desired, and I was certainly no better than he at enduring pain. It would have been easy. We could have looped the bedroll rope through the bars on the window and hanged ourselves. But I couldn't bear to part from the children, and anyway that was not the way I wanted to go. We were living evidence – for Hu Feng, for the case, and for the many friends who had been implicated. I resolved to live on, so we could emerge from behind those four walls alive.

I sat down beside him, grasped his matchstick-like hands, stroked his chiselled features, and said, choking back the tears,

'Do you see what you've done to yourself?' 'I can't carry on like this. I'm causing you too much pain.' Tears rolled down his cheeks. It broke my heart, but I said, 'You must be strong. You have to pull yourself together. Stop these stupid fantasies. You always told me to stay firm and carry on living. Now you must do all in your power to survive. If you can survive, we will have won. You must live.' He gazed at me with deep feeling, as if he had understood. But then he pushed me away and said in a cold voice, 'Go, let me think.'

I realised I would soon no longer be able to hold out. My physical condition had deteriorated. I suffered dizziness and palpitations, and I feared I might collapse. I asked the administrator to let me see a doctor. A female doctor came. She asked about my health. That was easy to answer, but not so my emotional state. Sitting in front of her, I poured out my pain and heartache. I almost burst into tears, but she kept on comforting me and telling me not to get upset, so I held back. She said, 'Don't worry, you're not seriously ill, you're just run down and stressed. I'll give you a blood tonic. You have to stop being so nervous.' I was grateful for her kindness, which I had not experienced in recent years. I kept on thanking her as I saw her off and watched the gate close behind her.

When I returned, I was surprised to see F standing at the door waiting for me. He asked, 'What did the doctor say?' To scare him, I said, 'She told me I get too little sleep and I'm under too much stress. I have heart disease and anaemia, and unless things change I might die.' He hesitated, and then said in a tone of deep sincerity, 'I won't disturb you in future, I'll make sure you get a good night's sleep.' 'You too should try to sleep like a normal person, and to live like a normal person.' He nodded emphatically.

His condition did improve. He began to eat the meals I took him and no longer spent all night out in the open. He told me, 'The talking's finished, now all we can do is wait for them to release us.'

Inevitably, I had been too optimistic. I had forgotten there would be an anxious wait. On waking, I would see a travel bag and clothes outside his door. He told me a helicopter was coming to pick him up, and I should get ready to go with him. 'How do you know this?' 'I was told through the air.' When I brought his breakfast, sometimes he looked disappointed and sometimes he seemed to be listening to someone talking, nodding from time to time in agreement.

The administrators, who only had a superficial view of what was going on, didn't believe he was still ill. They thought the 'fire' was spent and he would soon be better. One day the administrator forgot to close the door and F ran out. I shouted and the administrator gave chase, but F ran really quickly, goodness knows where he got the energy from. He reached another door and bolted it. In the end, the administrator brought him home. They didn't punish him, but they told me to keep a closer eye on him. Can you imagine! How exactly was I to keep an eye on him?

He again started eating irregularly. He said he was seriously ill. He went into the kitchen and urinated in a bowl, saying he'd been told through the air to do so, that his urine was a curative. He drank it, and tried to make me drink it. When I refused, he got angry, and said I didn't know what was good for me. Then he started keeping his urine in a thermos flask to send to Beijing. I had to tell the administrator, who made him pour it away. But the next day, he continued as usual. A few days later, he collapsed, and had no option but to eat the meat gruel and egg noodles I spooned into his mouth.

By the time he was back on his feet, he had forgotten what had happened, and sat quietly in the house. The beans we had planted had gone to seed. The administrator said we should keep them for planting next year. I got F to help me harvest the pods. We collected ten pounds of beans, and he seemed happy. Apart from sitting in his room writing secret notes to himself, everything seemed in order.

I didn't dare take him the newspaper, and he never asked for it.

His illness started shortly after the attack on Deng Xiaoping. He was very sensitive to the political situation. However, he never asked to see the paper. I told him about the Tangshan earthquake, and showed him Xiaofeng's letter. He wasn't in the least shocked, it was as if he was in another world. I discovered the draft of a new poem in his underwear pocket, about characters in *Dream of the Red Chamber*. Only by writing poetry could his imagination be diverted to another plane.

September in Sichuan. When the sun was out, you could feel a slight chill. At 3 p.m. on September 9, with F sitting on the stone bench staring blankly ahead of himself, we heard that Chairman Mao had died. This was an even bigger shock than the death of the Premier. We fell into a state of deep sorrow, and felt even more anxious about the future of the country. We each heaved a sigh, but we didn't dare speculate or comment, since we were surrounded by high walls and ignorant of what was going on in the outside world.

33

Taking Part in the Exposure Campaign

Three of the Party's stars had fallen, how could one not feel shocked? How could we be indifferent? F was restless and disturbed. He no longer wrote, and each day waited for the news-paper. We read the names of those who kept the death-watch, and speculated on their significance. The newspaper announced that the memorial meeting would be held on September 18, and the entire country would observe a three-minute silence.

At 3 p.m. on that day, it was drizzling. On hearing the sirens, we went out and stood silently under the eaves. F got drenched, deep in thought. He had much to recall, from the first time he met Chairman Mao in Chongqing right up to the instructions he received in the Chairman's own handwriting, all of which was connected with events in his later life. I gently pulled him back into the house, where he continued to sit deep in thought.

We were allowed to watch TV. We were profoundly moved to see the one million people participate in the memorial meeting in Tiananmen Square. Jiang Qing was escorted to the balustrade by young girls – against the stream, against the authority of teach-ers. F got angry when he saw her coquettishness and false genial-ity. Back in the house, he said, 'the villains really have taken over, who knows what bad things they will get up to.'

One afternoon, I heard a broadcast exposing Di Ke, a pen name Zhang Chunqiao had used. I told F to listen. It was about an article Zhang had written in the thirties, which made unwarranted charges against Xiao Jun's *Village in August*. Lu Xun had written

'The International Settlement in March' as a response, to reprimand Zhang. However, the *Complete Works of Lu Xun* published in 1958 hadn't explained who Di Ke was and nor had the broadcast, which merely exposed some of Zhang Chunqiao's recent activities. I said, 'It seems Zhang Chunqiao is about to fall.' It was the day after the 40th anniversary of Lu Xun's death. It saddened us to think he had been dead for 40 years, 20 of which we had spent in confinement. For years there'd been nothing commemorating him, this was a new development. In the Cultural Revolution, people like Zhang Chunqiao, Yao Wenyuan and Jiang Qing had used Lu Xun's words to attack people, distorting them at will. Usually F didn't bother to read articles of that kind, and if I saw them I didn't dare tell him, for fear of angering him. Today, however, we both felt things had changed, and history was about to restore Lu Xun's true features.

F had always felt that Zhang was the main instigator of the campaign against F. F had personally sent Lu Xun's 'The International Settlement in March' to *Nightingale Monthly*, and Zhang Chunqiao must have known this. I have no doubt he had a hand in F's life sentence. If Zhang Chunqiao really had been ousted, that would be good for us and for everyone.

The next morning, F asked the correctional officer, 'Has something happened to Zhang Chunqiao?' 'How do you know?' I said, 'They exposed his past on the radio yesterday.' 'Ah, so you heard. Yes, big things have been happening in Beijing, they've uncovered a Gang of Four.* They've been arrested.' He told us the masses in Beijing had demonstrated in celebration, and the nation was elated. Who could not be, now this nest of vipers had been cleared out? He told us some of the terrible things the Gang of Four had done. Finally he said, 'Keep an eye on the newspaper, all will be revealed.'

---

* The name given to a political faction that came to prominence in the Cultural Revolution. They were Mao Zedong's last wife Jiang Qing and her associates Zhang Chunqiao, Yao Wenyuan, and Wang Hongwen.

We were left surprised and happy.

The campaign to expose and criticise the Gang of Four took over from the Cultural Revolution. F was fascinated by the exposures and was no longer interested in pursuing his 'revelations'. Every day he waited eagerly for the paper to arrive, and he chatted with the administrators if the chance arose. In the past, he had either avoided them or pestered them to help solve his problem by expediting a decision. Now he was a changed man. His self-esteem, self-confidence and interest in national affairs had returned.

Early in December, the correctional officer called him to go to the office. A couple of hours later, he came back in wearing a smile of the sort I had never seen on him before. He told me, 'Beijing sent some people to talk about the Gang of Four with me. Political Commissar X of Prison No. 3 affirmed what I wrote about the death of Chairman Mao and other things. The Political Commissar raised the question of the Gang of Four and said he hoped I could "expiate by performing meritorious service". The Beijing people seemed earnest, sincere, serious and conscientious, unlike previous interrogators. One said he hoped I would boldly expose the Gang of Four. I said I knew three of them, but I had never spoken with them. There was nothing I could say about them. They asked me about Lu Xun's funeral and Yao Pengzi and his son Yao Wenyuan, as well as about Zhang Chunqiao. They showed concern for my health, and told me to have no misgivings.'

'So they want you to write exposures rather than confessions. They want you to join in criticising the Gang of Four!' I started shouting for joy.

'Don't rejoice too soon. After all, what can I expose? All I know about Jiang Qing is what I heard Old Nie's family say, which was largely based on what Song Zhidi and his wife said. I'm not going to start acting like the Gang of Four, exaggerating people's mistakes to take revenge on them. I have to seek truth from the facts, so there's not really much I can say.'

'We'll recall things together, I'm sure there are things you know that would help the Central Committee.'

His first exposé was about Jiang Qing and the love letters Tang Na had written her, which she published in the thirties, in an attempt to grab the limelight. It almost drove Tang Na to suicide. Then there was something about Yao Pengzi and Yao Wenyuan. F had gone to Yao Pengzi's home and seen the then 12-year-old Yao Wenyuan. He was in bare feet, and his mother was telling him off. Later we saw him a couple of times in Shanghai, but we never spoke with him. Yao Pengzi's son had joined the Communist Party, as a result of an introduction by an underground member who worked in Yao's shop. As for Zhang Chunqiao, there was the business discussed by Lu Xun in 'The International Settlement in March' and Zhang's fight with Xiao Jun. That's all we knew.

After we handed in the exposures, they invited F for several chats, all of them very polite. The administrator gave us several slips of paper each containing one question, and asked me to participate in the exposure.

I only remembered one thing. In 1952 or 1953, Nie Gannu was passing through Shanghai on his way to the birthplace of Shi Naian to do some research about *Water Margin* and he wanted to meet Zhang Chunqiao, who had contributed articles to *Trends* when Nie was editor. By that time, Zhang was director and editor-in-chief of *Liberation Daily*, and Nie wanted to ask him whether the newspaper's library had any materials on the book. I accompanied him to Zhang's reception room on the fifth floor. Old Nie introduced me, but Zhang merely nodded. I just sat and listened. Nie asked him for materials, but Zhang denied there were any. Nie said this was where Shi Liangcai had built up the *Shanghai News* library, there must be lots of important holdings. But he ended up with nothing. Outside, he cursed Zhang Chunqiao. In the old days, in Shanghai, when Zhang was writing newspaper fillers, he couldn't thank Old Nie enough when he published one of Zhang's articles. I said to Old Nie, 'Now the nonentities have the upper hand, look how arrogantly they behave.' We couldn't help laughing. Such was my experience of Zhang Chunqiao and his ugly face, about which I was now writing a report. We wrote a number of these exposures. The administrator told us the leadership was pleased and he hoped we would continue writing them.

Then something unexpected happened. The correctional officer, who was trying to get us to expose Yao and his father, asked us whether we knew that Yao Wenyuan had a godfather. We said we didn't, so he told us that Yao Pengzi had told Yao Wenyuan to call Xu Enceng, the KMT spy chief, father and to call Xu's wife mother. He asked us whether Yao Wenyuan had any other godfathers. We were baffled, and could come up with nothing. Finally, the administrator asked me whether Yao Wenyuan had a relationship of any sort with Hu Feng. 'Of course. Yao made his career in literature and art by criticising Hu Feng.' 'But some people say Yao Wenyuan is Hu Feng's godson.' I was astonished. Were they still out to frame F? I asked him to explain. He said, 'Someone in prison who used to work at Yao Pengzi's Writers' Studio as a cook says he heard Yao Wenyuan call Hu Feng father.' 'That's impossible. But I'll ask Hu Feng.' I knew F could easily relapse into phobia, so I raised the question as casually as possible. 'Did Yao Wenyuan come to town regularly? Did he used to visit you?' 'No. But Feng Xuefeng told me that Yao Wenyuan had gone to Chongqing to ask his father for money, and had stayed there for a few days.' I suddenly realised what must have happened. Yao Wenyuan said 'Feng aba' to Feng Xuefeng, which means Uncle Feng in Zhejiang dialect. The cook heard him and thought he was saying 'Hu aba', or Father Hu. The idea that Hu Feng was Yao Wenyuan's godfather was too ridiculous for words. I told the correctional officer, and he said the cook must have made a mistake.

On December 25, the correctional officer called F to the office. On his return, he said, 'My materials are "very good", they want us to go to Chengdu to expose the Gang of Four's criminal activities. Isn't that strange? After all, we've written everything we know. What else do you think they might have in mind?'

The female doctor came to check F's health. The next day, she called him to the office. The military doctor was there. They asked detailed questions and made a careful diagnosis. I was instructed to pack a suitcase, and to bring bedding and cooking implements.

Section Chief X came to tell us we could board the train when we were ready. The sky was heavy with snow and the temperature had dropped. F had been six years behind bars and might not be able to stand the cold, so I asked the Section Chief to open the suitcase and get out F's fur coat, hat, scarf and gloves. I kept on remembering the night-time journey to Miaoxi. If he got ill because of the cold, things might go wrong.

We climbed into the jeep. The doctor got in with us, while the Political Commissar travelled in front. We set off at high speed, and although the wind rushed in, we didn't feel cold. The driver told us he had put the heating on. F even had to unbutton his coat. The maize on either side of the road was covered with snow. The peach and apricot trees were starting to blossom, in a red and white spring display.

Driving through Linshui County, we got caught by the market crowds. It was still a long time until Spring Festival, but there were huge numbers of people on the road. The entire street was crammed with wicker baskets, so we slowed to walking pace, constantly stopping and starting. Most of those going to market carried homemade bamboo products, poultry, eggs and vegetables to exchange for farm tools and sun-cured tobacco leaves. We eventually squeezed through and sped off to Tankou, where we stopped for lunch.

They left F and me in the vehicle. The doctor brought two bowls of dumpling soup. 'There's more if you need it.' F wolfed it down. I tasted it, but it contained no meat and tasted of nothing. However, F seemed to like it. After all, he hadn't eaten in a restaurant for more than ten years.

Just before three, we crossed the Jiangbei Bridge into Chongqing, where we parked in front of the Public Security

Bureau's guesthouse. We were taken to the fifth floor, where there were seven or eight beds, two of which were occupied by cadres. The loudspeaker was broadcasting Chairman Mao's 'On the Ten Great Relationships'. We were nervous, but we discovered there was nothing terrible in it, he just said it was wrong to kill people, people's heads were not like leeks, if you cut them off by mistake, they wouldn't grow back again (or something like that). I secretly poked out my tongue, and F smiled wryly. 'If you're worried about mistakes, that means you probably made some,' he said.

The administrator brought us two bowls of rice, cabbage and beans, and a bowl of fried turnip. It was too spicy for F, with his piles. I fetched some boiled water to rinse away the chilli. However, they were outside leaves, too tough for him to chew, so I picked out some turnip slices and rinsed them off. The rice was only half cooked. F said, 'Lucky I ate more than two bowls of dumpling soup.' I laughed.

The administrator explained that it was not easy to buy food in Chongqing and they had had to go to the villages to buy the cabbage and turnips. I was surprised. In the past, you could buy all sorts of vegetables in Chongqing. They said it was because the Gang of Four had ordered the peasants to 'cut off the tail of capitalism', so no one dared grow them. Not only vegetables were in short supply – so were other farm products. The two cadres on our floor had been in Guiyang. They said there would be food shortages in Guizhou.

That evening at eight, we were taken to the train station at Caiyuanba to get the train to Chengdu. We went by soft sleeper. The carriage was beautiful, but there was no boiled water and the attendants seemed oblivious. So we took an early night. At eight the next morning, we arrived in Chengdu. The Political Commissar, the doctor and the two of us got into a car and passed through Xindu and Guanghan on the outskirts on our way to Qingjiang in Jintang County, where we were taken to a basement room in the provincial hospital directly under the Reform

Through Labour Bureau. The doctor brought some food, which she said was for patients. F said, 'Finally I can eat what ordinary people eat, for the first time in almost ten years.' His words stirred my heart.

34

In the Reform Through Labour Hospital

The hospital was below a hill, like a big ship moored against a bank, surrounded on three sides by water. At the back were hills, where fruit trees grew. If you included our basement, there were three floors. Inside the main entrance were consulting rooms, laboratories and an X-ray chamber, and above that were the wards. It had once been a temple. Although we were in the basement, there were half-submerged windows through which we could see out onto the road and passers-by could see in. Outside the window was a main thoroughfare along the river bank, and on the opposite bank was a small village. The Political Commissar sent someone to paper over the windows, leaving just a small strip at the top and bottom for the sun to shine through. The room was 14 or 15 square metres, with a double bed, a small bed, and a desk and benches. We had a charcoal stove to keep us warm. F was very pleased, and the next morning he started work.

He had already written quite a few poems under the titles 'Concerto on Female Tragic Sentiment' and 'Symphony on Tragic Sentiment in the *Dream of the Red Chamber*'. He threw himself into his work and was unaware of what was happening around him. The effect on his spirit was unmistakable. The next day, we read Chairman Mao's 'On the Ten Great Relationships'. It talked about the Hu Feng question and the *Dream of the Red Chamber*. However, this had little effect on F's spirit – if anything, it made him even more determined to finish his Symphony.

I was happy to have got him admitted to hospital. My dream of many years had finally come true. Whatever he was doing – writing exposures or doing research – at least he was in a real hospital. Was his bodily machine still sound? What must I do to ensure it ran smoothly? I wanted him to have a comprehensive physical check-up.

Just before New Year's Day, the doctors gave him a physical examination and took an electrocardiogram and a chest X-ray. The next morning, a nurse took blood samples.

I was allowed to go to town to do shopping. There was a main street, and the department store and the food store had everything you might want. Huge numbers of people flocked to the market. I didn't need much, so I went straight to the bookshop, which had lots of books and comics. It also had a stationery counter, where I bought some envelopes and letter paper. I couldn't help noticing a diary with a brown plastic cover embossed with a long-horned deer and the word 'Happy'. I bought it as a New Year gift for F, I knew he would like it. I also bought some peanut brittle and sesame cake, which he loved. Administrator W urged me to buy some alcohol. I chose a bottle of wine, so F could enjoy New Year in a way he hadn't for many years.

The diary made F very happy. He turned to the first illustration, of Lu Xun's tomb in Hongkou Park and a bronze statue of the seated Lu Xun. There were others of the International Hotel, the Broadway Mansions and Shanghai Library. All this took us back to Shanghai, after an absence of more than 20 years. Shanghai, how you have changed! Much of our past is bound up with you, how we miss you!

In the first few pages of the diary, F wrote down some important events from 1975 and 1976. His memory was quite vivid, much to my admiration. However, he concluded thus: 'I have confessed everything, in addition to what I've already said. So in 1976 I admitted my ideological guilt in the literary sphere.' Once again, he was comprehensively repudiating himself. I almost burst into tears. How could he not relapse?

He steeped himself in his 'Concerto'. He added 12 sections, and put them together as one collection. I advised him to rest for a few days and take it easy over New Year, but he didn't listen and carried on writing the afterword to his *Dream of the Red Chamber Symphony*. He had reached the point where he was oblivious of self.

Ever since our arrival, the administrator had fetched our meals. I asked whether we ought not to buy some meal tickets, but was told to leave it for the time being. However, I was unhappy about them fetching our food. I wanted to do it myself, but they said it would be inconvenient. So I had to leave it at that.

On New Year's Eve, the two administrators brought us chicken and seaweed soup and steamed pork. Food was more plentiful than it had been for years. F and I sat up until midnight, and we heard the bells ring in the New Year. Welcome, 1977! We had never entered the new year with such hope and anticipation.

On New Year's Day, the female doctor arrived in the company of a young doctor from the Chengdu College of Chinese Medicine. He took F's pulse and questioned him in detail. This was the so-called four methods of diagnosis, 'watch, smell, ask and feel'.

F was still trying to write the 'Explanation' of his *Dream of the Red Chamber Symphony*. I was escorted to the market, where I bought some oranges. Nearly all the houses were surrounded by orange trees, and they saved the fruit until New Year to up the price a little. F happily took his medicine and peeled an orange. Suddenly, the orange fell from his hands. I rushed to pick it up, only to find his head collapsed against the back of the chair, staring blankly. He seemed to have lost consciousness. I ran out to alert the administrators. Administrator W rushed to the door. He flung on his overcoat and fetched the doctor.

Director Lei and a nurse arrived. F was unconscious. They carried him to the bed and gave him an intravenous cardiotonic injection. Director Lei told the nurse to give him a glucose shot, while taking his blood pressure. He took it several times, as if there were a problem. Slowly, F came round, and was surprised to find himself surrounded by so many people. I told him what had happened. At first, he didn't believe me. Later, the Political Commissar came to visit him, and told him to have a good rest.

I asked Director Lei whether it was anaemia. I had discovered his piles were bleeding again. Director Lei said he couldn't say for certain, and F would need another check-up.

In the evening, they showed a documentary mourning Chairman Mao. The doctor told the administrator it would be better if we didn't go, in case we caught cold. However, I thought I had to go, because it was about whether we cherished and loved the Chairman. It was a recent documentary, but the scenes showing the special group of mourners walking in front had been cut out. After my return I told F, and he asked whether I had seen any scenes from when the Chairman was ill. I said no, just that I had seen many people among the millions of mourners choked with tears.

Within a few days, he returned to normal. Director Lei came almost daily, to remind him to take his medicine. He talked about the differences between Western and Chinese medicine, and told him to stop doubting his treatment. The investigation had revealed a high level of cholesterol. Director Lei prescribed two patent medicines and Yishouning capsules, and told him to start taking them immediately.

The female doctor also came. I asked her whether F's shock was due to heart failure or myocardial infarction. She said, 'It's not so serious. But he mustn't eat foods high in fat, it's easy to get your cholesterol down.' This set my alarm bells going. I had always thought he was anaemic, so every morning I had fried him eggs in pork fat. Perhaps I was feeding him too much meat and fat. It upset me. All I could think about was getting his cholesterol down as soon as possible.

He also seemed to have some sort of a premonition. He refused to rest, and devoted himself even more single-mindedly to his writing.

Director Sun, of the Reform Through Labour Bureau, and
Section Chief He came to talk with him. They told him his understanding of the Gang of Four was correct, but he should continue
to expose them. They said he had been divorced from society for
too long and didn't understand the objective situation, he should
mobilise all positive factors and rely on his own internal dialectic.
Although they merely mouthed generalities, F was moved,
perhaps because they weren't rude and arrogant, like his previous
interrogators. He asked permission to finish his article on *Dream
of the Red Chamber*. They said yes, but told him not to overtax his
brain and to pay attention to his health.

This conversation had a big effect on F, and I felt much happier.
Originally, after the shock, he was worried about how long he
had to live. He hadn't yet finished what he needed to finish, or
said what he needed to say. The thought that he might die without having done so filled him with despair. Now, he was relieved,
and decided to relax and recuperate while at the same time finishing his article.

After F had been writing for a few days, Administrator L
looked at the bits I had copied and asked me privately, 'What's
the point of all this?' I told him that in 1954 Hu Feng had been
criticised for his views on '*Dream of the Red Chamber* studies'. In
prison in Beijing, he had re-read it and was moved by some of the
characters, so he had written the 'Symphony on Tragic Sentiment
in the *Dream of the Red Chamber*'. The 'Explanation' expressed
his views on it. When Administrator L handed back the manuscript, F asked him what he thought of it. Administrator L said
that unless F transformed his world view, he would only be able
to consider problems from an idealist standpoint. F was disappointed, though fortunately this didn't affect his writing.

They said their tactic was for him to render meritorious service
in the struggle to expose and criticise the Gang of Four, so that
they could remove his hat. I was told to help transform him. They
asked how he had been recently. I said, in good spirits. His
phobias seemed to have lifted. He still heard things, but he was

able to ignore them. I implored them to remove the political pressure on him, to prevent a repeat of his old illness.

They talked with him for about two hours. In his diary, F noted down the main points:

1. The materials I'm writing on the *Dream of the Red Chamber* materials aren't necessary, but I can quickly finish them. Lots of people are doing research on the *Dream of the Red Chamber*. Chairman Mao has written about it.
2. I shouldn't get caught up in problems from the past, all that belongs to the past, it's not important. I should lay down the burden.
3. I don't think I'm capable of doing anything apart from literature, I am obsessed with it.
4. Historically, I separated myself from the Party. Lu Xun completely subordinated himself to the Party. [Here, he cited Guo Moruo's participation in the struggle against the Gang of Four.] I should grasp the main problem, lay down my burden, and go into battle with a light pack.
5. I must immediately join in the struggle to expose the Gang of Four. All the rest can wait. I mustn't let slip this 'great opportunity'.

He was anxious for me to finish copying his 'Explanation'. He put much devotion and effort into the 'Symphony'. But in my heart of hearts I would have preferred him not to write these things. I knew he had always loved *Dream of the Red Chamber*. Writing these pieces was his long-held aim. His fainting made him even more determined. I felt in the circumstances that there was no urgent need to copy and submit 'materials' other than the exposures. The Government might even think he was neglecting his obligations. Wouldn't it make more sense to wait until he had the chance to see various editions and get hold of more specific information? But he ignored me. In fact, I also valued these materials, and made sure to keep the manuscript in a safe place.

Director He brought him the newly published *Letters of Lu Xun* and *Complete Works of Lu Xun*. The *Complete Works* were based on an edition published before Liberation, and it was printed in the old way, in vertical columns. He started reading the *Letters*. In the 'Publishers' Statement' was a reference to 'Hu Feng and other bad people', which angered him. I pointed out that it had probably been written while the Gang of Four was in power. Among the letters was one to Kaji Wataru, which also made him angry.* Following Lu Xun's request, he had made an oral translation of Lu Xun's essays for Kaji and arranged for Kaji to stay on in Shanghai, thus sacrificing his own writing time and creating inconveniences for himself. To his surprise, Kaji secretly wrote the then sick Lu Xun a letter requesting personal instruction, of the sort Masuda Wataru had received.† This hurt F. He decided to write some materials about Kaji. He mentioned the translating he did for him and how he had helped him with his living arrangements. I reminded him that his main task was to expose the Gang of Four. He gave a wry smile. 'How can I expose them? I never even spoke with them. I'm not going to follow their methods. I'm not going to engage in wild speculation and link everything to the two-line struggle.' I started talking about some things I'd read in the newspaper, in the hope of triggering some memories. As a result, he wrote 'Once More on Zhang Chunqiao' and 'Two Supplementary Points on Zhang Chunqiao'.

Later, he asked whether someone could bring him the *Complete Works of Lu Xun* (the 1958 edition), so he could consult the annotation. I said, 'You criticise yourself for having an occupational disease, but you're at it again, you can't stop.' He later wrote 'Once More on Jiang Qing', 'Once More on Yao Pengzi', and 'Yao Father and Son'.

He had been taking Chinese medicine, which I decocted for him three times a day, but his condition didn't improve and his

---

* Kaji Wataru was a Japanese translator of Lu Xun's works.
† Masuda Wataru was a Japanese scholar of Sino-Japanese relations.

piles were still bleeding. I told the administrator, who brought two doctors. They examined F and said he had an enlarged prostate, the size of a hen's egg. I didn't understand, but I knew it was bad news. An operation to remove it was apparently out of the question.

Dr Huang, who practised Chinese medicine, took his pulse and examined the coating on his tongue, which was yellow and white, probably as a result of the inner fire. He prescribed five medicines, together with Yishouning tablets to lower the cholesterol.

I could see F was inwardly anxious, and so was I. The leaders who came to visit him repeatedly urged him not to let the opportunity slip. This implied that we might achieve the freedom we so yearned for. I knew we might still have to pay a big price, but I didn't dare say this. I was scared of demoralising him, and causing a relapse. He asked Administrator L for his views on the materials he had written, and whether Director He had found time to review them. The Political Commissar told him Director He had not yet finished reading them. He should put the emphasis on exposing the Gang of Four and transforming his standpoint.

Spring Festival was not far off, so I cleaned the house, swept the passageway, and washed the padding in F's quilt and the sheets. I did the washing in a nearby stream. It was early spring, and the water was very cold. A wind blew up and I had to run back into the house, where there was a warm fire. Once the washing was done, I took it out to dry. Because of the alternation between hot and cold and the constant rushing back and forth, my body ached and my mouth and tongue went dry. Director Lei took my temperature, which was nearly 40. He decided to inject penicillin. I slept until the next day, by when the burning had ceased. However, my limbs were weak, and I had a sore throat and a cough. F continued to write his 'Random Thoughts', even though I was ill. He still hid his writings in a drawer. This surprised Administrator L, who asked him, 'All that writing, what's it about?' He replied it was about the Gang of Four.

I was feeling a little less ill, so F asked me to do some copying. He was anxious and kept on at me, and read it through as soon as I had finished. I spent eight hours a day copying, apart from food breaks. My whole body was aching, especially my hands, but I had to resume copying as soon as I got up the next day. After he had finished proofreading, he wrote an additional two-page report and handed it to Administrator L. What did this haste mean? That 'it is the eve of Spring Festival, and I have completed my task'.

The thoughts were random. They included a study of the Gang of Four's crimes, and insights gained from reading Lu Xun's *Letters* and *Complete Works*. He used the dagger with which Lu Xun had pricked the vestiges of feudalism to expose the monsters who had infiltrated the world of literature and art. He said Lu Xun had long ago put a name to it: 'nihilistic posing'. He analysed some of the annotation in the *Complete Works* and Yao Wenyuan's early articles and used them to expose Yao. Finally he wrote, 'Originally I intended to explain my views on the concrete subjective and objective conditions on the basis of which the Gang of Four developed, but schizophrenia and fatigue prevented me from making my main point clear. I have written this to clarify my position and thinking, so it can be consulted by those who will instruct me. If I have committed errors in defending myself, I will examine myself anew, criticise myself, and confess.'

Although I worked hard to copy these 'Random Thoughts', I was not happy about them, for they did not take account of Director Sun's point that F had been out of society too long and didn't understand the objective situation. What might be the consequences? While the outside world was in the early stages of a return to calm after the wind and waves, people like us, isolated for more than two decades, should keep their opinions to themselves. For him, it was a question of baring his heart to the Government. But it seemed unlikely that the Government would welcome it, and even the administrator felt he had gone too far.

All I could hope was that he wouldn't stray from the point, split hairs, and have a relapse.

New Year in the hospital wasn't fun. Most of the patients and medical staff went home. Dinner on New Year's eve was very simple, so I prepared some extra dishes and gave F a glass of wine. At midnight, people on the opposite bank let off firecrackers. We had not heard from Xiaofeng, and I hadn't written to her. How were our children? Were they having a good time? It was ages before I got to sleep.

Early next morning, it was noisy outside. I stood on tiptoe and looked through the window. Crowds of people were walking along the street towards the hospital. The hospital had once been a temple. For years local people used to go there to worship at New Year, to gain the Buddha's protection. Even though it was now a hospital, they still came to pray, swarming through every floor of the building. The hospital sent guards to bar the wards with wooden railings.

I went out to chat with the mothers and girls. They had been out since early morning, after a meal of rice dumplings. Their pockets were full of peanuts, beans and sunflower seeds, which they ate as they walked. They walked all over town, until three or four in the afternoon, when they returned home for a meal of boiled noodles. There was no cooking that day – it was women's day off.

There were carved Buddhas on the cliff alongside the hospital. The big ones were several feet high, the little ones no more than a foot. They were hard to make out, but local people came to stand beneath them and put their palms together in an act of worship.

Spring had arrived, so we opened the windows to let the breeze in. F sometimes stood at the window watching the passers-by. Newly wedded couples returning to the bride's home strolled by. The husbands carried bamboo baskets, full of presents and cakes wrapped in red paper. The new brides were dressed in red. F said, 'The people in this region live quite well. Few are raggedly dressed.'

Administrator L had told F, 'You're in poor health, you mustn't catch cold, so don't go to the square to watch films.' In fact, he was afraid problems might arise. Local people often came to watch the films and sometimes got into fights with prisoners about seats. But whenever there was a film, he invited me. I also saw a performance by hospital staff and their families, including children. It was simple but lively and innocent. I told F about it, and he listened happily.

After reading the essays in Lu Xun's *Letters* and *Complete Works*, F decided to write an article on 'Issues Concerning Me in Lu Xun's Correspondence'. He said, 'There are lots of things no one will know unless I talk about them. The errors will be compounded, and who knows where it will end up. My body is already warning me. If I don't write this down, it will be too late.' I urged him to finish as soon as possible, and said I would do my best to assist his memory. So he read the correspondence and added notes. He started on February 21, and had finished by the 28th. He admitted the annotation was incomplete, but for the time being he would leave it at that. He spent another week reading it through, reflecting on what he had written, remembering what he could remember, and revising where necessary, until finally, on March 4, he handed it to me for copying. He had written 30,000 words.

Administrator L accompanied me to the market. He said the weather was warming up, and it was not as good a place to live as Dazhu. I said, 'But his health is much more likely to improve here than there.' I bought F a pair of elasticised green corduroy shoes, and some small fish and a pound of fresh mushrooms, his favourite foods. He was delighted, and recalled how I had bought him a similar pair before leaving Beijing (Xiaoshan called them 'lazy shoes'). That day, he over-ate. He slept badly and said his back hurt. He hadn't complained about his back for years, except for when he was in the big prison, when his feet swelled up. I think it must have been his kidneys. All I could do was give him a painkiller.

I kept on thinking of what Administrator L had said. Did it mean we would be sent back to Dazhu? How would that effect his illness and his chance of a way out? It was my job to strive for a better environment for him. I wanted to ask the leadership for permission to make a family visit, so we could see the children and get to know what was happening in the outside world, and to discuss a new future path for F. Or for them to let me go back to the brigade. Naturally that was a more passive approach, but perhaps they could be persuaded to make other arrangements for him, or even let him stay here so he no longer had to return to the big prison.

I told F and he looked stunned, as if I were about to abandon him. He said coldly, 'You are a free person, how can I comment?' I thought it best not to tell him all I had been thinking, for fear of making him angrier. Even so, I made a report to the administrator. If he was forced to return behind the high walls he might suffer a relapse, and I couldn't guarantee he would survive. I couldn't explain this to F, and it churned me up.

The next day, the doctor gave him another check-up, adding that he had consulted with the first doctor. More than that he didn't say.

In the afternoon, Administrator L called me over. Bureau Chief X of the Reform Through Labour Bureau, Section Chief X of the Public Security Bureau, and another cadre I had never met before had a talk with me and said they didn't agree with my report. I said, 'I haven't seen the children for more than ten years, I want to see them, I have the right. If you carry on letting him and me live alone together, can you guarantee my safety? I want to join the Reform Through Labour Brigade so I can be reformed and strive to remove my hat, surely that's something positive? He's your prisoner, his reform and safety should be your responsibility, not mine.' They realised a hard-line approach would not work, so they tried to persuade me to cooperate. They said they wanted to save Zhang Guangren and free him when the time was right, and they hoped I wouldn't upset their plan. There was no point in insisting, and anyway I had never really wanted to leave him, I just wanted to find a way out for him, so since their plan was that we should go back and wait for a decision from the

Central Committee, I could not but agree. At the end of the conversation I cried and felt greatly wronged.

Later, they called F out. They told him the materials he had written were useful and he had accomplished the task and should now return to Prison No. 3 to strengthen his ideological reform. F said he would first like another meeting with Director He and Section Head Yang to receive instructions on what he had written, so he could make a better self-criticism.

While we were packing, Administrator L told F that the Party wanted him to transform his world view. The Central Committee would decide whether the problems had been resolved, but basic levels would report on their investigation.

Administrator X and the female doctor from No. 3 Prison had already arrived, and told us we were to leave the next day.

F was supposed to have another check-up, but by now it was too late. There was only time for the doctor to measure his blood pressure and give him three tablets. That afternoon, the hospital ambulance, with some administrators from No. 3 Prison and Political Commissar X, took us to Chengdu's Public Security hostel.

We had dinner in the hostel, and left by car for the station. The Public Security cadres escorted us, so we didn't have to queue. For three months now, the hospital had taken great care of us, and I was grateful. I was even reluctant to leave. My fond thoughts about our life there and my worries about the future made me want to cry again.

At seven the next morning we reached Chongqing, where a vehicle from No. 3 Prison waited. Half-way through the journey we stopped for breakfast at the Young Prisoners' Correctional Centre in the outskirts north of the river. F said he would like to visit the Centre, because he had read Anton Makarenko's *Pedagogical Poem* and wanted to learn more about the subject. But permission was not granted, to his disappointment. From there we drove to No. 3 Prison.

35

Waiting

On the afternoon of 20 March 1977, we arrived back behind the same four walls. F had put aside his ideological burden, so he even felt happy, as if returning home. His meeting with the duty administrator was like a family reunion, with none of the old reserve.

Our small courtyard had been planted with a dozen or so peach trees, each three or four feet high and the thickness of an arm. There were a few lines of asparagus lettuce. Our three months away had brought us hope, and I no longer felt troubled by my surroundings. Even the four high walls no longer looked as frightening. The first thing I asked for was a pot to decoct his medicine in, and for them to continue his medical treatment. As long as he remained mentally stable, the rest could be easily cured.

I bought him a book of photos of Premier Zhou; two volumes of *Lu Xun's Letters*; and two books on health care, one on high blood pressure and one titled *Health Care Through Massage*. These helped him in his study and his physical health, and he liked them.

Every day he read the newspapers. He read a talk by the model worker Wang Jinxi that moved him deeply. A report on 'the iron and steel drilling worker Wu Quanqing' also filled him with admiration. This was all part of his response to the real world after the smashing of the Gang of Four.

The administrator told him to write about what he had gained ideologically from his three months in the Reform Through

Labour Hospital. Perhaps because he lacked interest, it took him several days to write just a couple of pages.

People's Daily published three poems by Vice-Chairman Ye Jianying. F responded with a poem ('Thinking of Old Friends') based on the rhyme sequence of 'Seeing From Afar', and he wrote other poems based on Vice-Chairman Ye's work. He also annotated them, and constantly revised the annotation. I was fed up with copying them, but he wouldn't stop. Although writing poems was not a 'proper occupation' for a person in prison, he insisted on doing it, and since they were about commemorating Vice-Chairman Ye, praising the revolutionary people, and praising the Long March, they could hardly be regarded as bad. As for the report on what he had learned in the Reform Through Labour Hospital, he put it to one side. In the end, the administrator said it would be all right if he just wrote a few thousand characters on the subject. He added there was no time limit and he could write more if he wanted, but the main task was to study Mao Zedong's 'On the Ten Great Relationships' and the fifth volume of his *Selected Works*.

The fifth volume had already been distributed throughout the country. *People's Daily* published some propaganda materials, including 'In Refutation of "Uniformity of Public Opinion"', but mentioned no one specifically. However, an editorial quoted the 'Editor's Note', which saddened F.* It meant his problem would not be easily resolved. I too was depressed. Once again, a ray of hope was enveloped in thick fog. Was Hu Feng being criticised?

He decided to abandon his self-criticism and start again. Fortunately, his interest had switched to poetry, which took up a lot of brain power and left him no time to think about other things.

After the editorial, there was bound to be an article. It was a law of nature. A few days later, an article linked the 'Hu Feng counter-revolutionary clique' with the Gang of Four, which angered us. How could they speak of 'seeking truth from the facts'? I didn't dare betray my feelings, for fear of affecting F.

---

* 'Editor's Note' was an anti-Hu Feng text.

Two days later, we read a report on 'The similarities and differences between the Gang of Four and the Hu Feng clique'. F said coldly, 'It's hard to know what to say about a theory that ignores concrete circumstances and facts.' 'They could easily make you the target again. It's commonplace to wash your hands or dye your hats red in other people's blood. Forget about it. What can they do? Just think about getting better. The main thing is to stay alive.'

The correctional officer came to see us. He asked F whether he had read the criticisms and what he thought of them, adding that they were meant to encourage F to progress. F answered, 'I have nothing to say. What's the point in making distinctions if they can write an article like that? All I can do is take responsibility for myself.' 'The provincial leadership doesn't want to talk with you again, you no longer have a problem. You must transform your world view, so you can contribute to the socialist cause.' 'I don't even have citizenship.' 'That's why you must study hard.'

That afternoon, he brought us the fifth volume of Mao's *Selected Works*. He said it wasn't yet publicly available, but they were giving us two copies so we could get on with our study. I thought it was wrong to get special treatment, so we just kept one, to read together.

The book fully absorbed F's attention. That evening, he read 18 articles, and he didn't sleep until deep into the night. For days, all he did was read Mao. He was unable to contain his excitement. He believed that it was his problem that had led to the slogan 'let a hundred flowers bloom and a hundred schools contend' in 1956–7. Chairman Mao had formally criticised Stalin's wrong interpretation of the dialectic, and F felt the need to study it carefully, because it raised numerous difficult questions.

The county was holding a mass rally, and loudspeakers boomed across the walls. It was a trial of criminal elements. The list of offences was long, more than 100. In addition to murder, robbery and rape, a new crime had emerged: trafficking in human beings. A woman in her twenties had trafficked five little girls to Fujian, for more than 1,000 yuan. We couldn't understand how there could be so many criminals. When the correctional cadre came, we asked him. 'It's due to the Gang of Four, many of the crimes were committed under the banner of rebellion. Now the clearing up has started, many have come to light, most of them committed by people in their twenties.'

I couldn't help thinking of our younger son, who had gone down to the countryside nearly a decade ago. Our daughter had written to say he was still working in the villages on seed improvement. Quite a few of his companions had been transferred back to Beijing, but he was happy to stay in the countryside. This saddened me – he had already lost ten years. Listening to the rally made me feel uneasy, how I longed to see my little boy.

I didn't dare tell F, for fear of setting him off. Fortunately, he paid no attention to what was happening in the world outside his head. He dedicated himself heart and soul to reading Mao and writing poetry. He was supposed to be writing a self-criticism, but he ignored it. The more he wrote, the harder it was to stop. He wrote dozens of pages, but still he hadn't got to the point. I was worried, because all that sitting made his piles bleed.

I harvested the lettuce and planted some aubergines and peppers. In my spare time, I made a copy of F's self-criticism, which he didn't finish until June 1. It was 40 or 50 thousand characters long. After that, he began his 'Lessons Learned', which the administrator kept asking for.

The correctional cadre told me, 'Zhang Guangren doesn't know how to do practical writing, if you're writing a self-criticism a few points are all you need.' I couldn't help smiling. 'He's spent his whole life writing articles, he's not an administrator. His goal is to write everything in great detail.' All he needed was to say that the medical treatment he had received had proved to him how great the Party was, that his understanding had made great strides, etc., etc., but he was incapable of that, and instead he analysed himself and strove hard to recall past events. Even his draft of 'Lessons Learned' was more than ten pages long. I couldn't convince him, all I could do was tell him what the administrator thought. He got upset, but then he said, 'I'll ignore them, I'm not writing it for them anyway. In future there will be people who understand. I have no choice: I have to write that way.'

I went to buy him some food and a small bamboo high-back chair, so he could relax and cool off. A female cadre went with me. People even thought I was her relative. But there was an unbridgeable gap between us. She was cold to me, and I to her, although I treated her with courtesy and respect.

F was busy writing about Chairman Hua's speech. He had no materials apart from what he read in the paper. Based on these, together with his own envisioning of the qualities a leader should possess and the contrast between Chairman Hua and the Gang of Four, he wrote and wrote. He grew ever more tired, and his piles bled. Because he stayed up so late, he caught a cold and lost his appetite. He kept on falling asleep. Did he have a fever?

His general health was good. He had chronic illnesses, but rarely coughs and colds. Now, however, his physical resistance seemed to have declined. He was constantly exhausted – who wouldn't be, with 10,000 words to write and so little time to do it in? After all, he was 76.

I told the administrator. The doctor came. He took F's pulse, measured his blood pressure, and said there was nothing to worry about, it was caused by external factors. If he took Western medicine, he'd start sweating and that wouldn't do him any good. He prescribed him two traditional remedies.

After taking them, F became more relaxed and started eating and drinking normally, but the haemorrhoidal cream didn't work. Despite his bad health, he still wanted to write more than 1,000 words a day. The doctor gave him an injection and some Chinese medicine and the bleeding stopped, except for occasional recurrences.

After working day and night on 'Lessons Learned', he finished it. He called it 'A Preliminary Understanding of the Wise Leader Chairman Hua'. After copying it, I did a count – it was 40,000 characters long. How much blood he had shed because of his inability to write practical Chinese! Even so, what he wrote would still not please the authorities.

He was summoned to the office. Two people from the Central Committee questioned him about his contact with Qiao Guanhua and said Qiao had later joined others opposed to Premier Zhou. They wanted F to tell them about Qiao, and to put it in writing. The administrator called me in as well. The visitors asked me to help Hu Feng recall his dealings with Qiao and what Qiao had said about Premier Zhou. How had we got to know Qiao?

We were amazed that the Qiao Guanhua affair had become so serious, especially the claim that he had opposed Premier Zhou. They had asked us to write materials, but we stuck to the facts. I had met Qiao on the ferry from Kowloon to Hong Kong. We also met later, in Chongqing, but very infrequently, and all I did was listen to him and F chat together. He gave me the impression of being talented, but showed subtle signs of pride and arrogance. He supported F when he was running *Hope*, and he translated Marx's *Theses on Feuerbach* for it. The first issue of *Hope* contained Shu Wu's 'On Subjectivism', which stirred up a storm, so F decided against turning it into a general publication. But Qiao still seemed to appreciate it and disagreed with its critics (though he might have said something different behind our backs). So F always considered him a friend.

However, in 1947, Qiao published an article criticising F in *Mass Art and Literature*. This surprised F. I was giving birth, and Qiao Guanhua got someone coming back from Hong Kong to bring F a tin of 555 Cigarettes (perhaps it was Zhou Erfu), some apples and a copy of *Mass Art and Literature*. When F came to the hospital to see me he brought me the apples, which is why I knew about it. He didn't tell me at the time about the article. Even some of his friends thought it was wrong of Qiao not to show him the article in advance and to get someone else to give it to him. F said, 'This has become a problem. How can we work together in future? If people want to impute crimes to me, they must discuss the rights and wrongs of it.' So he wrote a reply, and other writers did too. After that, F and Qiao viewed each other differently.

A few days earlier, F had recalled in 'A Preliminary Understanding of Chairman Hua' that Qiao Guanhua had said, 'There's nothing mysterious about the masses, they're a "tool" of the struggle', and had criticised F for saying that 'writers should write about real people'. According to Qiao, 'if real people are so important, why aren't real masses and their actual struggle important'? F had replied, 'Can there be real masses if there are no real people?' I reminded him of this, and said, 'Isn't that an example of cheap tricks and intimidation?'

'These are theoretical questions. What really needs clarifying is his moral character. If he was dazzled by fame and fortune and opposed the Premier, who was always so good to him, that would be unforgivable. However, I saw no signs of such behaviour. He was always full of admiration for the Premier. We can only write what we know.'

Next morning, Section Chief X asked how much he had written, and said the people from the Central Committee were waiting. F continued writing until midnight, and slept only at my insistence. The next day, they again tried to hurry him up, and took away what he had written. I didn't finish copying until the night of the fourth day, by which time it had grown to 20,000 words.

The Central Committee people asked him to clarify bits. Later, they talked with F about our elder son, Xiaogu, and told him Xiaogu was fine. The Government was 'seeking truth from the facts' and F should concentrate on reforming himself.

After the notes had been revised and re-copied several times, they asked F to affix his seal to the transcript. F didn't have a seal, so he used a fingerprint. He said, 'They were really conscientious. It shows they're serious about "seeking truth from the facts". They want to avoid wronging people. I wrote down what I know. I still have a favourable impression of Qiao. He has weaknesses and shortcomings, but he would never degenerate like the Gang of Four.'

The materials were good research and excellent commentary. His memory was clear, and he didn't try to kick Qiao when he was down. Sadly, it was not published.

F returned to his 'Lessons Learned'. His piles had not healed, and his blood pressure was low. The doctors gave him another tonic and some traditional medicine. As well as decocting medicine, cooking and looking after the vegetable garden, I had to do his copying. In the summer heat, he returned to writing poetry. His teeth started aching again, and it affected his sleep.

The Eleventh Congress was convened, and people celebrated with fire-crackers, gongs and drums. F focused on the documents published in the press, especially the remarks by Deng Xiaoping. He wrote some poems about it, which he revised several times and annotated before handing them over to the administrator. Then he returned to writing 'Lessons Learned'. Because of the heat, he often didn't start writing until after midnight.

The correctional cadre raised 22 questions about Lu Xun's *Diary* and *Letters*, which were to take precedence over all else. F had already dealt with some of the questions in his notes on Lu Xun's *Letters*. They weren't hard to answer, but thinking about them put him in a bad mood. Lu Xun hadn't told F about many of the things that happened.

F was again summoned to the office. The Political Commissar told him it was important to answer the 22 questions in detail. Section Chief X said it didn't matter if it took a long time, the main thing was to write down everything he knew.

Five days later, after lots of editing and revision, F handed me what he had written. After I had copied it, he revised a couple of points, read it through again, and added some afterthoughts.

He then returned to his 'Lessons Learned', and I to my cabbages. F and I had done the planting together, and we had also pulled up the peppers, hoed the soil, and sown the radishes. It was regarded as F's contribution to manual labour.

I had already copied 120 pages of 'Lessons Learned', but he was still nowhere near finishing. I said, 'That's not a report about what you learned in hospital, it's an account of your entire life. You mention your own mistakes, but you also say a lot about other people's shortcomings. That's inappropriate for someone of your status. If you're not careful, it will end up as another 300,000-word memo.'

He was surprised at my own opinion, but he kept his temper. 'Do you think I take it lightly? I'm much harsher on myself than I am on others. This is my self-criticism for the Party, I'm writing it before I die.' This touched me to the heart. Spiritually I was worlds away from him. Compared with him, I was base and selfish. From then on, I gladly copied for him.

In mid-November, the prison cadres had a private talk with me. They said I had progressed, and that my materials exposing the Gang of Four were useful. If I wanted to go out all I had to do was ask permission, I no longer needed an escort. That meant I had freedom of movement.

The correctional administrator called F to the office. They talked mainly about how to strengthen his ideological reform and plan for his release. When they came back to fetch 'Lessons Learned', they had another chat. I interrupted to say 'You've made big strides' (meaning F no longer need write about the past). The administrators said yes, why don't you leave it at that? After they had gone, F was furious. He said my comment could endanger him. 'The Government will be waiting for me to take the big step. I have to negate myself. Don't you realise that?' This upset me. Again I had put him in an awkward situation.

The office got some prisoners to plant grapes in our courtyard and put up trellises. We had already planted peach trees, so the courtyard was turning into an orchard. Watching the peaches ripen while sitting in the shade of the vine, I felt we were living an idyll.

In late December, I finished copying 'Lessons Learned'. It was 444 pages long and organised in 11 sections. It was about the lessons F had learned since first going to gaol in 1955. However, I was afraid it might offend some power holders, since bits of it were quite blunt. But F said, 'I wrote this for the Party, I must loyally submit it.' Twenty years in prison had taught him little.

After submitting 'Lessons Learned', he relaxed. He began to read the pictorial newspapers the administrator brought him and to sort out his old newspapers. Out shopping, I found a four-volume set of the *Selected Works of Marx and Engels*, which we had read earlier. He re-read some of their letters on literature and said proudly, 'So there's nothing wrong with my memory.'

On the last day of 1977, the cadres told him he had made progress. Department Head X said literature and art can't be divorced from politics and talked about who should be loved and who should be hated. The correctional cadre proposed that I write a summary. This was new: previously, they had not concerned themselves with me.

At New Year, we enjoyed a glass of beer together, for the first time in years. However, I felt not the least bit festive. I was thinking about how to write the summary, and he was probably thinking about whether he would be released in 1978.

The administrator told F his 'Lessons Learned' was too long, and the Political Commissar didn't have time to read it. He said F should write about manual labour and implementing prison rules, that was what prisoners usually did in their summaries.

After I had finished my own summary, I showed it to F. It was straightforward – a few general points about study and manual labour. I found it hard to talk about regulations, so I simply said I might have breached the rules unknowingly. F disapproved, but I said, 'It doesn't matter, I didn't compromise my character.' So I submitted it.

In January, F spent a fortnight working on his summary, which was 36 pages long. He also did some manual labour – he moved the vegetables I had cut, and planted some lettuce seedlings and did some watering.

One morning, I went out shopping. When I got back, the bell on the door wasn't working and no one answered. I panicked. What should I do? I walked round the prison wall to the main gate, where there was a small door and a PLA post. But it was deserted. I carried on along the wall, but the path was interrupted by a ditch. I walked across a single-plank bridge, but the door was shut and I was stopped from going further by barbed wire.

I screamed, 'You won't let me go, but you won't let me in either.' I returned the way I had come and started walking through the town. I was too embarrassed to ask the way, so I just headed in what I thought was the right general direction, and luckily I found the entrance. Because I was carrying a basket, the guard wouldn't let me in. Prisons can be just as hard to enter as to leave. I said I needed to speak with Administrator XX in the small prison. After much to-ing and fro-ing, another administrator arrived to take me there. By the time I got 'home', it was midnight. F was waiting anxiously. It turned out there had been a power failure and the bell had stopped working. They had forgotten there was a 'controlled element' roaming around outside.

I was busy preparing for New Year when a woman doctor came to tell F the results of his blood test. His cholesterol was down to 170, which was more or less normal.

I was called to the office and told that the prison authorities had decided to remove my 'element of the Hu Feng counter-revolutionary clique' hat. I was surprised, but not particularly happy. I had been wearing it for 20-odd years, and had long since become anaesthetised against it. That Party Secretary's wife had once said, 'Even if we take it off, we can always put it back on again.' I remained silent for a while, to show I wasn't about to shout 'long live this or that'. However, with so many eyes on me I had no choice but to say 'I'm very happy, I thank the Party for giving me the opportunity to lead a normal life, from now on I'll study even harder to repay the Party for the favour it has done me.' I worried that what I had said sounded inadequate, so I added, 'From now I will work even harder to help Zhang

Guangren, so he can start a new life as soon as possible, like me.' That did the trick. 'You are right. You're different from him, he doesn't sufficiently acknowledge his guilt and try to reform himself. We will do everything possible to help him, and so must you. Our Party's policy is to give people a way out.' They said that from February I would get the lowest wage scale, just over 30 yuan. Again, I expressed my gratitude.

I told F what had happened. 'They mean that if you reform your world view, they'll give you a way out.' 'Congratulations on reforming your world view and becoming a citizen. Reform my world view? Given their requirements, I'll never manage it!'

I wrote to tell the children. I knew they would be even happier than I was, for the distance between us had shortened.

I told them my hat been removed, but I didn't hail it as a big event or make sycophantic comments. I said I wasn't optimistic, that you could never tell what might happen. Administrator L returned the letter and said it did not comply with prison regulations. He also talked about F's refusal to admit his guilt. I was supposed to have had my hat removed, but I still had to abide by prison regulations. It was because of F, of course. So I was left suffering.

36

Emerging from Behind the High Walls

Even though I had learned of my political rehabilitation, which I had dreamed of for years, I was like someone who had starved for such a long time that when he sees nice food he has no appetite. F's sarcasm increased my feelings of bleakness. Their giving me special treatment wounded his self-esteem and increased his despair. He had put so much effort into finishing his 'Lessons Learned' only to be ordered to cut it to a summary, and he had not received the slightest positive comment.

He wrote a brief appendix that brimmed with trust in the Party:

After the ruling of Beijing's Supreme People's Court in 1965, I wrote 'After the Judgment'. I declared that just as I had not requested a defender or defended myself, I would not now appeal. However, I hoped 'After the Judgment' could be copied to the General Office of the Central Committee of the Chinese Communist Party and its Propaganda Department.

I was ignorant of the law, and the Court had not shown me any of the legal provisions used in my case. I look at my problem solely from the point of view of my understanding of the Party's principles and the spirit of its policies. I will not try to argue about it. Please forward 'After the Judgment' to the Central Committee, to show that my refusal to appeal is because I trust the Party. Although the Ministry of Public Security and the Municipal People's Procuratorate told me that the Supreme People's Procuratorate would not hear my case, I made no appeal to the Supreme People's Court.

I adopted the same position in regard to the decision of the People's Security Team of the Sichuan Provincial People's Congress in February 1970 to change my sentence to one of life.

My present attitude remains the same.

Whatever steps are taken in my regard will be on the basis of the Central Committee's assessment of the Party's principles and what is in its best interests.

Prisoner Hu Feng, 14 December 1977

F sincerely believed in the Party, but in return he received coldness and displeasure. Of course he found it hard to accept the special treatment I had received. Fortunately, I showed no sign of joy, or a gap might have opened between us. It's understandable that his comments were sometimes barbed. My task, to help him reform, was a thankless one.

In March, Deng Xiaoping was elected chairman of the Consultative Conference, and at the same time we received a letter from Xiaofeng and Xiaoshan and a photo. Xiaoshan had passed the first college entrance examination after the reform of the admissions system. Xiaogu's wife was in the photo, an honest and healthy worker. F had long worried that his elder son was already 40 and still not married, so the marriage lifted a weight off his mind. Their son was already three, and Xiaofeng's second son was six. F fell quiet, stopped working, and couldn't sleep. He told me he couldn't stop thinking about them, so I persuaded him to rest for a few days. At that moment, the peach trees blossomed, so we could admire the flowers.

Two men in military uniform came on an inspection. The Prison Director asked F, 'Are you studying? You must study the documents of the Fifth National People's Congress.' Administrator L told F to write out his thoughts after doing so. That night, he invited us to watch TV, which was showing the closing ceremony of the National People's Congress and a music and dance event to commemorate what would have been Premier

Zhou's 80th birthday. As we watched scenes of Premier Zhou Enlai in Chongqing rebuking the KMT and leading the staff of *New China Daily* in song, it was as if we were back in wartime Chongqing. Time waits for no one!

F was convinced that China was heading for stability and unity. He often talked with me about the country's future, and his state of mind was good. Apart from helping me plant vegetables, he read the newspapers or revised his old manuscripts, 'In Praise of the Foolish Old Man' and 'In Praise of the Great Turtle'.

Xiaofeng wrote to tell me that Xiaoshan had been admitted by the Inner Mongolia Normal College, and enclosed a photo of him and another of Xiaogu's family. Xiaogu's three-year-old son and Xiaofeng's six-year-old second son looked lovely. But Xiaogu's wife worked in a small town 30 miles away, so they lived separately, which was difficult with such small children.

The Administrator told F that he should lay down his ideological burden now his child was at university, and he also talked about a recent science conference. F had seen reports about it in the press, and saw it as evidence of a new emphasis on science and knowledge. He had been excited by a report about the mathematician Chen Jingrun, and now he became even more excited. He spent all day and night writing 'In Praise of the Scientific Spirit'. He also made copies of 'In Praise of Dreams' and 'In Praise of Striving', to send to Xiaoshan. He did the copying himself, carefully and neatly, to show his love for his youngest born.

He did little other than write and revise his poems, and after finishing them he rushed to hand them over, as if the leadership would appreciate his sincerity and devotion.

Fortunately, there had been a series of power cuts at night, so he often couldn't work late, but at first light he was at the table ready to start. I couldn't persuade him not to, so I simply urged him to eat some breakfast and arranged for him to do some manual labour, to lure him away from his desk for a while.

After he had finished rewriting 'In Praise of the Foolish Old Man', he changed the title to 'Symphony on How the Foolish Old

Man Transformed China', as a tribute to National Day. The next day he wrote an eight-page supplement, and handed that in too. Administrator L told him they weren't interested in poems, only in transforming his world view, that the poems he had copied to Xiaoshan were no good, etc., etc. F argued a bit, but soon gave up. They also said that there were no problems to which he had not confessed.

One evening, Section Chief X summoned F to the office. Political Commissar X said someone wanted to ask F about the article 'Mao Zedong on Lu Xun', published in *July* in 1938. He also said he that F's materials were a meritorious achievement. I said, 'If your writing is a meritorious achievement, that means you've committed no mistakes.' We sat together trying to remember what had happened in 1938. It seemed to us there could be no problems.

The next morning, two cadres asked him for a full account of the matter. After F had answered, they told him to go home and write it down. By the time it had been written and copied, late that night, it was 12 pages long. F was then asked to write a simple summary, and also to write about A Ying (Qian Xingcun).

He reduced what he had written about 'Mao Zedong on Lu Xun' to a couple of pages, and put a fingerprint on two copies. Then he wrote some materials on A Ying. Why were higher levels in such a hurry? F asked the administrator if the visitors had left, but he avoided replying. When F said that Da Mo (who had recorded 'Mao Zedong on Lu Xun') had stuck to the facts, the administrator nodded and said it was unlikely that Da Mo was a bad person.

They then asked F to submit materials on the meetings and correspondence with him mentioned in Lu Xun's *Diary*. After he had finished, we were allocated to environmental hygiene. We took great pains to clean up the house, but members of the prison leadership were not satisfied, so four prisoners re-cut the grass, turned over the soil, and carried away huge amounts of rubbish.

On the other hand, it did seem as if we had become a centre of attention. People constantly came to ask F to write materials, which he dutifully did. On one occasion, the administrator brought a note from a member of staff of East China Normal University. This person asked F what he knew about various passages in Lu Xun's correspondence, and added that F already had the relevant manuscript. The note was written on ordinary paper and the signature was obscured by an ink blot. There was no official seal. After the smashing of the Gang of Four, people asking F for materials or interviews were always very polite, but this note made me uncomfortable. It reminded me of the Cultural Revolution, it was as if Hu Feng and Lu Xun had joined together in counter-revolutionary activity, and now Hu Feng was to confess. It was clear that the person who wrote the note had already read F's materials, but he wasn't prepared to copy them himself and instead wanted us to do so. He must have had backing in influential quarters. Well, they could force F to write, but they couldn't force me, I was a free agent. So I put it to one side. A few days later, the administrator told me to hurry up, but I objected. 'We're old people. Why can't they do their own copying?' The administrator continued badgering me, until I gave in. However, F had not written these materials for general release. Who knows what the visitors would do with them? So I omitted bits that might have adverse consequences.

A month later, the correctional cadre came to tell me that everything had to be copied. But if they knew I hadn't copied everything, why didn't they simply add the missing bits themselves? 'I won't copy it. If he knows I left bits out, why doesn't he copy them himself? I'm in my sixties. I've done so much copying my hands are calloused. I'm not going to work myself to death for him.'

The next day, the administrator told F that the provincial Party Committee had approved the copying, meaning we had no choice. So I did it while boiling over with resentment. It was just like the Gang of Four, intimidating people by flaunting your connections.

F told the Political Commissar that we didn't want materials we had written for the prison authorities copied to others. He also pointed out that we were old, and hoped that in future this sort of work would no longer be assigned to us.

Summer had started, so I got out the bed mat and mosquito net. Administrator W asked me if F needed any cotton-padded clothes. F said, 'I've been here seven years and they never asked me that before. Now I've got clothes to wear, and they start caring about my welfare.' However, Administrator W still brought him a pair of shoes and told him to sign for them in the 'special uses' book.

One afternoon, some people carried out an inspection. They asked F how old he was and what his health was like, and they seemed concerned about his teeth and vision. They noticed my bedroom was damp – I slept on a camp bed I had brought with me, and fungi were growing underneath it. They said the floor should be cemented over. I said, 'Sprinkle lime over it, that will get rid of the damp.' Later, they gave me a small prison bed.

When the newspapers published Chairman Mao's speech to the Central Committee Work Conference of the Seven Thousand in 1962, F said, 'This speech has now been published. My problem should enter the stage of resolution.' 'Let's hope so, but don't get your hopes up.' I still couldn't help saying something disheartening.

Two prison chiefs, some office cadres, and Section Chief X accompanied Bureau Chief Zhang of the Reform Through Labour Bureau and the Miaoxi Party Secretary's wife on a visit. Section Chief X asked me what had happened when the Rebels searched the house in Miaoxi. He said they were investigating the confiscation of my property.

They were holding a conference. They organised quite a few films. I could see them all sitting in the VIP seats.

The weather heated up a lot. F couldn't work, so he helped me water the tomatoes and look after the aubergines. The grapes had ripened and looked lovely. Section Chief X said we could pick some to eat, but I preferred to leave them hanging. F was most interested in the fig trees. Every morning I picked five or six figs for him. If I left it too late, a grey bird similar to a thrush would start pecking at them.

Xiaoshan returned to Beijing from Hohhot on leave and stayed at his sister's home, from where he wrote to us. Xiaoshan had joined the Foreign Languages Department, so F wrote an essay on 'how to study a foreign language on your own', which we sent to him.

The correctional cadre asked F to write a thought report on the Sino-Japanese Peace and Friendship Treaty. F wrote a 20,000-character essay looking back on Sino-Japanese relations before Liberation from the point of view of Sino-Japanese relations since Liberation. It dealt with music, painting, dance and literature. I couldn't help but marvel at his memory. Some of the things he mentioned had happened 50 years ago, others only recently. He specially mentioned Liu Qing. He greatly admired Liu Qing's *The Builder* and knew the Gang of Four had persecuted him and destroyed his family and that in July there was to be a memorial meeting for him. Now, he took the opportunity to evaluate some theoretical aspects of *The Builder*, and to voice his contempt for what had happened to Liu Qing. I was close to tears as I copied it.

One afternoon, the Political Commissar talked with him for more than an hour, but stalked out at the end. 'They want me to confess things, and if I don't, it will mean I haven't reformed my world view. If it was that simple, why did I have to spend 20 years in prison? I won't barter my principles.' He had tried to explain his state of mind and his understanding of the issues to the administrators, but they had ignored him. They didn't even ask me to watch TV any more. Five or six days later, the correctional cadre asked F, 'Is there anything you want to talk about?' 'I am confident the Party will resolve my problem by seeking truth from the facts.' The administrator hurried away without a word.

F continued writing his materials, which got longer and longer. But his 'lack of progress' had angered them. When the correctional cadre came to fetch the newspapers of the previous three months, F asked to be allowed to keep them for a few more days so he could go through them again. The cadre took no notice and walked off with them.

The snub was planned. The next day, Administrator W brought *Red Flag*, which carried an article criticising Yao Wenyuan but also smearing Hu Feng. F told the correctional cadre, 'This article doesn't distinguish between good and bad, what sort of writing is that.' The administrator made no direct reply, merely remarking that Administrator L had twice gone to Shanghai on an assignment.

It seemed to us this visit to Shanghai had to do with F. F was writing his materials on the Gang of Four, which the Central Committee must have checked. An investigation that sought truth from the facts would be to our advantage and we should be grateful. Rumours and frame-ups would not stand up to genuine research.

F refuted numerous inaccuracies and untruths in the article about our relationship with the Yaos, and the administrator was unable to respond. It was obvious to Hu Feng that someone was trying to tie him to the Gang of Four. He didn't start fantasising, so there was no panic and no recurrence of his illness. But the situation remained precarious.

He wrote 'Another Brief Statement on Yao Pengzi and His Son' and I wrote 'On My Relationship with Yao and his Wife and the Writers' Studio'. We were duty-bound to clarify a number of claims that did not accord with the facts.

After F went to Hong Kong in 1948, I often went to Yao Pengzhi's Writers' Studio by myself, but most of my conversations with him had taken place downstairs. Mainly they were about publishing books and the money for books and publications they had sold on commission. Sometimes, Yao's wife told me Feng Xuefeng was upstairs, or some other acquaintance of mine, in which case I would pop up for a chat and to hear the 'inside' news. After Liberation, Yao Pengzi stopped coming to the shop. I went to his house, but I never once saw Yao Wenyuan. After the liberation of Shanghai, a sign saying 'dependants of an honoured revolutionary family' appeared on their door and I asked Yao Pengzi if his son had joined the army, but he said he was working for the Youth League's Municipal Committee. After 1950, when Hu Feng returned to Shanghai, I never went again. I was familiar with his shop assistants, who were all from the same place as he. Some of the young ones wanted social progress but thought Yao Pengzi wasn't interested in getting corrupt people to confess. When we moved to Beijing, three of his staff came to see me, hoping we would let them have our house, so I gave them the house and asked them only for what I myself had spent on fittings. This had nothing to do with Yao. However, we were criticised for 'letting Yao Pengzi turn [our] accommodation into a dormitory for the staff of the Writers Studio'. Other articles said Yao Wenyuan (a middle-school student at the time) received instructions from Yao Pengzi to act as a go-between for Hu Feng and Yao Pengzi.

These allegations insinuated that Hu Feng had engaged in clandestine activities with Yao Pengzi since before Liberation, using Yao Wenyuan as a middleman. But their authors had forgotten that Yao Wenyuan made his career by criticising Hu Feng. They probably thought Hu Feng had long since 'disappeared from sight', so they could say anything they liked about him and win the approval of those who hated him.

Luckily, a year earlier F and I had written materials exposing the Gang of Four and Yao Pengzi. F got angry and wrote a statement analysing the claims and criticising the smears. 'Criticisms of this sort harm the principles and spirit of the Party and the Party's prestige among the masses.'

F spent October on his 'Starting from Reality, Once Again on the Attitude to the Speech at the Yan'an Forum on Literature and Art'. He had already written more than 100,000 characters and had still not finished. I wanted him to write a clear and simple account of the facts, but he insisted on putting everything in its theoretical context. I was afraid he would upset the leadership, and that they might even launch another campaign against him. But I couldn't stop him.

In November, a commentator in a newspaper said it was important to 'rectify errors by seeking truth from the facts', which reassured me. I had found the trend of the previous few months chilling and was beginning to worry that the campaign to expose and criticise the Gang of Four might directly implicate Hu Feng.

A few days later, the correctional cadre gave F a copy of *China Youth Daily*, which reported that Xiaoshan had been admitted to university. There was no mention in the report of F's hat and he figured in it as an ordinary person, which had never happened before. So we had two reasons to be excited: Xiaoshan was going to university; and the chance of a new life glimmered before us.

Recently we had read a review of Cao Yu's play *From the Silence* and they had let us watch TV again. F was moved by Tao Siliang's tribute to her father Tao Zhu. It was vivid and touching, and we were overwhelmed by her sadness and sincerity. Before he was purged, Tao Zhu had written an eight-line *qilü* poem for his wife Zeng Zhi, on which F planned to base three poems titled 'Thoughts'.

After F had finished 'Starting from Reality', the correctional cadre said it was too long and told him to make a summary. F wrote one, of 12 pages. When the administrator told him to write his year-end report, he pointed to a stack of paper on the table. 'That's it.' But they still made him write his thoughts on Sino-US diplomatic relations, which came to several thousand characters.

I bought him a new diary, in the hope of a new start in 1979. Just as I was handing it to him, we heard a broadcast of the communiqué of the Third Plenary Session. Its policy decisions caused us to rejoice. The next morning, there was a broadcast of the Central Committee's memorial meeting for Peng Dehuai and Tao Zhu.

A female dental surgeon arrived from Chengdu to check F's teeth. She said some had broken off, leaving just the root, which couldn't be pulled out. A couple needed extracting, which she would arrange in the next few days. So F could finally look forward to an end to his years of toothache.

The correctional cadre told F to write down his thoughts on the Third Plenum communiqué. F gave him his three poems. 'These are my thoughts.' The cadre left in a hurry. F and I carefully read the communiqué. The more we read, the better we felt. The paper carried the text of a speech by Secretary-General Hu Yaobang at a tea party organised by the Federation of Literary and Art Workers. It seemed as if the resolution of the Third Plenum was to be thoroughly implemented.

On January 11, I was called to the office. Administrator L told me he had received a phone call from the Provincial Public Security Department telling him to release F and let him go to Chengdu. The news caught us by surprise – we had expected it, but not so soon. At three, F was escorted to the office. Huang, Director of the Provincial Public Security Department, told him that the Department had been notified by telephone by the Central Public Security Bureau that he was to be released. Other things could be dealt with in Chengdu. They said we could leave as soon as we were ready. They asked F for his reaction. 'I have already written three sets of materials. My ideological understanding is set out in my past materials.' The Political Commissar said he had helped expose and criticise the Gang of Four and had supported Chairman Mao and Chairman Hua, and although his poems were not published, they contained good sentiments, etc., etc. They escorted him to the door. Director Huang suggested we might first go to the County Committee guest house for a few days, but we said it was unnecessary and we would stay where we were.

I wrote to Xiaofeng. The next afternoon, I went with F to have a look round Dazhu county town, and he went to the post office to send his son a telegram.

The prison sent some prisoners to pack for us, and told us to sit in the TV lounge.

On the morning of 14 January 1979, we went to the office to bid farewell. F thanked everyone for their help. The Political Commissar mentioned errors Chairman Mao had made in handling cadres, and he also mentioned Qu Yuan, King Wen and Confucius. But he said past problems were not necessarily someone else's fault, and in future a conclusion would have to be reached about errors and achievements. F said it was important to observe principles.

We set out at nine, accompanied by the doctor and the correctional cadre. While leaving through the prison gate, I experienced indescribable feelings. I had been there six years, and F had been there nine years. Goodbye! We were finally leaving the high walls, still alive, having obtained our freedom.

Epilogue

On 17 January 1979, we arrived in Chengdu and stayed in the Provincial Committee's No. 2 Guest House. Not long afterwards, our son came from Beijing to see us, and we spent Spring Festival together. The Sichuan Public Security Department sent someone to tell Hu Feng he could request work, and they told me I could get a job in the Cultural Bureau. Hu Feng said, 'I've been locked up for more than 20 years, and now I'm supposed to look for a job. I'm in my seventies. Aren't I allowed a break?' So he didn't go. In Chengdu, we revisited some historical sites. I queued up to buy cinema and theatre tickets and bought some literary publications, to fill the gap left by all those years.

In February, the life sentence passed by the Revolutionary Committee of the People's Security Team was revoked. In June, Hu Feng was appointed to the Provincial People's Political Consultative Conference in Sichuan, and I was allocated work as an archivist in the Provincial Museum. Hu Feng had already begun corresponding with his friends. He was reading a lot, and writing an account that went on for hundreds of thousands of characters of his literary views and of some still widespread misconceptions and criticisms concerning organisational affiliations and personal connections. This was for submission to the Central Committee.

He looked robust, and he even accompanied his elder son's family on a trip to Mount Emei. However, more than 20 years of prison life had taken a toll on his health, in addition to which he was

77. In the guest house, seeing the doctor and getting medicine was not so easy. In the autumn, they discovered he was suffering from severe and incurable prostatitis. He was so busy writing that he never took a rest. In the early winter, he suffered a urinary obstruction and haematuria. He underwent surgery, but he continued to bleed heavily for six days, and needed a second operation. They removed his prostate, but his brain was not getting enough blood, so he became mentally confused again. Later I learned this is known as 'psychogenic psychosis'. The children took turns to come from Beijing and Nanjing to help me care for him. Hu Feng wasn't put in a senior cadres' ward but was kept the whole time in an observation room. Even if they had let him out of hospital, he had no home to go to and would have had to go back to the guest house, which was completely inappropriate. The children wrote to the Central Committee asking for him to be allowed to return to the capital for medical treatment. The matter was quickly resolved. In late March 1980, I went back with him to Beijing. Various departments concerned themselves with his case, and he was admitted to Friendship Hospital and later transferred to a centre for the prevention and treatment of mental illness. That September, the Central Committee rehabilitated the 'Hu Feng counter-revolutionary clique' and appointed Hu Feng as an adviser to the Ministry of Culture's research institute. I was allocated to be a writer stationed at the Writers' Association. His illness came and went, and after a period of treatment in Shanghai, his mental state returned more or less to normal. He was appointed to the Standing Committee of the National People's Political Consultative Conference and to the committee of the National Federation of Literary and Art Workers, and was made an adviser to the Chinese Writers' Association. In 1982, we moved to a new house. At last we had our own home again and he could walk around the light and spacious living room leaning on his stick. He started writing copious recollections, and his creative springs began to flow.

Just as he was planning to recover lost time and apply his remaining years to working for the Party, his health went from bad to worse. He went to hospital and was diagnosed with cardiac cancer, at an advanced stage. At his age, surgery was out of the question. The cancer cells spread to his liver and lymphoid tissues. We didn't tell him the whole truth, we simply said he had stomach ulcers and pneumonia. He trusted his doctor and submitted to any treatment, without ever complaining. Later on, he found it ever harder to swallow. Every mouthful of food and medicine was a struggle, but he put up with the pain and forced himself to eat, because the doctor told him that food was even more important than medicine for getting better. How he longed to stay alive!

The children wouldn't let me nurse him through the night, I too was old and unable to support him. So I only went to see him during the day. Once, he grabbed my hand and said, 'Someone's trying to frame me, this is a terrible mess!' 'Don't be afraid, it's not possible. Besides, I'm here! I can help you make things clear.' 'Can you, can you really?' 'Yes, I can, believe me . . .' I couldn't say any more because of the tears. I realised his paranoia was back. My daughter gave me a meaningful look, and I quickly went to the toilet, where I cried my heart out.

The next time I went, he was dying and couldn't speak any more. That was 8 June 1985.

He left no last words, but his deathbed worries were not irrational. To ensure he received a fair and unprejudiced funeral oration, we had to overcome a number of artificial obstacles. Not until the start of the second year was a memorial meeting held for him, under the auspices of the Ministry of Culture. He received a just evaluation of the sort that he could not have dared to expect in his lifetime but was his due. The entire family stood in front of the bier. I was not fully conscious and thought I was in a dream, but faced with the hundreds of leaders and old and new friends who had come to the hall to mourn him, I realised everything was indeed real. Many past friends I had not seen for years gripped my hand. Some smiled and tried to console me. The strong handshakes and smiling faces showed me they understood Hu Feng and respected him. Many had been implicated in the past because of him. Friends he had always felt guilty about came, peered painfully at his portrait, bowed deeply before him, shook my hand, and spoke words of comfort. Young literary workers who felt gratitude and admiration for his incorruptible spirit came forward to pay tribute. And then . . . and then . . .

If he could have stepped down from the photo, he would have embraced these friends with all his heart and soul. Sadly, it was too late. He could only look down with his smiling face on the crowd. He must have been overjoyed at the thought that he would never again experience those terrors and could at last sleep deeply and in peace.

My promise to him is still far from fulfilled, but I dare say this to him: 'I assure you that I will spend the rest of my life washing the remnants of dirt from your face and showing your true features to the world!'